W9-BDE-249

# Vegetarian & More!

## Versatile Vegetarian Recipes with Optional Meat Add-Ins

**Linda Rosensweig**

author of the best-selling cookbook ***New Vegetarian Cuisine***

Printed in the United States of America on acid-free ♾, recycled paper ♻

Cover and Interior Designer: Lynn N. Gano
Cover Illustrator: Dave Albers



**Library of Congress Cataloging-in-Publication Data**

Rosensweig, Linda.
Vegetarian & more! : versatile vegetarian recipes with optional meat add-ins / Linda Rosensweig.
p. cm.
Includes index.
ISBN 1–57954–112–7 hardcover
1. Vegetarian cookery. I. Title.
TX837.R82624 2000
641.5'636—dc21 99–089916

**Distributed to the book trade by St. Martin's Press**

2 4 6 8 10 9 7 5 3 1 hardcover

Visit us on the Web at www.rodalecookbooks.com, or call us toll-free at (800) 848-4735.

*"Nothing will benefit human health and increase the chances for survival of life on Earth as much as the evolution to a vegetarian diet."*

—Albert Einstein, physicist

# A Tale of Two Tastes

A VEGETARIAN COOKBOOK WITH nonvegetarian alternatives? Why would anyone tackle such a project? For me, the answer is simple: I eat vegetarian, but my family still loves meat.

This book grew out of need, really. I needed to relieve my own dinnertime stress! I had been cooking two separate meals every night: a vegetarian dinner for me and a meat meal for my husband and daughters. We're also a family with different food tastes and timetables. My husband, Daniel, loves mushrooms, but Rachel and Samantha can't stand them. Daniel has an early breakfast, but the kids eat later. Providing satisfying, healthy meals for everyone—every day—became quite a challenge.

But, as they say, "Every obstacle is an opportunity." Over time, I developed a way to please us all. Instead of making two meals, I started creating recipes that could be converted from vegetarian to nonvegetarian with a few simple steps. In most cases, a little browned beef, sausage, or cooked chicken could be added to half of the recipe near the end, creating a dual vegetarian/nonvegetarian meal. I also found that many of my old meat-based standbys could go the other way: from nonvegetarian to vegetarian. Soon I was converting recipes from vegetarian to nonvegetarian—and back again—with no problem.

I like to call this flip-flop cooking. What a change it made in my life as the family cook! Suddenly, there were fewer dishes to clean up. There was more time for other activities. And everyone was happier with our food. I decided, why stop there? To make things even easier, I began tagging my recipes for quick reference. I tagged the recipes that my daughters would eat as "kid-friendly." I tagged the "freezable" recipes, so we could have ready-made meals. I also tagged the "microwaveable" recipes for the times when we need food really fast. These tags appear on the recipes in this book and are explained further on pages 16–17.

Once I got comfortable cooking this way for my immediate family, it carried over to bigger family gatherings and get-togethers with friends, too. These days, there's a mixed crowd of vegetarians and meat-lovers almost everywhere you go. Some people want to eat less meat. Some people love meat and want to eat more of it. And some folks just want to eat more healthfully. I found that flip-flop cooking appealed to just about everyone. The recipes can be vegetarian, nonvegetarian, or both.

But here's what I like most about this way of cooking: I know that this food is healthy for my family. Secretly, I want them to eat more vegetables and fruits and grains and all the other things that are good for them. But they still want their meat loaves and hamburgers. No problem. Now, we start our meals with a foundation of plant foods and add meats, poultry, and seafood in simple ways. This gives us all what we want: taste, convenience, variety, and good health.

# Acknowledgments

*To Elaine Molzahn,*
*thank you for helping me to follow my dream to cook*

# Contents

# *Acknowledgments*

YEARS OF TRIAL AND ERROR, wonderful discoveries, and the culinary influences of many people have resulted in the book you now hold in your hands. Much of the credit goes to behind-the-scenes people too numerous to mention by name. But I would like to express my sincere thanks to:

Barbara Farrell, for helping me through the toughest days of writing

David Joachim, my editor, for providing insightful suggestions and for guiding this book with a steady hand at every stage

Carol Munson, of Winter Springs Editorial Services, for her meticulous recipe editing

The Rodale Test Kitchen, for retesting these recipes to make them as perfect as possible

The rest of the staff at Rodale Books, for their publishing acumen and their enthusiasm for this book

Jodi Weber, Lori Palmer, and Laurie Salis for all their laughs

Daniel Rosensweig, my husband, for encouraging me to take on this project, for his excitement, and for his support

And, last, my daughters, Rachel and Samantha, my real-life recipe testers

# A Tale of Two Tastes

# Contents

# What's So Good about Eating This Way

**THE AVERAGE AMERICAN EATS** more plant foods than ever before. Well . . . at least in recent history. According to the U.S. Department of Agriculture (USDA), the typical American ate 40 percent more grain products, 20 percent more fruit, 3 percent more vegetables, 6 percent less meat, 13 percent fewer dairy products, and 37 percent fewer eggs in 1994 than in 1978.

Why are people changing the way they eat? For most folks, it's a health issue. In a major Roper Center survey, 88 percent of respondents said the main reason they choose meatless meals is for better health. But consider this: A study of female physicians found that more than 40 percent who ate vegetarian did it for taste. And that's why I do it. Vegetarian food tastes great! Take a look at pizza, for example. It's mostly plant foods and totally vegetarian (unless you add meaty toppings). And it's one of the most popular foods in America. Potato salad is another American classic that's completely vegetarian. Grilled cheese is another. Even newcomers like bean burritos and chips and salsa are usually 100 percent vegetarian. There are dozens of popular foods you may already enjoy that you might not think of as vegetarian. The best thing about these foods is that many of them can easily include meat if you want them to. That flexibility is the basis of this book. I learned to cook both vegetarian and nonvegetarian meals at the same time because my family still likes to eat meat.

## Less Meat, No Mystery

Eating and cooking vegetarian may seem like the ultimate challenge. But, really, cooking with plant foods is simple. You do it every time you make pancakes, cook pasta, or throw together a salad. Let's answer some of the most common questions about cooking and eating this way.

**Won't it taste bad?** The fact is, vegetarian foods are some of the most popular foods in the United States. But, in all honesty, staunch meat-eaters will miss the meat if you simply pull the ol' switcheroo on them. To satisfy meat-lovers who are trying to eat less meat or who may be hesitant about eating a vegetarian meal, try serving "meaty" foods like grilled portobello mushrooms or roasted eggplant at first. These foods have a chewy texture and flame-kissed flavor that mimic those of meat. Eggplant Lasagne (page 183), Eggplant and Roasted Red Pepper Lasagna (page 228), and Grilled Portobello Sandwiches (page 132) would be good recipes to start with. Or just follow the "Quick Conversions" in the recipes throughout this book to add small amounts of meat to a vegetarian dish. That way, the meat-lovers will still get the meat, and you'll feel better knowing it's cooked into a healthy recipe.

You can also try the endless variety of meatless sausages, hot dogs, and burgers now available in supermarkets. Many of these products are indistinguishable from their more "carnivorous" counterparts. I often include meatless sausage links at breakfast and my whole family loves them.

**Doesn't it take longer to cook?** Nope. I'm a working mom, so I don't have time for fussy recipes. In fact, it takes less time because you're cooking one meal instead of two. Most of the dishes in this book are ready to eat in less than 45 minutes. If you're making a meat version of a recipe, it's usually a simple matter of tossing in the meat, then finishing the recipe as directed. Cooking times rarely vary for the "Quick Conversions." And when you need super-quick recipes, turn to the chapter Fast Five-Ingredient Main Dishes (beginning on page 143). Every recipe has only five ingredients. I rely on these recipes when I come home dog tired, or when I just don't feel like cooking.

**Doesn't it require strange ingredients?** Pasta, canned beans, cream cheese, sliced provolone, mustard, sun-dried tomatoes, jarred roasted peppers, balsamic vinaigrette, soy sauce. . . . These are not strange ingredients and are available in most supermarkets. I made a point of making sure that all of the ingredients in this book are familiar and available in the average grocery store. There's only one recipe that may throw you for a loop: Grilled Tempeh with Sour Cream (page 171). Tempeh is a traditional Asian food

## What's a Vegetarian?

Nearly 14 million Americans call themselves vegetarians. Some are not vegetarians in the strict sense of the word. Strictly speaking, vegetarians eat no animal meats—no beef, pork, lamb, veal, chicken, turkey, game meats, fish, or shellfish. However, many vegetarians do eat dairy products and/or eggs. And there are many people who eat no *red* meat but occasionally fish or poultry. Technically, these folks aren't vegetarians. Plus, there are many "part-time vegetarians" or "semivegetarians" who eat vegetarian some of the time (which includes just about everybody). Below are a few definitions that should help clear things up. The two types of semivegetarians are listed first, then come the last four "true" types of vegetarians.

**Pollo-vegetarian:** They eat plant foods plus eggs, dairy products, poultry, and perhaps fish. They do not eat red meats.

**Pesca-vegetarian:** They eat plant foods plus eggs, dairy products, fish, and shellfish. They do not eat red or white meats.

**Lacto-ovo-vegetarian:** They eat plant foods, eggs, and dairy products. They do not eat any animal meats. This is the most common type of vegetarian in the United States.

**Lacto-vegetarian:** They eat plant foods and dairy products. They do not eat any animal meats or eggs.

**Ovo-vegetarian:** They eat plant foods and eggs. They do not eat any animal meats or dairy products.

**Vegan:** They eat only plant foods. They do not eat any animal meats, eggs, or dairy products. May also avoid honey and other animal by-products such as gelatin. They may even exclude yeast.

made from soybeans. It has a strong flavor that many longtime vegetarians simply love (including me!). Fortunately, tempeh is now available in many large supermarkets as well as health food stores.

There are also a few recipes for tofu, which is familiar to most folks by now. If you still haven't tried it, or if you haven't liked what you've tried, give tofu another shot. Tofu is like an egg. The flavor and texture depend mostly on how it's prepared. And tofu is widely available in different flavors and textures in the refrigerated produce section of most supermarkets.

**Won't it be boring?** No way! My kids and my husband tell me straightaway if they're bored with our food. Variety has become the cornerstone of our family diet. Without it, I'd be sunk. Variety and simplicity are the two key factors that keep my family coming back to the dining table. Scan the recipe lists at the beginning of each chapter to see how varied vegetarian food can be. Or check out the "Vegetarian Food Guide Pyramid" on page 10.

## Plant Foods Boost Your Health

Vegetarian food can be quick, innovative, and satisfying. But the major long-term benefit of eating this way is a boost in your health profile. Studies show that vegetarians live longer, weigh less, and have fewer chronic diseases than their meat-eating counterparts. No wonder so many people are eating more plant foods. Here are some of the specific benefits you can expect.

***Weigh less.*** People who switch from a meat-centered diet to a vegetarian diet often lose weight. We know *that* this is true, but no long-term study has conclusively proven *why*. One theory is that vegetarians tend to exercise more. Another is that they eat fewer calories because the diet is lower in fat and higher in fiber. (When you eat more fiber, you tend to feel full sooner, so you eat less food and fewer calories, too). But there are no studies that prove any of these theories. However, at least one study has shown that even when calorie intake and exercise were constant, vegetarians *still* weighed less than meat-eaters. Researchers at Purdue University studied the average meat-eater, who ate 2,225 calories a day and weighed 158 pounds. In comparison, the average vegetarian ate 2,340 calories (nearly 125 calories more) and weighed 143 pounds—or 15 pounds less! And the vegetarians had the same exercise habits as the meat-eaters. It's still something of a mystery why vegetarians often weigh less than omnivores. But with all the other health bonuses, cutting back on meat is certainly worth a try if you want to drop a few pounds.

***Reduce risk of heart disease.*** Cholesterol is a fatlike substance that can build up on the inside of your heart's arteries. The higher your blood cholesterol, the more likely you are to suffer from heart disease. Note that cholesterol exists only in animal foods and not in plant foods. And cholesterol usually comes along with saturated fat, which is the real culprit in raising your blood cholesterol levels. Several studies have shown that a vegetarian diet, because it is lower in saturated fat, can cut the risk of or even help *reverse* the effects of heart disease.

## Soy to Your Health

More than 40 human studies have shown that eating soy-based foods like tofu and soy milk can reduce the risk of heart disease, the leading cause of death in the United States. Soy foods are high in protein but low in saturated fat, and they contain no cholesterol. Soy-based foods contain mostly polyunsaturated fats, which don't raise blood cholesterol. Research shows that soy protein can reduce blood cholesterol by 10 to 15 percent in people with elevated cholesterol. What's more, soy foods can reduce the blood cholesterol of people who already eat a low-fat diet. See page 18 for tips on adding soy foods to your diet.

In an Australian study, researchers tracked three groups: one group's diet was high in fat and contained meat; the second was lacto-ovo-vegetarian (including dairy and eggs, but no meat); and the third was a variation of lacto-ovo-vegetarian, but 60 percent of the plant protein was replaced with lean meat. Both the vegetarian and lean meat diets significantly lowered blood cholesterol. But the totally vegetarian diet lowered cholesterol *twice* as much as the lean meat diet (10 percent versus 5 percent). Statistically, that simple 10 percent reduction in cholesterol reduces the chance of having a heart attack by 20 to 30 percent. Plus, vegetarian foods (like black beans, chickpeas, spinach, and asparagus) are high in folate, which helps protect your heart even more by keeping levels of a substance called homocysteine low. Homocysteine is a by-product of eating meat and dairy foods.

***Cut cancer risk.*** Seventh Day Adventists follow a mostly vegetarian diet for religious reasons. Health researchers began studying this group in the 1960s and have found that Adventists are consistently healthier than the average American. According to the Center for Disease Control and Prevention (CDC), Adventists have significantly lower death rates from heart disease, diabetes, and many forms of cancer, including lung and breast cancers. "The most striking result of our work is that no matter what cancer site we examine, there seems to be a very strong protective association with the consumption of fruits and vegetables," says Paul Mills, Ph.D., a researcher who studied cancer among the Seventh Day Adventists for 8 years at Loma Linda University in California.

*(continued on page 8)*

## Foods That Heal

Nutrition scientists have uncovered a world of beneficial substances in foods beyond the traditional vitamins and minerals. These substances are called phytochemicals, literally "plant chemicals." Phytochemicals can help prevent heart disease and many different cancers. Some phytochemicals are antioxidants (which help boost your immune system and prevent heart disease). To get the full benefit of these substances, experts recommend eating more fruits, vegetables, and whole grains. Here are some of the best foods you can eat for better health.

| Food | Substance It Contains | Health Benefits | Uses |
|---|---|---|---|
| Alliums (onions, garlic, shallots, leeks, scallions, and chives) | Allium and sulfur compounds | May help prevent cancers, cut cholesterol, and help dissolve clots | Fresh or cooked |
| Apples, onions, celery, cranberries, grapes, broccoli, endive, and red wine | Flavonoids | May help prevent heart disease and cancer | Fresh or cooked |
| Beans (chickpeas, kidney beans, lentils, and soybeans) | Isoflavones | May help prevent hormone-based cancers and lower levels of harmful estrogen | Cooked or canned |
| Berries, nuts, and grapes | Ellagic acid | May help prevent cancers | Fresh salads and snacks, cooked main dishes, sprinkled on top of dishes |
| Cherries and citrus fruits | Monoterpenes | May help prevent cancer | Fresh or frozen |
| Cruciferous vegetables (broccoli, cauliflower, brussels sprouts) | Glucosinolates and indoles | May help prevent cancers | Fresh, steamed, stir-fried, and in casseroles |

| Food | Substance It Contains | Health Benefits | Uses |
|---|---|---|---|
| Dark-green leafy vegetables (spinach, kale, collards) | Beta-carotene, lutein, zeaxanthin | May help prevent cancer, heart disease, and macular degeneration | Fresh or cooked |
| Flaxseed | Lignans and omega-3 fatty acids | May help prevent cancers and lower blood cholesterol | Add flaxseed oil or freshly ground flaxseed to food or take a dietary supplement |
| Green and black teas | Polyphenols | May help prevent cancers | Hot or cold beverage |
| Orange fruits and vegetables (carrots, sweet potatoes, winter squash, cantaloupe) | Beta-carotene | May help prevent cancers | Fresh or cooked |
| Potatoes, tomatoes, spinach, beans, nuts, and oats | Saponins | May help prevent breast, prostate, and colon cancers | Fresh or cooked |
| Soy foods (tofu, soy milk, veggie burgers, soy flour, soybeans) | Isoflavones and saponins | May help prevent certain cancers and lower cholesterol | Fresh, baked, grilled, broiled, stir-fried; in casseroles and baked goods; for drinking |
| Tomatoes | Lycopene | May help prevent prostate and other cancers and heart disease | Fresh or cooked |
| Watermelons | Glutathione | May help prevent cancer and boost immunity | Fresh or pureed into cold soups or smoothies |

Although the dietary link to cancer is still under intense study, experts believe that if every person reduced his or her intake of fat to no more than 30 percent of calories and ate foods high in fiber (20 to 35 grams a day), there would be a 50 percent reduction in colorectal cancer, a 25 percent reduction in breast cancer, and a 15 percent reduction in cancers of the prostrate, endometrium, and gallbladder. A study of women in 21 countries, for example, found that those who ate high-fat diets (45 percent of calories coming from fat) had more than five times the risk of breast cancer than women who got only 15 percent of calories from fat. Not surprisingly, a balanced vegetarian diet fits the bill perfectly because it is low in fat and high in fiber. A typical vegetarian eats about two to three times as much fiber as a nonvegetarian.

***Lower blood pressure.*** High blood pressure is the "silent killer" in the United States because experts estimate that nearly half of the more than 50 million Americans who have it don't even know it. A stroke or heart attack is often the first sign. Studies have shown that eating a plant-based diet can help lower your blood pressure. Research from Harvard Medical School and Brigham and Women's Hospital in Boston compared meat-eaters with two groups of vegetarians. The first vegetarian group ate mostly grains and vegetables. The second vegetarian group also included dairy products. Both vegetarian groups had blood pressure approximately 10 to 15 points lower than did meat-eaters. And the stricter vegetarian group had blood pressure even lower than that of the vegetarians who included dairy products.

***Plenty of protein.*** Vegetarians don't need to take protein pills or eat "complementary proteins" at the same meal. According to the American Dietetic Association's official *Position on Vegetarian Diets*, "Plant sources of protein alone can provide adequate amounts of essential amino acids (protein) if a variety of plant foods are consumed and energy needs are met." Vegetarians just need to eat a varied, balanced diet like everyone else. For some surprising sources of protein, turn to page 160.

***Lots of calcium.*** For vegetarians who include dairy products and eggs, adequate calcium intake is no problem. "Lacto-ovo-vegetarians have calcium intakes that are comparable to or higher than those of nonvegetarians," says the American Dietetic Association. Even if you choose not to eat dairy products, you can meet your calcium needs by including high-calcium plant foods in your diet, such as dried figs, fortified soy milk and orange juice, tofu, and legumes like white beans, chickpeas, and vegetarian baked beans.

***More vitamins and minerals.*** Most of the world's vitamins and minerals are contained in plant foods. Eat more of these foods and you'll increase your intake. It's that simple. Vegetarians eat more vitamins A, C, and E, thiamin, riboflavin, magnesium, folate, and carotenoids than nonvegetarians. By eating more plant foods, you'll also get important phytochemicals, which researchers have found to play an important role in immune function and disease prevention.

***More energy and stamina.*** It's difficult for the human body to convert the main components of meat (protein and fat) into carbohydrates. And carbohydrates are our best source of body fuel. By replacing meat with complex carbohydrates like vegetables and grains, your body gets its fuel more readily and it burns more steadily for hours. This extra energy helps many vegetarians exercise more, which in turn builds stamina and provides even more energy!

## Building Balance

Vegetarians are generally a healthy group of folks. But a vegetarian diet isn't *automatically* good for you. If you think about it, a diet of ice cream, cookies, doughnuts, and potato chips is entirely vegetarian. But it's certainly not healthy! Vegetarians who rely too heavily on eggs, cheese, and other whole-milk dairy products can do more harm than good to their health.

A good-for-you vegetarian diet is very similar to the diet outlined by the USDA's Food Guide Pyramid. It's built on balance, variety, and moderation. Even the recommended number of servings in each food group is the same as for a healthy diet that includes meat. The only exception for vegetarians is that in the protein group, plant proteins (like beans, eggs, and tofu) replace meat proteins (like beef, pork, and chicken).

To help vegetarians plan meals, the American Dietetic Association developed a daily food guide pyramid (see page 10). Eating the recommended number of servings in each food group will result in a perfectly sound diet that's nutritionally complete. Look inside the pyramid to find a few examples of the foods in each group. Notice also what counts as a serving of each food. If you're a part-time vegetarian, you can still use this pyramid to plan your daily meals. Just replace some of the plant proteins with meat proteins. To further boost your health, the American Dietetic Association offers the following tips.

- Choose a variety of foods, including whole grains, vegetables, fruits, legumes, nuts, seeds, and, if desired, dairy products and eggs.
- Choose whole, unrefined foods often and minimize intake of highly sweetened, fatty, and heavily refined foods.

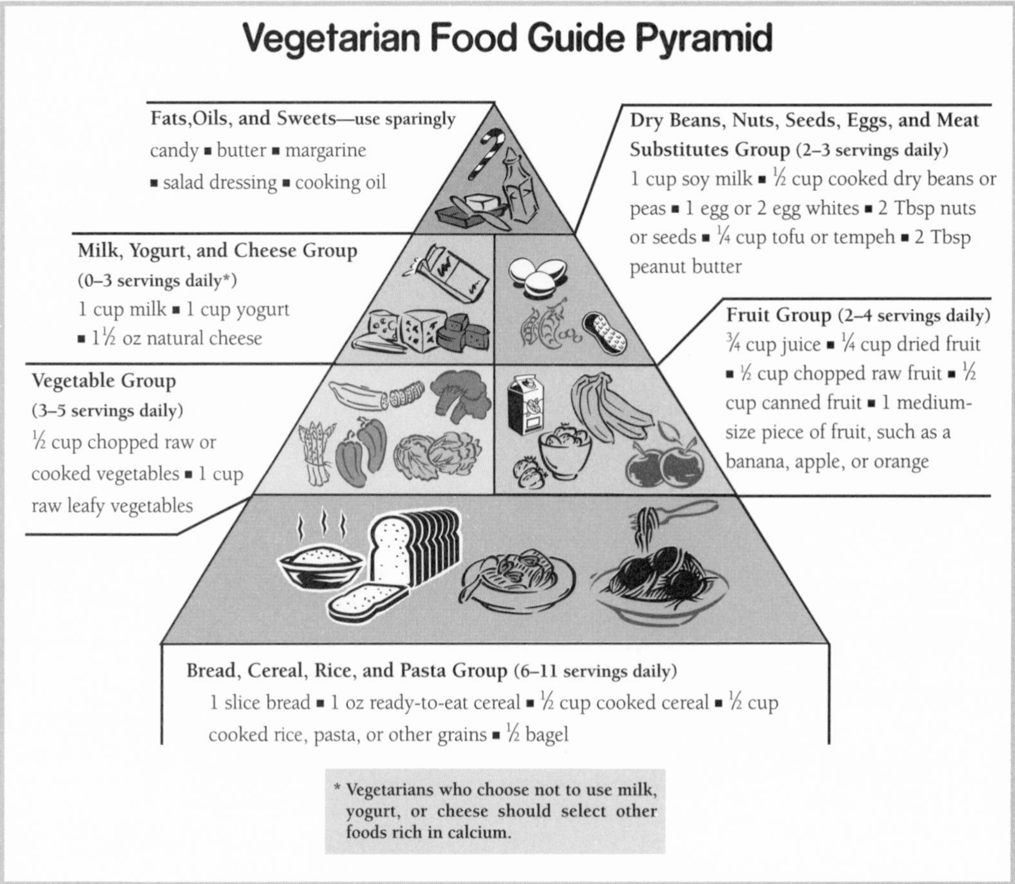


● If animal foods such as dairy products and eggs are used, choose lower-fat versions of these foods. Cheeses and other high-fat dairy foods and eggs should be limited in the diet because of their saturated fat content and because their frequent use displaces plant foods in some vegetarian diets.

● Vegans should include a regular source of vitamin $B_{12}$ in their diets along with a source of vitamin D if sun exposure is limited.

● Solely breast-fed infants should have supplements of iron after the age of 4 to 6 months and, if sun exposure is limited, a source of vitamin D. Breast-fed vegan infants should have vitamin $B_{12}$ supplements if the mother's diet is not fortified.

● Do not restrict dietary fat in children younger than 2 years. For older children, include some foods higher in unsaturated fats, such as nuts, seeds, nut and seed butters, avocado, and vegetable oils, to help meet nutrient and energy needs.

## Enjoy Your Food

The bottom line is that the closer you can come to a plant-based diet, the better off you will be. But most people don't eat for health. They eat for pleasure. For satisfaction. And because food tastes good! I can tell you my recipes taste good until I'm blue in the face, but the only way you'll know is to try them. Also, I *do* want you to know that every recipe has been tested and retested on my husband, my kids, myself, and our friends. And they were tested again at the publisher's expense.

I hope you enjoy this food as much as my family does. Think of this book as a starting point. Once you get comfortable with converting recipes from vegetarian to nonvegetarian (and vice versa), you can do the same thing with your old favorites. By then, you'll be well on your way to a healthier way of eating.

*"The only real stumbling block is the fear of failure. In cooking, you've got to have a what-the-hell attitude."*

—Julia Child, cooking expert

# Converting To and Fro

I BEGAN COOKING THIS WAY out of love: a love for my family, a love of good cooking, and a love for a healthy way of life. I wanted to please my family with their favorite meat-based foods while at the same time providing them with a healthy diet founded on vegetables, fruits, grains, cereals, and nuts.

Eventually, I developed a supply of vegetarian recipes that could be easily converted for meat-lovers. Most of the recipes in this book can be converted from vegetarian to nonvegetarian in a few simple steps. Look for the following "Quick Conversion" symbol at the bottom of recipes to quickly identify these "convertibles."

The "Quick Conversion" directions will tell you exactly how to convert each recipe. Note that only changes for the meat version are specified. Everything else in the vegetarian recipe remains the same. For most recipes, that means you start the vegetarian recipe, divide it in half toward the end, then stir in the cooked meat, poultry, or fish and finish cooking as the recipe directs. It's that simple. Here are a few other tips to help you get the most versatility out of this book.

**You don't have to convert.** If you follow the main recipe as written, you will end up with a vegetarian dish that serves four (some casseroles may serve a few more). Only follow the "Quick Conversion" directions at the bottom of the recipe when you want to make a nonvegetarian dish in addition to the vegetarian one.

**Each conversion makes a dual meal.** When you follow the conversion directions, *half* of the recipe will be converted for meat-lovers. The other half remains vegetarian. I wrote the conversions this way so that you can make a single meal for a mixed crowd. Many people told me that this is their biggest challenge. As written, the conversions allow you to serve a dual vegetarian/nonvegetarian meal at the same time.

**You *can* make a total conversion.** If you'd like to convert the *entire* recipe for meat-lovers, simply double the amounts given in the conversion directions and mix the meat into the entire dish instead of just half. For instance, the conversion for Tortellini Lasagna on page 148 adds 6 ounces cooked sausage to half of the

## A Note on Vegetables

All vegetables called for in the recipes in this book are assumed to be medium-size. If a different size is needed, the recipe will specify "large" or "small." In most recipes, slight variations in vegetable size don't make a huge difference to the final product. When size does matter, exact weights or volume amounts will be specified.

casserole. You could add 12 ounces sausage to the entire casserole to make the recipe completely for nonvegetarians.

**Read the entire recipe first.** This step is essential to making a dual vegetarian/nonvegetarian meal. As you read the conversion directions, note the additional ingredients needed and when they will be added to the main recipe. For example, the sausage in the Tortellini Lasagna is sprinkled on before topping with the cheese. Then the entire dish is baked.

**Conversion cooking times rarely change.** If they do, each recipe conversion specifies the exact cooking time needed. For food safety, I keep an instant-read thermometer on hand to check meat doneness. You can also do a visual check. If you're unsure of when a particular type of meat is cooked, refer to "Doneness Temperatures" on page 22.

**Be flexible.** Use whatever meat you or your guests like best. In many recipes, the animal protein (beef, pork, poultry, or seafood) can be substituted. Just replace the meat called for with the same amount of your favorite meat. For instance, if you prefer ground beef to sausage in the Tortellini Lasagna, replace the 6 ounces of sausage called for with 6 ounces of ground beef.

**Keep meat pans on hand.** You may need to cook bacon, brown beef, or grill chicken to complete the meat version of any given recipe. I keep a lightweight medium nonstick skillet on hand specifically for this purpose. It also makes cleanup easier to line roasting pans with foil.

**Use the same pan.** To save time, you can cook the meat in the same pan that the vegetables were cooked in once the vegetables have been removed (but not the other way around if the vegetarians at the table are squeamish).

**Try one dish for oven-baked recipes.** Most of the baked recipes in this book call for the almost-completed mixture to be divided and placed in two smaller baking dishes instead of one large dish. Then, meat is added to one of the dishes and both are baked. I call for separate dishes because

## Vegetable Shelf Life

Freshness is the key to great-tasting vegetables. Most fresh vegetables are firm and crisp with no signs of wilting or browning. (Avocados, which are really a fruit, are the exception; fresh avocados should "give" slightly to gentle palm pressure.) It also helps to store vegetables properly so that they hold on to their freshness as long as possible. Here's how to get the most life and the best flavor from your fresh produce.

| Fresh Vegetable | Best Storage Place | Use Within . . . |
|---|---|---|
| Artichokes | Refrigerator | 3 days |
| Asparagus | Refrigerator | 1–2 days |
| Avocados | Refrigerator (once ripened) | 3–5 days |
| Bean sprouts | Refrigerator (in water to cover) | 3 days |
| Beets | Refrigerator (after tops are removed) | 1 week |
| Broccoli | Refrigerator | 3–5 days |
| Broccoli raab | Refrigerator | 2 days |
| Brussels sprouts | Refrigerator | 2 days |
| Cabbage | Refrigerator | 7 days |
| Carrots | Refrigerator | 2 weeks |
| Cauliflower | Refrigerator | 5 days |
| Celery | Refrigerator | 7 days |
| Corn | Refrigerator | 1 day |
| Cucumbers | Refrigerator | 1 week |
| Eggplant | Refrigerator | 1 week |
| Green beans | Refrigerator | 2–5 days |
| Greens | Refrigerator | 2 days |
| Mushrooms | Refrigerator | 1 week |
| Onions | Cool, dry place with good circulation | 1 month |
| Parsnips | Refrigerator | 2 weeks |
| Pea pods | Refrigerator | 2 days |
| Peppers | Refrigerator | 1 week |
| Potatoes | Cool, dark place (away from onions) | 3 weeks |
| Scallions | Refrigerator | 5 days |
| Turnips | Refrigerator | 2 weeks |
| Winter squash | Refrigerator | 2 weeks |
| Zucchini | Refrigerator | 3–5 days |

many vegetarians don't want meat anywhere near their food. But if you're serving vegetarians who don't mind the meat being in the same dish (not touching, mind you), then you can simply add the meat to half of the mixture in the large dish called for in the main recipe. This makes cleanup much easier. Just remember which side of the pan has the meat! I sometimes mark the meat side with a toothpick.

**Prep first.** As with all cooking, it saves time to have the ingredients chopped, measured, and ready to go before you actually start cooking. And in the case of certain recipes (like a stir-fry, for example), it's a must because the cooking time is so short.

**Convert your own recipes.** Use the tips and recipes in this book as examples of how to convert your own recipes. Stuffed peppers are a good example of a favorite dish that can be vegetarian, nonvegetarian, or both. To completely convert a traditional stuffed pepper recipe made with beef, replace the beef with cooked lentils or crumbled cooked veggie burgers. To make a dual meal out of it, replace *half* the beef with lentils and divide the two mixtures among the bell pepper shells. Many of your favorite recipes may be easily converted from nonvegetarian to vegetarian or vice versa.

## Useful Symbols in This Book

When my kitchen was undergoing renovations, I had a hard time feeding my family. The only appliance I could use was my microwave! It sure would have been nice to have my microwave recipes marked so that I could find them at a glance. With that in mind, I've done just that in this book. I've marked recipes according to their particular usefulness. In addition to "Quick Conversion" recipes, I've added symbols for three other types of recipes: Microwaveable, Freezable, and Kid-Friendly. These are important things to know when you're trying to satisfy finicky young eaters or make a meal ahead of time so that it can be reheated whenever needed. Look for the following symbols to quickly find the recipes you're looking for.

***Microwaveable recipe:*** These recipes are super-fast. Look for these when time is really short. They can be cooked from start to finish in the microwave oven. Microwave directions are included with the recipe under the heading "Tip." Keep in mind, too, that almost all the recipes in this book can be *reheated* in the microwave oven (bread recipes are a notable exception).

***Freezable recipe:*** This symbol is for recipes that freeze well for make-aheads or long storage. Having ready-made meals in the freezer is a real lifesaver on nights when I come home tired. Freezing directions are included with these recipes under the heading "Tip."

***Kid-friendly recipe:*** Here's one that parents will love. This symbol appears before any recipe that kids like to eat. I've tested these recipes on my two picky daughters, Rachel and Samantha, and on my neighbors' kids. Only when I got their seal of approval did I mark the recipe "kid-friendly." These are mostly mild-flavored or handheld foods that kids tend to like, such as sandwiches, pasta, vegetables, and fruits. Many of these recipes are easy for kids to help prepare, too. To make other dishes in the book kid-friendly, try replacing strong-flavored ingredients with mild-flavored ones. For instance, replace watercress with romaine lettuce or blue cheese with Parmesan cheese.

## Kid-Friendly Foods

Keep the following kid-friendly staples on hand to satisfy even the pickiest junior eaters. These keep my little ones coming back to the table.

**Assorted healthy cereals:** Pack them in food-storage bags, and great nutritious snacks are ready anytime, anywhere.

**Breads, muffins, and bagels:** Bagels make great pizza, too.

**Fruit snacks:** Stock all-fruit versions in various shapes and sizes.

**Granola bars:** Look for reduced-fat varieties.

**Hot dogs:** These are available in all varieties—turkey, chicken, beef, and veggie.

**Ketchup:** A kid staple, just about anything can be dunked in it or slathered with it.

**Macaroni and cheese:** Show the kids how to make their own.

**Parmesan cheese:** This is the answer for my kids, who shake it on just about anything.

**Pasta:** All shapes and sizes are available.

**Pizza dough:** Kids love to make their own pizza—just supply their favorite toppings.

**Soups:** Stock all kinds, especially noodle soups.

## The Versatile Vegetarian Kitchen

To make flip-flop cooking a success, it helps to know what you're adding in and what you're taking out. Many vegetarians are unfamiliar with cuts of meat and how to cook them. Likewise, meat-lovers may not know the first thing about tofu. Here's a guide to vegetarian and meat products to keep on hand for converting recipes from vegetarian to nonvegetarian and back again. Not all of these foods are used in the recipes in this book, but I included descriptions of foods like soy milk in case you choose to use them. All of these foods can be found in large supermarkets or health food stores.

## Conversion Foods

Here are a few foods I use to convert my vegetarian recipes for meat-lovers. In most cases, I just add the cooked meat to half of the recipe near the end of the cooking time. Sometimes it's necessary to add a little more seasoning to the meat version. This applies mostly to simmered dishes like stews because the added meat will "dilute" the seasoning already in the dish. Taste before you bring any dish to the table. In the case of foods you don't eat, get a family member or friend to taste it. Your tongue (or their tongue) will tell you whether the food needs a little more salt, pepper, chili powder, lemon zest, vinegar, hot-pepper sauce, and so on.

**Beef**
- Ground beef
- Beef tenderloin
- Beef hot dogs

**Pork**
- Bacon (strip, Canadian)
- Ham (smoked, lean deli slices)
- Pastrami
- Pepperoni
- Pork tenderloin
- Prosciutto
- Sausage (hot Italian, kielbasa)

**Poultry**
- Chicken (boneless breasts, bone-in parts, smoked)
- Turkey breast (ground, smoked deli slices)
- Turkey sausage
- Turkey bacon

**Fish and Shellfish**
- Anchovies (canned)
- Clams
- Mussels
- Salmon (steaks)
- Scallops
- Shrimp
- Tuna (canned)
- White fish (halibut, snapper, cod, flounder)

**Broth**
- Chicken broth
- Beef broth

Soy-based foods like tofu have been making headlines lately because of their potential health benefits, among them fighting heart disease and cancer. Although "soy" still has a negative connotation to many, you may already be eating it. Soy is widely used as a meat extender in things like canned chili. It's often labeled as vegetable protein. Soybean oil is also used in many canned and jarred foods because it costs less than other oils. Check the labels of the foods you eat and you're likely to see vegetable protein or soybean oil quite often. If you'd like to get more soy foods into your diet, here are descriptions of a few and how to use them.

***Regular tofu (Chinese tofu; bean curd):*** Made from ground and boiled soybeans, tofu is essentially curdled soy milk. It is made into rectangular blocks much like curdled cow's milk is made into cheese. Regular tofu comes in three textures: soft, firm, and extra firm. Look for it packed with water in plastic tubs in the refrigerated produce section of your supermarket. Tofu is generally very mild and takes well to marinades before cooking. Premarinated and baked tofu is now available in many supermarkets.

Once opened, tofu can be refrigerated for about 5 days. Place the tofu in a container, cover with water, and put on the lid. For best freshness, change the water every 1 to 2 days. Before using, drain the tofu and squeeze it dry for a firmer texture. Wrap the tofu in several layers of paper towels and gently press between your hands over a sink to remove excess water.

Regular tofu can also be frozen for a firmer texture. Wrap the drained block of tofu in plastic and freeze for up to 6 months. The color will change to a darker beige and the consistency will become more crumbly. Thaw and squeeze dry before using.

*Uses (fresh):* Marinated and grilled, broiled, baked, browned, sautéed, or stir-fried

Mashed for use in casseroles (as you would use ricotta cheese)

*Uses (frozen):* Crumbled and browned in a skillet for use in soups, stews, or casseroles (as you would use ground beef)

***Silken tofu (Japanese tofu; bean curd):*** This is a softer version of regular tofu. The soy milk for silken tofu is strained through silk to produce a more creamy, silky texture. This type of tofu is not as well suited to marinating and dry-heat cooking as regular tofu. But it is very well suited to creamy soups, dips, sauces, and dressings. It comes in aseptic packages that do not need refrigeration until after opening. Once opened, silken tofu should be stored as regular tofu is: Place it in a container, cover with water, put on the lid, and refrigerate for 3 to 5 days. Change the water every 1 to 2 days.

*Uses:* Cubed for use in soups

Pureed for use in creamy soups, sauces, and dips

Pureed for use in baking (as you would use sour cream or yogurt)

***All-vegetable protein products:*** Available in the freezer or refrigerated sections, these foods are made from vegetable protein (translation: soybeans) and come in several varieties. Beef-flavored ones come in burgers or "crumbles," which can be used as a substitute for ground beef. Sausage flavors come in links or patties with varieties such as Mexican or herb-flavored. Chicken flavors come in breaded nuggets or patties. Once you get them home, these meat substitutes can be frozen for about 4 months. Quality and flavors vary widely, so try different brands to find your favorite.

*Uses:* Cooked and served according to package directions

Added to pasta sauces, casseroles, soups, and stews

***Soy milk:*** A creamy liquid made by boiling soybeans and pressing out the "milk." The milk is then cooked further to remove the strong bean flavor. Most soy milks are made from organically grown soybeans and are sometimes fortified with calcium and vitamin D. Soy milks also come in vanilla or chocolate flavors. Again, the quality and flavors vary widely among brands. Experiment to find a soy milk that tastes good to you.

Soy milk can be found in most large supermarkets and health food stores. Often packaged in aseptic containers, it can be stored unopened until the expiration date on the label. After opening, refrigerate for up to 1 week. When adding cold soy milk to hot liquids (such as coffee), warm the milk first in the microwave oven so that it doesn't curdle when it hits the hot liquid.

*Uses:* For drinking, in coffee, or over cereal

In baking, as a replacement for cow's milk in a 1 to 1 ratio

***Soy butter:*** Soy butter is like peanut butter but made from roasted soybeans. The flavor is similar to that of peanut butter but stronger. Use soy butter however you would use peanut butter. Store in the refrigerator after opening.

*Uses:* In sandwiches, sauces, and spreads

***Soy flour:*** Soy flour is made from dried soybeans ground into flour. When added to baked goods, this flour adds additional protein. Soy flour also contains a bit more fat than most flours, which makes it a good addition to low-fat baked goods because it tenderizes the final product.

***Texturized vegetable protein (TVP):*** TVP, also referred to as vegetable-protein crumbles in the recipes, is soy flour that is compressed into dried chunks or small grains. It is low in fat and high in calcium. Use it in place of ground beef. Meat-lovers tend to like TVP because it has a chewy, meaty texture. TVP comes dry, so it must be reconstituted in hot, flavored liquids or simmered in soups or stews. It takes on the flavor of whatever it's cooked

## Lean Cuts

Many vegetarians don't know the first thing about buying meat. And people who want to eat more healthfully often ask me to point them toward the leanest cuts. Here they are. I use these to keep fat and calories low when adding meat to a vegetarian dish.

**Beef:** Tenderloin, sirloin, top round, eye of round, tip round, flank steak, chuck shoulder

**Pork:** Tenderloin, sirloin chops, top loin chops, loin roast, and lean boneless ham

**Lamb:** Loin chop, blade chops, sirloin roast, foreshank, whole leg

with. Most health food stores and some large supermarkets carry it. Store TVP in an airtight container at room temperature indefinitely.

*Uses:* Simmered in chili or sloppy joes (as you would with ground beef)

Reconstituted in hot flavored liquids to make loaves, patties, or meatballs (as you would with ground beef)

***Tempeh (TEM-pay):*** A traditional Indonesian soy food made from cooked fermented soybeans that are pressed into patties. Sometimes grains such as rice are mixed in. Because it is fermented, tempeh has a stronger flavor and firmer texture than tofu. Tempeh is also higher in fiber and lower in fat than both tofu and soy milk. It takes well to marinades and tends to absorb the flavor of whatever it's cooked with. Health food stores and large supermarkets stock it in the refrigerator or freezer sections. Don't be alarmed if you see tiny black spots on the surface of tempeh. This simply means that the beneficial enzymes are still intact.

*Uses:* Cooked and served according to package directions

Crumbled into soups, stews, or chili

***Miso:*** Fermented soybean paste with a sharp, salty flavor. Miso is made by fermenting soybeans in cedar kegs with grains such as rice or barley for several years. It can be found refrigerated in large supermarkets, health food stores, or Asian markets. Once opened, miso can be stored in the refrigerator for up to 8 months. When using with hot liquids such as soups, add miso near the end of the cooking time by transferring some of the liquid to a small bowl, dissolving the miso in the liquid, then adding the mixture back to the pot.

## Doneness Temperatures

Here's a key rule in food safety: Thoroughly cook your food. Most recipes come with cooking times (including mine). But cooking times can change as a result of varying oven temperatures, slow or fast clocks, and other factors. It helps to have a doneness test, especially if you don't cook meat often (or even if you do!). To be on the safe side, here are doneness tests for beef, pork, poultry, fish, shellfish, and lamb.

The most accurate test is done with an instant-read thermometer to get a temperature reading. These thermometers are available in kitchen stores. You can also do a visual or tenderness check. One or both methods are listed below for common foods. When using an instant-read thermometer, insert it into the center or thickest portion of the meat for the most accurate reading. Note that roasts and whole birds should stand 10 minutes before slicing.

| Meat | Doneness Test |
|---|---|
| **Beef** | |
| Ground (loose) | No longer pink |
| Ground (in loaf or patties) | 160°F, no longer pink |
| Roasts | 145°F (medium-rare) |
| | 160°F (medium) |
| | 165°F (well-done) |
| Long-cooking pot roasts | Fork-tender |
| **Pork** | |
| Chops | 160°F, juices run clear |
| Roasts | 155°F, juices run clear |

*Uses:* Stirred into soups, sauces, gravies, or dressings (as you would soy sauce, anchovy paste, or salt)

Pureed into pesto (as you would Parmesan cheese)

***Meats:*** For those who don't buy meat often, it's somewhat comforting to know that today's meat labels are standardized. Meat labels will always list the weight of the package, price per pound, cost, and name of the cut.

| Meat | Doneness Test |
|---|---|
| **Chicken** | |
| Boneless breasts | 160°F, juices run clear |
| Bone-in parts | 170°F, juices run clear |
| Whole | 180°F (breast), juices run clear, 165° for stuffing |
| Ground (loose) | No longer pink |
| Ground (in loaf or patties) | 165°F, no longer pink |
| **Turkey** | |
| Breasts | 170°F, juices run clear |
| Whole | 180°F for breast, 165°F for stuffing |
| Ground (loose) | No longer pink |
| Ground (in loaf or patties) | 165°F, no longer pink |
| **Fish** | |
| Fillets | Fish flakes easily |
| Steaks | Fish is just opaque |
| **Shellfish** | |
| Shrimp, scallops, lobster | Shellfish is opaque |
| Clams, mussels, oysters | The shells open (discard any unopened shells) |
| **Lamb** | |
| Chops, roasts | 145°F (medium-rare) |

The name of the cut will include the part of the animal that the cut comes from. I often look for lean cuts, such as tenderloin or sirloin. I also trim off any visible fat from the surface. Good-quality meat is marbled with enough interior fat to keep it tender, so trim the surface of these cuts the best you can. Plan on buying about 4 ounces of meat (uncooked) per person.

*"No meal is as good as when you have your feet under your own table."*

—Scott Nearing, U.S. naturalist

# *Menus for Everyday Occasions*

A GREAT MEAL is not always the result of spending long hours in the kitchen. Sometimes, the best meals are the simplest. One of the most memorable meals I've ever eaten consisted only of Feta Bruschetta (page 63), red wine, and a piece of Dried-Cherry Spiral Bread (page 273). Late one afternoon, a close friend had stopped by unexpectedly and I pulled together the bruschetta for us to munch on. We got to talking, enjoying the bruschetta, and laughing about who knows what. Just as the sun was setting, I cut us each a piece of the dried cherry bread (which I had made the previous day for my kids). There was a brief lull in the conversation when we both sat back, looked out the window at the sunset, and simply enjoyed the act itself of eating.

It's not always the food that makes a meal memorable, but the people with whom you share it. I always try to keep that in mind, whether I'm putting together an impromptu lunch for 2 or a holiday dinner for 12.

Here are a few of the everyday menus that I rely on for family dinners and casual get-togethers with friends. I included one or two more elaborate menus for special occasions. Think of these menus as starting points and personalize them as needed.

Notice that bread or biscuit recipes appear with many of the meals here. Most of these are pretty simple, like Skillet Oat Bread (page 262). But if the thought of making any kind of bread scares you, you can always pick up a similar type of bread at your local bakery.

These menus will serve four people generously. If you need to serve more, just double or triple the recipes. And if you have a mixed crowd of vegetarians and meat-lovers, satisfy everyone at the table by following the "Quick Conversions" in each recipe.

**Mexican Night**

Pepper Salsa (page 289)
Tortilla chips
Vegetable-Tortilla Bake (page 115)
Mixed-Bean Tacos (page 130)
Fresh fruit drizzled with honey and lime juice

**Casual Pasta Dinner**

Crispy Caesar Salad (page 97)
Hearty Vegetarian Bolognese (page 215)
Italian bread
Cheesecake with fresh berries

**Come Over for the Game**

Eggplant Spread (page 293)
Pita triangles
Bean Chili over Grilled Polenta (page 88)
Roquefort Focaccia (page 149)
Popcorn Balls (page 58)
Assorted cookies

**Spring Lunch**

Gazpacho with Avocado Salsa (page 78)
Cheddar Crisps (page 260)
Grilled Portobello Sandwiches (page 132)
Watercress-Apple Salad (page 101)
Lemon bars

**Brunch**

Muesli (page 41)
Yogurt
Cheesy Eggs (page 170)
Skillet Oat Bread (page 262)
Dried Fruit Butter (page 291)
Fresh melon wedges

**BBQ**

Macaroni-Bean Salad (page 100)
Grilled Tempeh with Sour Cream (page 171)
Lemon-Marinated Vegetable Kabobs (page 113)

Parmesan Cheese Flatbread (page 261)
Brownies

### Sit-Down Dinner

Ricotta-Stuffed Tomatoes (page 50)
Creamy Mushroom Soup (page 74)
Onion Flatbread (page 61)
Shells with Radicchio and Romano (page 206)
Rainbow of fruit sorbets

### Kids' Favorite Meal

Cheddar Cheese Bread (page 269)
Baked Elbows with Three Cheeses (page 226)
Carrot and celery sticks
Peanut Butter Oat Snacks (page 59)

### Asian Evening

Wonton Soup with Ginger (page 80)
Spicy Asian Slaw (page 96)
Rice-Filled Pot Stickers (page 244)
Sesame Dipping Sauce (page 286)
Fortune cookies

### Pizza Night

Salad greens with Berry Vinegar (page 286)
Caponata Pizza (page 120)
Baked Ziti Pizza (page 119)
Biscotti

### Pack a Kid's Lunch

Peanut Butter and Raisin Spirals (page 138)
Ranch Snack Mix (page 57)
Apple slices with Dried Fruit Butter (page 291)
Juice box

### Cold Winter's Night

Roasted Red Pepper Soup (page 73)
Whole Wheat–Caraway Biscuit Squares (page 268)
Lentil and Vegetable Shepherd's Pie (page 256)
Apple pie

### Monday through Friday Dinner

Skillet Rice and Beans (page 156)
Good-for-Toasting Wheat Bread (page 276)
Cauliflower with Citrus Vinaigrette (page 104)
Berry Applesauce (page 47)

### Summer Supper

Honey-Melon Soup (page 77)
Southwestern Wrap (page 138)
Tangy Potato Salad (page 99)
Frozen yogurt with fresh berries

### Fall Dinner

Stuffed Acorn Squash (page 112)
Quick Cassoulet (page 193)
Honey-Rye Bread (page 278)
Brussels Sprouts with Roasted Red Peppers (page 106)
Pumpkin pie

### Special Winter Dinner

Feta Bruschetta (page 63)
Creamy Tomato Soup (page 75)
Braised Winter Vegetables (page 111)
Polenta Torte (page 187)
Poached pears

### Kid's Birthday Party

Spicy Sweet Potato Chips (page 57)
Peanut Butter Spread (page 69)
Fruit and Nut Sandwiches (page 137)
Egg Salad Cone Cups (page 69)
Ice cream cake

### Special Spring Dinner

Field greens with Berry Vinegar (page 286)
Cavatelli with Asparagus (page 213)
Molasses-Corn Yeast Bread (page 280)
Yogurt-Cheese Tomato Spread (page 292)
Assorted crackers
Mixed berries

### Spaghetti Night

Sliced tomato and mozzarella
Sun-Dried Tomato Triangles (page 56)
Hot cooked spaghetti with Mexican Marinara Sauce (page 285) and Veggie Meatballs (page 173)
Assorted cookies

### Soup and Sandwich

Quick Noodle Soup (page 83)
Hummus-Pumpernickel Club (page 135)
Sliced bell peppers
Fruit juice bar

### Light Dinner

Papaya Quesadillas (page 62)
Cauliflower with Citrus Vinaigrette (page 104)
Iced herbal tea
Arrowroot cookies

### Come Over for the Oscars

Air-popped popcorn
Hot Pizza Dip (page 51)
Sliced Italian bread
Eggplant Lasagne (page 183)
Frozen yogurt sundaes

### Breakfast on the Go

Sunflower Granola (page 42)
Orange Muffins (page 39)
Banana
Hazelnut coffee

*"Measure your health by your sympathy with morning and spring."*

—Henry David Thoreau, U.S. philosopher, author, and naturalist

# Fresh Starts



**Mornings in our house** change from day to day. During the week, it's usually pretty rushed. I'm busy getting our daughter Rachel to school. And my husband, Daniel, rushes around getting himself to work (in between tickling our younger daughter, Samantha). But weekends are another story. I make breakfast more special on Saturday and Sunday, even if we have other things to do. This chapter has recipes for both time-crunched and laid-back mornings. Either way, many recipes can be made ahead. And if the early hours are not your time for trying out new recipes, who says you can't enjoy pancakes for dinner or a shake for a midday snack?

## Recipes

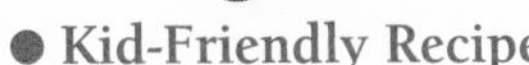

● Kid-Friendly Recipe

● Freezable Recipe

● Microwaveable Recipe

# Potato-Mushroom Omelette

- **1 teaspoon olive oil**
- **2 red potatoes, cut into small cubes**
- **1 red onion, finely chopped**
- **4 ounces mushrooms, sliced**
- **½ teaspoon dried thyme**
- **4 eggs**
- **4 egg whites**
- **⅓ cup 1% milk**
- **¼ teaspoon salt**
- **⅛ teaspoon ground black pepper**
- **¼ cup (1 ounce) shredded reduced-fat Swiss cheese**

WARM THE OIL in a large nonstick skillet over medium heat. Add the potatoes, onion, and mushrooms. Cook, stirring frequently, for 10 to 12 minutes, or until the potatoes are tender. Sprinkle with the thyme and cook for 1 minute longer.

MEANWHILE, in a medium bowl, combine the eggs, egg whites, milk, salt, and pepper.

TRANSFER THE POTATO MIXTURE to a small bowl. Coat the skillet with nonstick spray and warm over medium heat. Pour in one-quarter of the egg mixture and swirl the pan to coat the bottom. As soon as the bottom of the egg mixture is set, lift the edges with a small spatula and tilt the skillet, letting the uncooked egg run underneath. Cook for 30 seconds longer.

SPRINKLE ONE-QUARTER OF THE VEGETABLES and 1 tablespoon of the cheese over the egg mixture. Fold to enclose the filling. Transfer to a plate. Repeat with the remaining egg mixture, vegetables, and cheese, recoating the skillet with spray as needed.

**Makes 4**

***Per omelette:*** *186 calories, 15 g. protein, 15 g. carbohydrates, 7 g. fat, 216 mg. cholesterol, 298 mg. sodium, 1 g. dietary fiber*

## Quick Conversion

**Potato-Mushroom Omelette with Smoked Turkey:** For a dual vegetarian/nonvegetarian dish, prepare the recipe with the following changes. For each smoked turkey portion, arrange 3 ounces of minced cooked smoked deli turkey over the potato mixture. Top with the cheese.

# Tomato and Egg Muffins

- 8 eggs
- ¼ cup finely chopped scallions
- 2 tablespoons 1% milk
- 1 teaspoon Dijon mustard
- ⅛ teaspoon ground red pepper
- 1 teaspoon canola oil
- 4 sourdough or plain English muffins, split
- 1 large tomato, cut into 8 slices
- ½ cup (2 ounces) shredded reduced-fat Monterey Jack cheese

PREHEAT the broiler.

IN A MEDIUM BOWL, combine the eggs, scallions, milk, mustard, and pepper.

WARM THE OIL in a large nonstick skillet over medium heat. Add the egg mixture and cook, stirring occasionally with a spatula, for 4 to 5 minutes, or until scrambled.

MEANWHILE, place the muffin halves on a baking sheet. Broil for 1 minute, or until lightly browned. Remove from the oven.

DIVIDE THE EGG MIXTURE evenly among the muffin halves. Top each with a tomato slice and 1 tablespoon cheese. Broil for 1 minute, or until the cheese melts.

**Makes 4 servings**

***Per serving:*** *240 calories, 18 g. protein, 8 g. carbohydrates, 15 g. fat, 436 mg. cholesterol, 242 mg. sodium, 1 g. dietary fiber*

## Quick Conversion

**Tomato and Egg Muffins with Bacon:** For a dual vegetarian/nonvegetarian dish, prepare the recipe with the following changes. For the bacon portion, cook 4 strips of bacon in a medium nonstick skillet for 5 to 8 minutes, or until crisp. Transfer to a plate lined with paper towels. Divide the bacon among 4 of the muffin halves. Top with the eggs, tomato, and cheese and bake as directed. You can also use 4 slices of Canadian bacon in place of strip bacon.

# Italian Strata

- **2** **cups cubed Italian bread**
- **1** **package (10 ounces) frozen chopped broccoli, thawed**
- **1** **tomato, chopped**
- **1** **cup (4 ounces) shredded fontina cheese**
- **4** **eggs**
- **¼** **cup 1% milk**
- **2** **tablespoons (½ ounce) grated Parmesan cheese**
- **2** **tablespoons chopped fresh basil or 2 teaspoons dried**
- **¼** **teaspoon salt**
- **⅛** **teaspoon ground black pepper**

PREHEAT THE OVEN TO 375°F. Coat an 11" × 7" baking dish with nonstick spray.

COMBINE THE BREAD CUBES, broccoli, and tomato in the prepared dish.

IN A SMALL BOWL, combine the fontina, eggs, milk, Parmesan, basil, salt, and pepper. Pour over the bread cubes.

BAKE FOR 25 TO 30 MINUTES, or until set and the top is golden.

**Makes 8 servings**

***Per serving:*** *285 calories, 15 g. protein, 34 g. carbohydrates, 10 g. fat, 125 mg. cholesterol, 615 mg. sodium, 3 g. dietary fiber*

## Quick Conversion

**Italian Strata with Prosciutto:** For a dual vegetarian/nonvegetarian dish, prepare the recipe with the following changes. Divide the bread cubes, broccoli, and tomato between two 1-quart baking dishes. For the prosciutto portion, stir in ¼ pound slivered prosciutto. Divide the egg mixture between the 2 portions. Bake for 20 to 25 minutes, or until set and the top is golden. (To make both portions in one baking dish, arrange the prosciutto on one side of the dish underneath the vegetables. Pour on the eggs and bake as directed.)

# Baked French Toast with Crumb Topping

- 2 eggs
- ½ cup 1% milk
- ¼ cup orange juice
- 8 slices egg bread (½" thick)
- 1 cup crushed honey or plain cornflake crumbs

PREHEAT THE OVEN TO 350°F. Coat a large nonstick baking sheet with nonstick spray.

IN A SHALLOW BOWL, whisk the eggs, milk, and orange juice. Dip 1 bread slice at a time into the mixture, turning to coat both sides.

PLACE THE CRUMBS on a large piece of waxed paper. Coat the bread on both sides, pressing gently to ensure the crumbs stick.

BAKE FOR 6 TO 8 MINUTES, or until the underside is golden. Carefully turn and bake for 4 minutes longer, or until the top is golden brown.

**Makes 4 servings**

***Per serving (2 slices):*** *367 calories, 14 g. protein, 60 g. carbohydrates, 8 g. fat, 148 mg. cholesterol, 681 mg. sodium, 2 g. dietary fiber*

**Tip:** If you're using plain cornflake crumbs and want honey flavor, stir 1 tablespoon honey into the egg mixture. I sometimes stir ¼ teaspoon ground cinnamon into the eggs, too.

# Apple Pancakes

- 1 cup all-purpose flour
- ¼ cup whole wheat flour
- 2 teaspoons baking powder
- ½ teaspoon pumpkin pie spice
- 1 small green apple, pared and finely chopped
- 1⅓ cups 1% buttermilk
- 1 large egg
- 1 tablespoon vegetable oil
- 1 tablespoon honey
- Confectioners' sugar (optional)

IN A LARGE BOWL, combine the all-purpose flour, whole wheat flour, baking powder, and pumpkin pie spice. Gently stir in the apple.

IN A SMALL BOWL, combine the buttermilk, egg, oil, and honey. Stir into the flour mixture just until combined. Batter will be lumpy.

COAT A LARGE SKILLET or griddle with nonstick spray and warm over medium heat. For each pancake, pour ¼ cup batter into the skillet. Cook for 2 minutes, or until the tops are bubbly and the edges just begin to look dry. Flip and cook for 2 to 3 minutes longer, or until golden. Repeat with the remaining batter, recoating the skillet with spray as needed. Served topped with confectioners' sugar, if using.

**Makes 4 servings**

***Per serving (3 pancakes):*** *258 calories, 9 g. protein, 43 g. carbohydrates, 6 g. fat, 56 mg. cholesterol, 303 mg. sodium, 3 g. dietary fiber*

**Tip:** These pancakes can be frozen for up to 3 weeks. Stack cooled pancakes with waxed paper between each layer. Wrap the stack in foil or freezer wrap, or place in a freezer bag. To use, toast while still frozen.

## Quick Conversion

**Apple-Ham Pancakes:** For a dual vegetarian/nonvegetarian dish, prepare the recipe with the following changes. Divide the completed batter between 2 bowls. For the ham portion, stir 1 ounce minced lean deli ham (about 1 thin slice) into one of the bowls.

# Molasses-Bran Waffles

- 1 cup all-purpose flour
- ½ cup crushed bran flake cereal
- 2 teaspoons baking powder
- 1 teaspoon baking soda
- 1¼ cups 1% buttermilk
- 2 large eggs, lightly beaten
- 2 tablespoons butter or margarine, melted
- 2 tablespoons light molasses
- 1 teaspoon vanilla extract
- Confectioners' sugar

PREHEAT THE WAFFLE IRON according to the manufacturer's directions.

IN A LARGE BOWL, combine the flour, cereal, baking powder, and baking soda.

IN A SMALL BOWL, combine the buttermilk, eggs, butter or margarine, molasses, and vanilla. Pour into the flour mixture, stirring just until combined.

LADLE ENOUGH BATTER onto the waffle iron to come within 1" of the edges. Cover and bake according to the manufacturer's directions. To serve, sprinkle with the confectioners' sugar.

REPEAT with the remaining batter.

**Makes 8**

***Per waffle:*** *141 calories, 5 g. protein, 19 g. carbohydrates, 5 g. fat, 63 mg. cholesterol, 334 mg. sodium, 1 g. dietary fiber*

**Tip:** These waffles can be frozen in a freezer bag for up to 1 month. To use, toast while still frozen.

# Lemon-Poppy Muffins

- 2 cups all-purpose flour
- ⅓ cup sugar
- 1 tablespoon poppy seeds
- 1 teaspoon baking powder
- 1 teaspoon baking soda
- 1 cup (8 ounces) reduced-fat lemon yogurt
- 1 egg
- 2 tablespoons lemon juice
- 2 tablespoons vegetable oil
- 1 tablespoon grated lemon peel

PREHEAT THE OVEN TO 400°F. Coat 12 muffin cups with nonstick spray.

IN A LARGE BOWL, combine the flour, sugar, poppy seeds, baking powder, and baking soda.

IN A MEDIUM BOWL, combine the yogurt, egg, lemon juice, oil, and lemon peel. Stir into the flour mixture just until moistened.

DIVIDE THE BATTER evenly among the prepared cups. Bake for 12 to 14 minutes, or until the tops are golden and a toothpick inserted in the center comes out clean.

COOL IN THE PAN on a rack for 10 minutes. Remove the muffins and let cool completely on the rack.

**Makes 12**

***Per muffin:*** *146 calories, 4 g. protein, 25 g. carbohydrates, 3 g. fat, 19 mg. cholesterol, 159 mg. sodium, 1 g. dietary fiber*

**Tip:** These muffins can be frozen in a freezer bag for up to 3 months. To use, thaw in the refrigerator or wrap in a microwaveable paper towel and microwave on low power for 25 to 35 seconds, or just until thawed.

# Orange Muffins

- 2 cups all-purpose flour
- ¼ cup sugar
- 1 tablespoon grated orange peel
- 1 teaspoon baking powder
- 1 teaspoon baking soda
- ½ teaspoon ground cinnamon
- 1¼ teaspoons salt
- ½ cup raisins or fresh blueberries
- 1 cup (8 ounces) reduced-fat vanilla yogurt
- ¼ cup orange juice
- 1 large egg
- 2 tablespoons butter, melted

PREHEAT THE OVEN TO 400°F. Coat 12 muffin cups with nonstick spray.

IN A LARGE BOWL, combine the flour, sugar, orange peel, baking powder, baking soda, cinnamon, and salt. Gently stir in the raisins or blueberries.

IN A MEDIUM BOWL, combine the yogurt, orange juice, egg, and butter. Stir into the flour mixture just until moistened.

DIVIDE THE BATTER evenly among the prepared cups. Bake for 10 to 12 minutes, or until a toothpick inserted in the center comes out clean.

COOL IN THE PAN on a rack for 10 minutes. Remove the muffins and let cool completely on the rack.

**Makes 12**

***Per muffin:*** *156 calories, 4 g. protein, 29 g. carbohydrates, 3 g. fat, 25 mg. cholesterol, 208 mg. sodium, 1 g. dietary fiber*

**Tip:** These muffins can be frozen in a freezer bag for up to 3 months. To use, thaw in the refrigerator or wrap in a microwaveable paper towel and microwave on low power for 25 to 35 seconds, or just until thawed.

## Quick Morning Food

On some mornings, finding even 10 minutes to eat a bowl of cereal can be a struggle. That's when I whip up these easy fixes. I keep the Ricotta Spread in the fridge to top bagels or toast. The Peach Take-Along Shake comes together in no time for a quick on-the-run breakfast. And if you have children in tow, take along a kid-size breakfast of pita halves spread with flavored cream cheese and stuffed with their favorite dry cereal.

### Ricotta Spread

- **1 cup (8 ounces) reduced-fat ricotta cheese**
- **2 tablespoons 1% milk**
- **1 tablespoon confectioners' sugar**
- **½ teaspoon ground cinnamon**
- **½ cup raisins**

IN A BLENDER or mini food processor, combine the cheese, milk, sugar, and cinnamon. Blend or process until smooth, scraping down the sides as needed. Stir in the raisins.

**Makes about 1 cup**

***Per 2 tablespoons:*** *75 calories, 4 g. protein, 10 g. carbohydrates, 3 g. fat, 10 mg. cholesterol, 41 mg. sodium, 0 g. dietary fiber*

**Tip:** This spread can be refrigerated in a tightly covered container for up to 1 week.

### Peach Take-Along Shake

- **2 cups (16 ounces) reduced-fat lemon yogurt**
- **2 cups mixed fruit juice blend**
- **2 cups coarsely chopped fresh or thawed frozen peaches**
- **2 teaspoons honey**
- **2 ice cubes**

IN A BLENDER, combine the yogurt, juice blend, peaches, honey, and ice cubes. Blend just until smooth and creamy.

**Makes 2 servings**

***Per serving:*** *119 calories, 14 g. protein, 138 g. carbohydrates, 4 g. fat, 17 mg. cholesterol, 197 mg. sodium, 5 g. dietary fiber*

**Tip:** When I'm really busy, I pour this refreshing breakfast-in-a-glass into my travel mug and enjoy it on the way.

# Muesli

In a large bowl, combine the milk, dried fruit, oats, brown sugar, and cinnamon. Cover and refrigerate 15 minutes.

Spoon ½ cup yogurt into each of 4 parfait glasses. Top with the oat mixture and walnuts.

**Makes 4 servings**

***Per serving:*** *397 calories, 12 g. protein, 49 g. carbohydrates, 18 g. fat, 9 mg. cholesterol, 108 mg. sodium, 3 g. dietary fiber*

- **½ cup 1% milk**
- **½ cup coarsely chopped mixed dried fruit**
- **⅓ cup quick-cooking oats**
- **2 tablespoons packed brown sugar**
- **½ teaspoon ground cinnamon**
- **2 cups (16 ounces) reduced-fat vanilla yogurt**
- **¼ cup coarsely chopped walnuts**

# Cinnamon-Apple Cereal

In a 2-quart saucepan, combine the oats, apple juice, milk, apple or pear, vanilla, and cinnamon. Bring to a boil over medium heat. Reduce the heat to low. Cook, stirring constantly, for 2 to 3 minutes, or until the fruit is tender and the oats are cooked.

Stir in the yogurt. Cook for 1 minute over low heat, or until heated through.

**Makes 4 servings**

***Per serving:*** *176 calories, 6 g. protein, 32 g. carbohydrates, 3 g. fat, 4 mg. cholesterol, 54 mg. sodium, 3 g. dietary fiber*

- **1 cup quick-cooking oats**
- **¾ cup apple juice**
- **1 cup 1% milk**
- **1 apple or pear, chopped**
- **1 teaspoon vanilla extract**
- **¼ teaspoon ground cinnamon**
- **½ cup (4 ounces) reduced-fat vanilla or cinnamon-apple yogurt**

# Sunflower Granola

- **4** **cups rolled oats**
- **1** **cup honey-flavored wheat germ**
- **1** **cup oat bran**
- **½** **cup unsalted sunflower seeds**
- **¾** **cup coarsely chopped mixed dried fruit (such as apples and apricots)**
- **¼** **cup packed brown sugar**
- **2** **tablespoons melted butter or margarine**
- **2** **tablespoons thawed apple juice concentrate**

PREHEAT THE OVEN TO 300°F. Coat two 15" × 10" jelly-roll pans with nonstick spray.

IN A LARGE BOWL, combine the oats, wheat germ, oat bran, sunflower seeds, and dried fruit.

IN A SMALL MICROWAVEABLE BOWL, combine the brown sugar, butter or margarine, and juice concentrate. Microwave on high power for 1 minute. Stir well. Stir into the oat mixture.

SPREAD THINLY OVER THE PREPARED PANS. Bake for 15 to 20 minutes, or until golden brown, stirring once. Cool completely and store in airtight containers.

**Makes 8 cups**

***Per cup:*** *444 calories, 25 g. protein, 79 g. carbohydrates, 14 g. fat, 0 mg. cholesterol, 44 mg. sodium, 10 g. dietary fiber*

# Fruit Fritters

- 2 large eggs
- ⅔ cup 1% milk
- 2 teaspoons lemon juice
- 1 teaspoon + 3 tablespoons vegetable oil
- 1 teaspoon confectioners' sugar
- 1 cup all-purpose flour
- 1 teaspoon baking powder
- 5 cups fruit (bananas, apples, strawberries, peaches), cut into bite-size pieces

WHISK THE EGGS in a large bowl until light and lemon-colored. Gradually whisk in the milk, lemon juice, 1 teaspoon oil, and confectioners' sugar. Stir in the flour and baking powder until smooth. Refrigerate for at least 30 minutes.

Warm the remaining 3 tablespoons oil in a large heavy skillet over high heat. Pat dry the fruit pieces with a paper towel. Holding 1 piece of fruit at a time with a fork or tongs, dip the pieces into the egg-flour mixture, letting the excess drain back into the bowl. Carefully place in the skillet, making sure not to crowd the pieces. Cook in batches for 2 minutes on each side, or until golden brown. Transfer to paper towels.

**Makes 8 servings**

***Per serving:*** *192 calories, 5 g. protein, 27 g. carbohydrates, 7 g. fat, 54 mg. cholesterol, 76 mg. sodium, 2 g. dietary fiber*

**Tip:** To keep the fritters warm, place them in a preheated 250°F oven. I like these best when they're dusted with cinnamon sugar. You can also serve them with maple syrup or a sprinkling of confectioners' sugar.

# Couscous-Banana Breakfast Pudding

- 1 cup water
- ½ cup couscous
- 1½ cups (12 ounces) reduced-fat vanilla yogurt
- 2 small bananas, thinly sliced
- 2 peaches, sliced
- 1 tablespoon packed brown sugar
- 1 teaspoon lemon juice
- ½ teaspoon ground cinnamon
- 1 tablespoon shredded coconut, toasted

BRING THE WATER TO A BOIL over high heat. Remove from the heat and stir in the couscous. Let stand for 5 minutes. Fluff with a fork.

IN A LARGE BOWL, combine the couscous, yogurt, bananas, peaches, brown sugar, lemon juice, and cinnamon. Cover and refrigerate for 30 to 60 minutes to blend the flavors.

SPOON INTO INDIVIDUAL DISHES and top with the coconut.

**Makes 4 servings**

***Per serving:*** *262 calories, 8 g. protein, 55 g. carbohydrates, 2 g. fat, 6 mg. cholesterol, 71 mg. sodium, 4 g. dietary fiber*

# Soy Milk Smoothie

- 2 cups soy milk or 1% cow's milk
- 1 pint strawberries, hulled and halved
- 1 small frozen banana, cut into small pieces
- 2 teaspoons sugar
- ¼ teaspoon ground cinnamon

IN A BLENDER OR FOOD PROCESSOR, combine the soy milk or cow's milk, strawberries, banana, sugar, and cinnamon. Blend or process until smooth and creamy.

**Makes 4 servings**

***Per serving:*** *96 calories, 4 g. protein, 16 g. carbohydrates, 3 g. fat, 0 mg. cholesterol, 15 mg. sodium, 4 g. dietary fiber*

**Tip:** I keep a couple of ripe bananas in the freezer for shakes like this one. For ***Strawberry-Banana Soft Ice Cream***, use 2 frozen bananas, 2 cups frozen strawberries, and ½ cup to 1 cup milk as needed. Proceed as directed and serve immediately.

# Autumn Baked Fruit

- **2** **Bosc pears, peeled and sliced**
- **2** **apples, peeled and sliced**
- **1** **cup chopped mixed dried fruit**
- **1** **cup orange juice**
- **½** **cup apricot all-fruit spread**
- **1** **teaspoon pumpkin pie spice**
- **½** **cup crushed vanilla wafer crumbs**
- **Vanilla or lemon yogurt (optional)**
- **Pancakes or waffles (optional)**

PREHEAT THE OVEN TO 350°F.

ARRANGE THE PEARS, apples, and dried fruit in an 11" × 7" baking dish.

IN A SMALL BOWL, combine the orange juice, fruit spread, and pumpkin pie spice. Pour over the fruit.

BAKE FOR 20 TO 30 MINUTES, or until the fruit is tender, stirring occasionally. Sprinkle the crumbs over the fruit. Bake for 10 minutes. Serve plain or atop yogurt, pancakes, or waffles, if using.

**Makes 8 servings**

***Per serving:*** *226 calories, 2 g. protein, 50 g. carbohydrates, 4 g. fat, 0 mg. cholesterol, 65 mg. sodium, 4 g. dietary fiber*

**Tip:** This baked fruit compote warms up the kitchen on chilly fall mornings. I like it served simply over vanilla or lemon yogurt. My husband likes it on pancakes or waffles.

# Berry Applesauce 

- 6 **Golden Delicious apples, peeled and chopped**
- 2 **cups fresh or thawed frozen blueberries, raspberries, or strawberries**
- ½ **cup mixed-berry fruit juice blend**
- 3 **tablespoons packed brown sugar**
- ½ **teaspoon ground cinnamon**

IN A LARGE SAUCEPAN, combine the apples, berries, juice blend, brown sugar, and cinnamon. Cover and cook over medium-low heat, stirring frequently, for 20 to 30 minutes, or until the fruit is very tender.

TRANSFER TO A FOOD PROCESSOR and process until smooth. (If preferred, transfer to a large bowl and coarsely mash.) Cover and refrigerate until cold.

**Makes 8 servings**

***Per serving:*** *103 calories, 0 g. protein, 26 g. carbohydrates, 1 g. fat, 0 mg. cholesterol, 4 mg. sodium, 4 g. dietary fiber*

**Tip:** My kids love this fruity applesauce with pancakes and waffles.

*"'Nearly eleven o'clock,' said Pooh happily. 'You're just in time for a smackerel of something.'"*

—A. A. Milne, British author

# Great Little Bites

OURS IS A FAMILY OF NIBBLERS. Especially on weekends, we nosh here and snack there. Sometimes we have an appetizer before dinner. And we love to make a meal of nibbles when family or friends come over.

All of the snacks in this chapter are quick to assemble. The Popcorn Balls and Ranch Snack Mix make great midday munchies. Whet your appetite before the main event with Papaya Quesadillas or Feta Bruschetta. If guests are coming, Ricotta-Stuffed Tomatoes and Hot Pizza Dip are ready in no time.

I also included a few ultra-simple recipes for children to make. Whenever hunger strikes, kids can easily whip up Apple-Bagel Sandwich Melts or Egg Salad Cone Cups. For more spreads and sauces, see Dips, Dunks, and Slathers beginning on page 283.

## Recipes

● Kid-Friendly Recipe

● Freezable Recipe

● Microwaveable Recipe

# Ricotta-Stuffed Tomatoes

- **1 pint large cherry tomatoes**
- **½ cup (4 ounces) reduced-fat ricotta cheese**
- **¼ cup chopped fresh basil or 2 teaspoons dried**
- **2 tablespoons Italian salad dressing**
- **1 tablespoon marinated sun-dried tomato bits**
- **2 teaspoons chopped capers**
- **¼ teaspoon ground black pepper**

CUT A THIN SLICE OFF THE TOP of each tomato. Using a very small spoon or melon scoop, carefully scoop out the pulp, reserving a sturdy shell. Place the pulp in a medium bowl. Stir in the cheese, basil, dressing, sun-dried tomatoes, capers, and pepper.

SPOON INTO EACH TOMATO SHELL. Serve immediately.

**Makes 4 servings**

***Per serving:*** *84 calories, 5 g. protein, 6 g. carbohydrates, 5 g. fat, 5 mg. cholesterol, 169 mg. sodium, 1 g. dietary fiber*

**Tip:** These are good warm, too. Place the tomatoes in a baking dish. Bake at 350°F for 15 to 20 minutes, or until heated through.

## Quick Conversion

**Ricotta-Stuffed Tomatoes with Crabmeat:** For a dual vegetarian/nonvegetarian dish, prepare the recipe with the following changes. Divide the cheese mixture between 2 bowls. For the crab portion, stir in 2 tablespoons lump or imitation crabmeat.

# Hot Pizza Dip

- **8** **ounces reduced-fat cream cheese**
- **1** **teaspoon dried Italian seasoning**
- **¼** **teaspoon garlic powder**
- **½** **cup marinara sauce**
- **1** **can (4 ounces) mushrooms, drained**
- **1** **small red bell pepper, chopped**
- **1** **small tomato, chopped**
- **¾** **cup (3 ounces) shredded reduced-fat mozzarella cheese**
- **1** **tablespoon (¼ ounce) grated Parmesan cheese**
- **1** **tablespoon chopped fresh basil or 1 teaspoon dried**
- **Italian bread or crackers**

PREHEAT THE OVEN TO 350°F.

IN A MEDIUM BOWL, with a mixer at medium speed, beat the cream cheese, Italian seasoning, and garlic powder until smooth. Spread in a 9" pie plate. Top with the marinara sauce, mushrooms, pepper, and tomato. Sprinkle the mozzarella and Parmesan over the tomatoes.

BAKE FOR 15 TO 20 MINUTES, or until the cheese is melted. Top with the basil. Serve with the bread or crackers.

**Makes 8 servings**

***Per serving:*** *202 calories, 9 g. protein, 21 g. carbohydrates, 9 g. fat, 22 mg. cholesterol, 465 mg. sodium, 2 g. dietary fiber*

## Quick Conversion

**Hot Pizza Dip with Pepperoni:** For a dual vegetarian/nonvegetarian dish, prepare the recipe with the following changes. For the pepperoni portion, arrange 4 ounces thinly sliced pepperoni atop the tomatoes in half the pie plate. Top with the cheese and bake as directed.

# Chickpea Spread

- **1 can (15 ounces) chickpeas, rinsed and drained**
- **⅓ cup mixed-vegetable juice**
- **2 tablespoons fat-free plain yogurt**
- **2 tablespoons tahini or smooth natural peanut butter**
- **1 tablespoon chopped fresh cilantro or 1 teaspoon dried**
- **2 cloves garlic**
- **2 teaspoons balsamic vinegar**
- **2 scallions, chopped**
- **2 large pitas, cut into triangles**

In a food processor, combine the chickpeas, juice, yogurt, tahini or peanut butter, cilantro, garlic, and vinegar. Process until smooth, scraping down the sides of the bowl as necessary. Transfer to a small serving bowl. Cover and refrigerate for at least 30 minutes to blend the flavors.

Top with the scallions and serve with the pita triangles.

**Makes 8 servings**

***Per serving:*** *141 calories, 5 g. protein, 22 g. carbohydrates, 3 g. fat, 0 mg. cholesterol, 269 mg. sodium, 3 g. dietary fiber*

# Cilantro-Chile Dip

- **1** **cup (8 ounces) reduced-fat sour cream**
- **2** **ounces reduced-fat cream cheese**
- **¼** **cup chopped canned green chiles**
- **2** **tablespoons chopped fresh cilantro or parsley**
- **2** **tablespoons 1% milk**
- **1** **tablespoon lime juice**
- **1** **tablespoon minced onion**
- **⅛** **teaspoon ground red pepper**
- **Baked tortilla chips (optional)**

IN A SMALL BOWL, combine the sour cream, cream cheese, chiles, cilantro or parsley, milk, lime juice, onion, and pepper. Cover and refrigerate for at least 30 minutes to blend flavors. Serve with the tortilla chips, if using.

**Makes 4 servings**

***Per serving:*** *567 calories, 13 g. protein, 101 g. carbohydrates, 12 g. fat, 32 mg. cholesterol, 410 mg. sodium, 9 g. dietary fiber*

**Tip:** I like this mixture on top of baked potatoes, too.

# Hot Black Bean Picante Dip

- **1 can (15 ounces) black beans, rinsed and drained**
- **1 teaspoon olive oil**
- **6 scallions, chopped**
- **2 cloves garlic, minced**
- **1 teaspoon chili powder**
- **1 tomato, chopped**
- **½ cup picante sauce**
- **½ cup (4 ounces) shredded reduced-fat Cheddar cheese**
- **2 tablespoons chopped fresh cilantro or 2 teaspoons dried**
- **2 teaspoons lime juice**
- **¼ cup (2 ounces) reduced-fat sour cream**
- **Baked tortilla chips or pitas**

In a medium bowl, coarsely mash the beans.

Warm the oil in a medium nonstick skillet over medium heat. Add the scallions and garlic. Cook, stirring frequently, for 4 to 5 minutes, or until tender. Stir in the chili powder. Cook for 1 minute. Add the beans, tomato, and picante sauce. Cook over medium heat, stirring frequently, for 5 to 7 minutes, or until the mixture is thick. Remove from the heat. Stir in the cheese, cilantro, and lime juice.

Spoon into a bowl and top with the sour cream. Serve warm with the chips or pitas.

**Makes 8 servings**

***Per serving:*** *268 calories, 12 g. protein, 44 g. carbohydrates, 6 g. fat, 13 mg. cholesterol, 778 mg. sodium, 4 g. dietary fiber*

# Ricotta Toasts

- **8** **slices dry French bread (⅓" thick each)**
- **½** **cup (4 ounces) reduced-fat ricotta cheese**
- **¼** **cup seasoned dry bread crumbs**
- **2** **large egg whites, lightly beaten**
- **1** **tablespoon chopped fresh chives or 1 teaspoon dried**
- **1** **tablespoon (¼ ounce) grated Parmesan cheese**
- **¼** **teaspoon garlic powder**
- **¼** **teaspoon paprika**

PREHEAT THE BROILER. Place bread slices on a large broiler pan.

IN A MEDIUM BOWL, combine the ricotta, bread crumbs, egg whites, chives, Parmesan, and garlic powder. Spread over the bread slices. Sprinkle with the paprika.

BROIL FOR 2 TO 3 MINUTES, or until the ricotta mixture is golden and the edges of the bread begin to brown.

**Makes 4 servings**

***Per serving:*** *239 calories, 13 g. protein, 38 g. carbohydrates, 3 g. fat, 7 mg. cholesterol, 802 mg. sodium, 2 g. dietary fiber*

## Quick Conversion

**Ricotta Toasts with Ham:** For a dual vegetarian/nonvegetarian dish, prepare the recipe with the following changes. For each ham portion, place one 1-ounce slice of cooked ham on 4 of the bread slices (a total of 4 ounces of sliced cooked ham). Top with the cheese mixture. Broil.

# Sun-Dried Tomato Triangles

- **2 large whole wheat pitas**
- **½ cup creamy sun-dried tomato salad dressing**
- **½ cup jarred sun-dried tomato bits (optional)**
- **½ cup (2 ounces) shredded reduced-fat mozzarella cheese**
- **2 tablespoons (½ ounce) grated Parmesan cheese**

PREHEAT THE OVEN TO 350°F. Arrange the pitas on a large ungreased baking sheet. Spread the dressing over each. Top with the tomato bits (if using), mozzarella, and Parmesan.

BAKE FOR 6 TO 8 MINUTES, or until the cheese melts and the bread begins to brown. Let stand for 2 minutes. With a pizza cutter or sharp knife, cut each pita into 8 triangles.

**Makes 8 servings**

***Per serving:*** *109 calories, 5 g. protein, 12 g. carbohydrates, 5 g. fat, 4 mg. cholesterol, 260 mg. sodium, 2 g. dietary fiber*

**Tip:** These toasts can be frozen for up to 3 weeks. To use, thaw in the refrigerator overnight. Bake at 350°F for 3 to 6 minutes, or until warm.

## Quick Conversion

**Sun-Dried Tomato Triangles with Smoked Turkey:** For a dual vegetarian/nonvegetarian dish, prepare the recipe with the following changes. For each turkey portion, place 2 ounces thinly sliced smoked turkey breast on a pita after spreading with the dressing. Top with the tomato bits (if using) and cheeses. Proceed as directed.

# Ranch Snack Mix 

PREHEAT THE OVEN TO 250°F. In a 15" × 10" or larger baking dish, combine the crackers, pretzels, cereal, and peanuts.

IN A SMALL BOWL, combine the salad dressing mix, oil, broth, chili powder, and garlic powder. Pour over the cracker mix and toss to coat.

BAKE, STIRRING FREQUENTLY, for 15 to 20 minutes, or until the crackers begin to brown. Let cool.

**Makes 8 servings**

- **3 cups plain oyster crackers**
- **1 cup thin pretzel sticks**
- **1 cup wheat square cereal (such as Chex)**
- **¼ cup unsalted peanuts**
- **1 package (1 ounce) ranch salad dressing mix**
- **⅓ cup olive oil**
- **¼ cup vegetable broth**
- **1 teaspoon chili powder**
- **¼ teaspoon garlic powder**

***Per serving:*** *236 calories, 5 g. protein, 25 g. carbohydrates, 13 g. fat, 6 mg. cholesterol, 546 mg. sodium, 2 g. dietary fiber*

**Tip:** Store extra snack mix in an airtight container.

# Spicy Sweet Potato Chips 

PREHEAT THE OVEN TO 400°F. Coat 2 large baking sheets with nonstick spray.

IN A LARGE FOOD-STORAGE BAG, combine the cheese, chili powder or seasoning blend, garlic salt, and cumin.

ADD HALF OF THE POTATO SLICES to the bag, and shake to coat with the cheese mixture. Arrange in a single layer on the baking sheet. Repeat with the remaining slices.

DRIZZLE THE POTATOES with the oil. Bake for 15 to 20 minutes, or until crisp and golden brown.

**Makes 8 servings**

- **¼ cup (1 ounce) grated Parmesan cheese**
- **1 tablespoon chili powder or seasoning blend**
- **½ teaspoon garlic salt**
- **½ teaspoon ground cumin**
- **1 pound sweet potatoes, thinly sliced**
- **1 tablespoon olive oil**

***Per serving:*** *92 calories, 2 g. protein, 14 g. carbohydrates, 3 g. fat, 2 mg. cholesterol, 136 mg. sodium, 2 g. dietary fiber*

# Popcorn Balls

- **6** **cups air-popped or microwave popcorn**
- **½** **cup unsalted peanuts**
- **¼** **cup unsalted butter**
- **2** **cups (2 ounces) mini marshmallows**
- **1** **tablespoon corn syrup**

Coat a large jelly-roll pan with nonstick spray. Spread the popcorn and peanuts over the pan.

In a small microwaveable bowl, combine the butter, marshmallows, and corn syrup. Microwave on medium power for 2 minutes, stirring once, or until smooth and creamy. Pour over the popcorn mixture and stir to coat. Loosely cover with waxed paper. Refrigerate for 20 to 30 minutes, or until firm. Using 2 large spoons, form into balls and serve.

**Makes 8 servings**

***Per serving:*** *248 calories, 3 g. protein, 22 g. carbohydrates, 17 g. fat, 33 mg. cholesterol, 21 mg. sodium, 2 g. dietary fiber*

**Tip:** Marshmallows contain gelatin, an animal by-product avoided by some vegetarians. You can find gelatin-free marshmallows in many health food stores.

# Cinnamon-Apple Rice Mix

- **3** **tablespoons honey**
- **2** **tablespoons unsalted butter or margarine**
- **2** **tablespoons thawed apple juice concentrate**
- **½** **teaspoon ground cinnamon**
- **¼** **teaspoon ground nutmeg**
- **3** **cups puffed rice cereal**
- **2** **cups puffed wheat cereal**
- **1** **cup mini pretzel twists**
- **1** **cup dried cranberries, raisins, or other chopped dried fruit**

Preheat the oven to 250°F. In a 13" × 9" baking dish, combine the honey, butter or margarine, juice concentrate, cinnamon, and nutmeg. Place in the oven for 1 minute, or until the butter or margarine melts.

Add the rice cereal, wheat cereal, pretzels, and cranberries, raisins, or other dried fruit. Toss to coat. Bake, stirring frequently, for 10 to 15 minutes, or until crisp. Let cool completely. Store in an airtight container for up to 3 days.

**Makes 8 servings**

***Per serving:*** *248 calories, 4 g. protein, 50 g. carbohydrates, 4 g. fat, 0 mg. cholesterol, 627 mg. sodium, 2 g. dietary fiber*

# Peanut Butter Oat Snacks

- **1¼ cups quick-cooking oats**
- **1 cup crispy brown rice cereal**
- **½ cup crushed honey-flavored cornflakes**
- **½ cup smooth natural peanut butter**
- **½ cup honey**
- **1 teaspoon vanilla extract**
- **½ cup mini chocolate chips**
- **2 tablespoons confectioners' sugar (optional)**

PREHEAT THE OVEN TO 350°F. Coat an 8" × 8" baking dish with nonstick spray.

IN A MEDIUM BOWL, combine the oats, rice cereal, and cornflakes.

IN A SMALL MICROWAVEABLE BOWL, combine the peanut butter, honey, and vanilla. Microwave on medium power for 1 minute, stirring once, or until the mixture is smooth. Pour over the cereal and toss to coat. Gently stir in the chocolate chips. Spoon into the prepared pan, smoothing with the back of the spoon.

BAKE FOR 20 TO 30 MINUTES, or until firm and the edges begin to brown. Cool on a rack. Cut into squares. Serve slightly warm and dust with confectioners' sugar, if using.

**Makes 8 servings**

***Per serving:*** *300 calories, 7 g. protein, 43 g. carbohydrates, 13 g. fat, 0 mg. cholesterol, 40 mg. sodium, 3 g. dietary fiber*

**Tip:** These bars can be frozen for up to 1 month. To use, thaw at room temperature.

# Polenta Sticks

- 1 cup vegetable broth
- 1 cup water
- ½ teaspoon dried basil
- ½ teaspoon garlic powder
- ½ cup instant polenta
- 2 tablespoons (½ ounce) grated Parmesan cheese
- 2 large egg whites
- ½ cup plain dry bread crumbs
- 1 cup marinara sauce, warmed

LINE AN 8" × 8" BAKING DISH with a large piece of plastic wrap, allowing the excess to hang over the sides.

IN A MEDIUM SAUCEPAN, combine the broth, water, basil, and garlic powder. Bring to a boil over high heat. Gradually add the polenta, stirring constantly. Reduce the heat to medium. Cook, stirring constantly, for 5 minutes, or until the mixture pulls away from the sides of the pan. Stir in the cheese. Spoon into the prepared pan. Fold over the plastic wrap to cover the top.

CHILL FOR 30 MINUTES, or until very firm. Invert onto a cutting board. Cut in half, and cut each half into 16 strips.

MEANWHILE, preheat the oven to 425°F. Coat a large baking sheet with nonstick spray.

PLACE THE EGG WHITES in a shallow bowl and beat lightly. Place the bread crumbs on a large piece of waxed paper. Dip the polenta sticks into the egg whites, then coat with the bread crumbs. Place the sticks on the baking sheet. Bake for 15 minutes. Turn and bake for 10 minutes, or until the sticks are golden. Serve with the sauce.

**Makes 4 servings**

***Per serving:*** *195 calories, 8 g. protein, 32 g. carbohydrates, 4 g. fat, 6 mg. cholesterol, 886 mg. sodium, 3 g. dietary fiber*

## Quick Conversion

**Polenta Sticks with Hot Italian Sausage:** For a dual vegetarian/nonvegetarian dish, prepare the recipe with the following changes. For the sausage portion, cook 4 ounces hot Italian sausage in a large skillet over medium heat for 6 to 10 minutes, or until no longer pink. Slice thinly. Serve with the polenta sticks and marinara sauce.

# Onion Flatbread 

- **1 tablespoon olive oil**
- **1 red or sweet onion, sliced and separated into rings**
- **2 tablespoons parsley**
- **1 tablespoon sesame or poppy seeds**
- **1 tablespoon chopped fresh rosemary or 1½ teaspoons dried**
- **¼ teaspoon salt**
- **¼ teaspoon ground black pepper**
- **1 tube (11 ounces) refrigerated French bread dough**
- **1 tomato, chopped (optional)**

PREHEAT THE OVEN TO 350°F. Coat a large baking sheet with nonstick spray.

WARM 1 TEASPOON OF THE OIL in a large nonstick skillet over medium heat. Add the onion. Cook, stirring frequently, for 6 to 8 minutes, or until the onion is soft and golden. Remove from the heat, and stir in the parsley, sesame or poppy seeds, rosemary, salt, and pepper.

PLACE THE DOUGH on the prepared baking sheet. Roll or stretch and press into a 16" × 7" rectangle. Bake for 10 minutes. Drizzle with the remaining 2 teaspoons olive oil. Spread onion mixture over the dough, leaving a ½" border. Top with the tomato, if using.

BAKE FOR 15 TO 20 MINUTES, or until golden brown. Remove to a rack and let cool for 10 minutes. Cut into 8 slices.

**Makes 4 servings**

***Per serving:*** *199 calories, 5 g. protein, 31 g. carbohydrates, 6 g. fat, 0 mg. cholesterol, 455 mg. sodium, 3 g. dietary fiber*

**Tip:** This bread can be frozen for up to 3 weeks. To use, thaw at room temperature for 1 hour. Bake in a 350°F oven for 5 minutes, or until warm.

## Quick Conversion

**Onion Flatbread with Ham:** For a dual vegetarian/nonvegetarian dish, prepare the recipe with the following changes. For the ham portion, sprinkle 2 ounces finely chopped ham over half the dough on top of the onion mixture. Proceed with the recipe as directed. (I sometimes use 2 ounces smoked turkey in place of the ham.)

# Papaya Quesadillas

- 1 papaya, peeled and cubed
- ½ small red onion, chopped
- 2 tablespoons parsley
- 1 tablespoon lime juice
- 3¼ ounces reduced-fat cream cheese
- 2 tablespoons chopped jarred roasted red peppers
- 4 large flour tortillas (12" diameter)
- 1 tablespoon butter or margarine

IN A SMALL BOWL, combine the papaya, onion, parsley, and lime juice.

IN ANOTHER SMALL BOWL, mix the cream cheese and peppers. Spread over 2 tortillas to within ½" of the edge. Top with the papaya mixture and the remaining tortillas.

MELT 1½ TEASPOONS BUTTER or margarine in a large nonstick skillet over medium heat. Cook 1 tortilla stack at a time for 2 to 4 minutes on each side, or until golden brown. Use the remaining butter or margarine as needed.

CUT EACH STACK into 8 triangles.

**Makes 8 servings**

***Per serving:*** *115 calories, 3 g. protein, 16 g. carbohydrates, 5 g. fat, 10 mg. cholesterol, 130 mg. sodium, 2 g. dietary fiber*

## Quick Conversion

**Papaya Quesadillas with Chicken:** For a dual vegetarian/nonvegetarian dish, prepare the recipe with the following changes. Divide the papaya mixture between 2 bowls. For the chicken portion, stir 1 cup chopped cooked chicken into 1 bowl. Use in 1 tortilla stack.

# Feta Bruschetta 

PREHEAT THE OVEN TO 500°F. Place the bread on a large ungreased baking sheet. Bake for 3 to 4 minutes, or until lightly browned.

MEANWHILE, IN A SMALL BOWL, combine the tomato, cheese, olives (if using), basil, and vinegar.

REMOVE THE SLICES FROM THE OVEN, and while still warm, drizzle with the olive oil and rub with the cut side of the garlic. Top with the tomato mixture.

**Makes 4 servings**

***Per serving:*** *212 calories, 6 g. protein, 28 g. carbohydrates, 7 g. fat, 8 mg. cholesterol, 492 mg. sodium, 2 g. dietary fiber*

- **8 slices sourdough or Italian bread (⅓" thick slices)**
- **1 small tomato, chopped**
- **¼ cup (1 ounce) finely crumbled feta cheese**
- **2 tablespoons finely chopped pitted kalamata olives (optional)**
- **1 tablespoon chopped fresh basil or 1 teaspoon dried**
- **2 teaspoons red wine vinegar**
- **1 tablespoon olive oil**
- **1 clove garlic, cut in half**

## Quick Conversion

**Feta Bruschetta with Anchovies:** For a dual vegetarian/nonvegetarian dish, prepare the recipe with the following changes. Divide the tomato mixture between 2 bowls. For the anchovy portion, finely chop 1 small anchovy fillet (or use 1 tablespoon anchovy paste). Stir into 1 bowl. Spoon onto 4 bread slices.

# Feta and Green Olive Nachos

- **2 large pitas, split through the side**
- **1 tablespoon olive oil**
- **½ cup (2 ounces) crumbled feta cheese**
- **1 small tomato, chopped**
- **¼ cup coarsely chopped pimiento-stuffed olives**
- **2 tablespoons finely chopped scallions**
- **1 tablespoon balsamic vinegar**

PREHEAT THE OVEN TO 325°F. Cut the pita halves into 8 triangles each to make 32 triangles. Place the triangles on a large ungreased baking sheet in a single layer. Drizzle with the olive oil. Bake for 5 to 7 minutes, or until the edges begin to brown.

MEANWHILE, IN A MEDIUM BOWL, combine the cheese, tomato, olives, scallions, and vinegar. Spoon onto the pita triangles and bake 5 minutes, or until just warmed.

**Makes 4 servings**

***Per serving:*** *210 calories, 5 g. protein, 27 g. carbohydrates, 8 g. fat, 12 mg. cholesterol, 582 mg. sodium, 1 g. dietary fiber*

## Quick Conversion

**Feta and Green Olive Nachos with Beef:** For a dual vegetarian/nonvegetarian dish, prepare the recipe with the following changes. Divide the cheese mixture between 2 bowls. For the beef portion, brown ¼ pound extra-lean ground beef in a nonstick skillet, breaking up the meat with a spoon. Stir into one of the bowls. Spoon onto half of the pita triangles.

# Cajun Tofu

- ¼ cup all-purpose flour
- 1 tablespoon chili powder
- 1 teaspoon grated lime peel
- ½ teaspoon ground cumin
- ¼ teaspoon garlic salt
- ⅛ teaspoon ground red pepper
- 12 ounces firm tofu, drained, squeezed dry, and cubed
- 1 tablespoon olive oil
- ½ cup (4 ounces) fat-free plain yogurt
- 1 tablespoon honey
- 2 teaspoons lime juice

IN A LARGE FOOD-STORAGE BAG, combine the flour, chili powder, lime peel, cumin, garlic salt, and pepper. Add half the tofu cubes and shake to coat. Remove to a bowl. Repeat with the remaining tofu.

HEAT 1½ TEASPOONS OF THE OIL in a large nonstick skillet over medium-high heat. Add half the tofu and cook, stirring frequently, for 4 to 6 minutes, or until golden. Remove from the skillet. Heat the remaining 1½ teaspoons oil and repeat with the remaining tofu.

IN A SMALL BOWL, mix the yogurt, honey, and lime juice. Serve with the tofu.

**Makes 8 servings**

***Per serving:*** *84 calories, 5 g. protein, 8 g. carbohydrates, 4 g. fat, 1 mg. cholesterol, 54 mg. sodium, 1 g. dietary fiber*

## Quick Conversion

**Cajun Chicken:** For a dual vegetarian/nonvegetarian dish, prepare the recipe with the following changes. Use half the tofu. For the chicken portion, cut a ¾-pound boneless, skinless chicken breast into ¾-inch cubes. Coat with the flour mixture. After cooking the tofu, add the remaining 1½ teaspoons oil to the skillet and cook the chicken for 5 to 6 minutes, or until golden and no longer pink inside. Proceed with the recipe as directed.

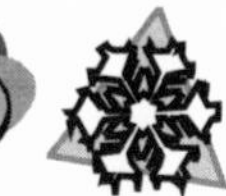

# Cabbage Spring Rolls

- **1 tablespoon peanut oil**
- **2 ribs bok choy, shredded**
- **¼ small head red cabbage, shredded**
- **3 scallions, chopped**
- **1 small green bell pepper, chopped**
- **½ cup finely chopped canned water chestnuts**
- **1 tablespoon minced fresh ginger**
- **1 tablepoon soy sauce**
- **2 large egg whites, lightly beaten**
- **12 egg roll wrappers**

WARM 1 TEASPOON OF THE OIL in a large wok or nonstick skillet over medium-high heat. Add the bok choy, cabbage, scallions, pepper, water chestnuts, and ginger. Stir-fry for 4 to 5 minutes, or until crisp-tender. Add the soy sauce. Stir-fry for 1 minute. Remove from the heat and let stand for 5 minutes. Stir in the egg whites.

WORKING WITH 1 WRAPPER AT A TIME, spoon ¼ cup filling near a corner of the wrapper. Brush the edges with water. Fold the corner over the filling. Fold the sides in and roll up. Repeat with the remaining filling and wrappers.

WIPE OUT THE WOK or skillet. Add the remaining 2 teaspoons oil and warm over medium-high heat. Add the filled wrappers (in batches if necessary) and cook for 4 to 5 minutes, or until golden, turning to brown on all sides. (Coat the wok or skillet with nonstick spray, if necessary.)

**Makes 4 servings**

***Per serving:*** *139 calories, 6 g. protein, 21 g. carbohydrates, 4 g. fat, 2 mg. cholesterol, 435 mg. sodium, 3 g. dietary fiber*

**Tip:** These spring rolls can be frozen for up to 1 month. To use, thaw in the refrigerator overnight. Wrap in waxed paper. Microwave on medium power for 1 to 2 minutes, or until heated through.

## Quick Conversion

**Cabbage Spring Rolls with Shrimp:** For a dual vegetarian/nonvegetarian dish, prepare the recipe with the following changes. Divide the cabbage mixture between 2 bowls. For the shrimp portion, stir in ½ cup chopped cooked peeled and deveined medium shrimp. Use the shrimp filling for 6 of the wrappers.

# Cold Eggplant Rolls

**½** **cup dry-pack sun-dried tomatoes**

**1** **large eggplant**

**1** **tablespoon olive oil**

**¼** **cup low-fat Italian salad dressing**

**6** **ounces reduced-fat mozzarella cheese, thinly sliced**

**½** **cup fresh basil leaves**

**Ground black pepper**

PREHEAT THE BROILER. Coat a broiler rack with nonstick spray.

SOAK THE TOMATOES in hot water to cover for 10 minutes, or until soft. Drain.

CUT THE EGGPLANT LENGTHWISE into 8 thin slices. Arrange on the rack and brush with the oil. Broil for 2 to 3 minutes on each side, or until tender. Brush with the dressing. Top with the cheese, tomatoes, and basil. Sprinkle with the pepper.

STARTING WITH THE SHORT SIDE, roll up. Fasten with a toothpick. Refrigerate for at least 30 minutes.

**Makes 4 servings**

***Per serving:*** *207 calories, 13 g. protein, 14 g. carbohydrates, 12 g. fat, 25 mg. cholesterol, 460 mg. sodium, 4 g. dietary fiber*

**Tip:** These appetizers also make a nice presentation when you leave them unrolled.

## Quick Conversion

**Cold Eggplant Rolls with Prosciutto:** For a dual vegetarian/nonvegetarian dish, prepare the recipe with the following changes. To make the prosciutto portion, divide 3 ounces of thinly sliced prosciutto among 4 of the broiled eggplant slices. Top with the cheese, tomatoes, and basil. Sprinkle with the pepper. Roll up and proceed as directed.

## Snacks That Kids Can Make

My kids are always munching, so I showed them how to make these simple recipes. The first few times my kids made these snacks, they felt such a sense of accomplishment. And I loved hearing them say, "Mommy, look what I made." At least the first time, you may want to guide your littlest ones through these recipes.

### Apple-Bagel Sandwich Melt

- **1 sliced bagel**
- **2 dried apple rings**
- **2 slices reduced-fat American cheese**
- **Ground cinnamon**

PREHEAT THE OVEN or a toaster oven to 350°F.

TOP EACH BAGEL HALF with a dried apple slice and a cheese slice. Sprinkle with the cinnamon. Place on a small ungreased baking sheet.

BAKE FOR 6 TO 8 MINUTES, or until the cheese melts.

**Makes 1 serving**

***Per serving:*** *198 calories, 8 g. protein, 41 g. carbohydrates, 1 g. fat, 0 mg. cholesterol, 484 mg. sodium, 3 g. dietary fiber*

## Peanut Butter Spread

IN A SMALL BOWL, combine the peanut butter and yogurt. Stir in the raisins. Spread over the rice cakes.

**Makes 4 servings**

- **½ cup smooth peanut butter**
- **¼ cup (2 ounces) reduced-fat vanilla yogurt**
- **¼ cup raisins**
- **8 rice cakes**

***Per serving:*** *301 calories, 10 g. protein, 31 g. carbohydrates, 17 g. fat, 1 mg. cholesterol, 162 mg. sodium, 3 g. dietary fiber*

## Egg Salad Cone Cups

IN A SMALL BOWL, mash the eggs until crumbly. Stir in the mayonnaise and relish. Using an ice cream scoop or spoon, fill the cones with the egg salad.

**Makes 2 servings**

- **2 hard-cooked eggs, peeled**
- **¼ cup reduced-fat mayonnaise**
- **1 tablespoon pickle relish**
- **2 flat-bottomed ice cream cones**

***Per serving:*** *178 calories, 7 g. protein, 11 g. carbohydrates, 12 g. fat, 220 mg. cholesterol, 288 mg. sodium, 0 g. dietary fiber*

*"There is nothing like soup. It is by nature eccentric: no two are ever alike, unless of course you get your soup from cans."*

—Laurie Colwin, U.S. cookbook author

# Big-Flavor Soups and Stews

THESE ARE AMONG my simplest recipes. Asparagus-Lemon Soup is absolutely delicious, and it's ready to eat in about 40 minutes. Or try the Gazpacho with Avocado Salsa, which takes no cooking at all.

If you can whirl a milkshake in a blender, you can create a delicious cold dish like Honey-Melon Soup. And if you can simmer vegetables, you can make hot and hearty stews like robust Greens and Beans Stew.

Most of these soups and stews make 4 servings. All you need is an ordinary 3- or 4-quart saucepan with a lid. Since I do have some bigger pots, I sometimes double these recipes and freeze the extras for fuss-free dinners on busy nights.

## Recipes

● Kid-Friendly Recipe

● Freezable Recipe

● Microwaveable Recipe

# Asparagus-Lemon Soup

- 1½ pounds asparagus, cut into 2" pieces
- 1 potato, peeled and chopped
- 1 teaspoon olive oil
- 1 small onion, chopped
- 1 rib celery, chopped
- 1 tablespoon all-purpose flour
- 2 cups vegetable broth
- ¾ cup 1% milk
- ¼ cup reduced-fat plain yogurt
- 1 tablespoon lemon juice
- ¼ teaspoon salt
- ¼ teaspoon ground black pepper
- 2 teaspoons dried basil or 2 tablespoons chopped fresh

PLACE THE ASPARAGUS AND POTATO in a large saucepan. Add water to cover. Bring to a boil over high heat. Reduce the heat to low. Cover and simmer for 8 to 10 minutes, or until the vegetables are tender. Drain.

WARM THE OIL in a large saucepan over medium heat. Add the onion and celery. Cook, stirring frequently, for 4 to 5 minutes, or until tender. Reduce the heat to low. Stir in the flour. Cook and stir for 1 minute. Gradually pour in the broth, stirring constantly. Cook and stir over medium heat for 5 minutes. Add the asparagus and potato.

POUR INTO A FOOD PROCESSOR or blender. Process or blend until smooth. Return to the saucepan. Stir in the milk, yogurt, lemon juice, salt, and pepper. Cook over low heat for 4 to 5 minutes, or until heated through. Sprinkle with the basil.

**Makes 4 servings**

***Per serving:*** *132 calories, 9 g. protein, 18 g. carbohydrates, 4 g. fat, 3 mg. cholesterol, 713 mg. sodium, 3 g. dietary fiber*

**Tip:** When I can't find fresh asparagus, I use broccoli instead. Sometimes, I save a few pieces of cooked asparagus or broccoli to place on top of the soup.

# Roasted Red Pepper Soup

- 2 teaspoons butter
- 1 onion, chopped
- 2 ribs celery, chopped
- 1 potato, peeled and finely chopped
- 1¼ cups vegetable broth
- 2 tablespoons all-purpose flour
- 2 cups 1% buttermilk
- 1 cup frozen corn, thawed
- ½ cup chopped roasted red pepper
- ⅛ teaspoon ground red pepper

MELT THE BUTTER IN A LARGE SAUCEPAN over medium heat. Add the onion and celery. Cook, stirring often, for 4 to 5 minutes, or until the onion is tender. Add the potato and 1 cup of the broth. Bring to a boil. Reduce the heat to medium and simmer for 15 minutes, or until the potato is almost tender.

IN A CUP, mix the flour and remaining ¼ cup broth. Stir into the soup and cook, stirring constantly, for 4 to 5 minutes, or until the soup thickens slightly. Reduce the heat to low. Stir in the buttermilk, corn, roasted red pepper, and ground red pepper. Cook, stirring frequently, for 6 to 8 minutes, or until the potato is tender.

**Makes 4 servings**

***Per serving:*** *168 calories, 8 g. protein, 29 g. carbohydrates, 4 g. fat, 10 mg. cholesterol, 465 mg. sodium, 3 g. dietary fiber*

**Tip:** After stirring in the buttermilk, do not let the mixture boil, or it will curdle.

## Quick Conversion

**Roasted Red Pepper Soup with Smoked Turkey:** For a dual vegetarian/non-vegetarian dish, prepare the recipe with the following changes. For the turkey portion, after stirring in the ground red pepper, transfer half of the soup to a medium saucepan. Stir in ½ pound cubed cooked smoked turkey breast. Cook until the potato is tender.

# Creamy Mushroom Soup

- **2 cups vegetable broth**
- **1 large potato, peeled and cubed**
- **1 tablespoon olive oil**
- **4 strips vegetable-protein bacon**
- **½ onion, chopped**
- **1 garlic clove, minced**
- **1 pound mushrooms, thinly sliced**
- **1¼ cups evaporated milk**
- **¼ cup (2 ounces) reduced-fat sour cream**
- **½ teaspoon dried thyme**
- **¼ teaspoon salt**
- **⅛ teaspoon ground white or black pepper**

In a medium saucepan, combine the broth and potato. Bring to a boil over medium heat. Reduce the heat to low, partially cover, and simmer for 10 to 12 minutes, or until the potato is tender. Let cool for 5 to 10 minutes. Transfer to a blender or food processor. Blend or process until smooth.

Meanwhile, warm 1 teaspoon of the oil in a large saucepan over medium heat. Add the bacon. Cook for 2 to 3 minutes on each side, or until browned. Transfer to a plate lined with paper towels. Crumble.

Warm the remaining 2 teaspoons oil in the same saucepan. Add the onion and garlic. Cook over medium heat for 4 minutes, or until soft. Add the mushrooms and cook for 5 minutes, or until tender. Stir in the milk, sour cream, thyme, salt, pepper, and pureed potato. Simmer over low heat for 5 minutes, or until heated through.

Top each serving with the bacon.

**Makes 4 servings**

***Per serving:*** *248 calories, 12 g. protein, 21 g. carbohydrates, 15 g. fat, 29 mg. cholesterol, 961 mg. sodium, 2 g. dietary fiber*

## Quick Conversion

**Creamy Mushroom Soup with Bacon:** For a dual vegetarian/nonvegetarian dish, prepare the recipe with the following changes. Replace half of the vegetable-protein bacon with smoked pork bacon, cooking the pork bacon in a separate skillet. Top 2 servings with vegetable-protein bacon and 2 servings with pork bacon.

# Creamy Tomato Soup

- **1 tablespoon butter**
- **1 small onion, chopped**
- **2 cloves garlic, minced**
- **2 cans (14½ ounces each) chopped tomatoes**
- **2 cups 1% buttermilk**
- **¼ cup chopped fresh basil**
- **¼ cup chopped fresh chives**

MELT THE BUTTER IN A MEDIUM SAUCEPAN over medium heat. Add the onion and garlic. Cook, stirring frequently, for 4 to 5 minutes, or until tender. Stir in the tomatoes (with juice) and cook for 10 to 15 minutes, or until the tomatoes begin to thicken. Transfer to a blender or food processor. Blend or process until smooth. Return to the saucepan.

STIR IN THE BUTTERMILK and simmer over medium heat for 10 minutes. Do not boil.

STIR IN THE BASIL. Top with the chives.

**Makes 4 servings**

***Per serving:*** *131 calories, 8 g. protein, 16 g. carbohydrates, 5 g. fat, 12 mg. cholesterol, 562 mg. sodium, 3 g. dietary fiber*

# Cabbage Borscht

- **4 cups vegetable broth**
- **½ cup low-sodium mixed-vegetable juice**
- **¼ head green cabbage, shredded**
- **1 carrot, shredded**
- **1 leek, white part only, chopped**
- **1 can (16 ounces) shoestring beets, drained**
- **2 teaspoons cider vinegar**
- **1 teaspoon packed brown sugar**
- **½ teaspoon dried tarragon**
- **⅛ teaspoon ground black pepper**
- **¼ cup (2 ounces) reduced-fat sour cream**

IN A LARGE SAUCEPAN, combine the broth and vegetable juice. Bring to a boil over medium heat. Stir in the cabbage, carrot, and leek. Cover and simmer over medium heat for 15 minutes, or until tender.

MEANWHILE, place 1 cup of the beets in a blender or food processor. Blend or process until smooth. Stir into the cabbage mixture. Stir in the remaining beets, vinegar, brown sugar, tarragon, and pepper. Bring to a boil over medium heat. Reduce the heat to low, cover, and simmer for 10 to 15 minutes to blend flavors.

REMOVE FROM THE HEAT and stir in the sour cream.

**Makes 4 servings**

***Per serving:*** *111 calories, 5 g. protein, 20 g. carbohydrates, 3 g. fat, 6 mg. cholesterol, 1,257 mg. sodium, 3 g. dietary fiber*

## Quick Conversion

**Cabbage Borscht with Ham:** For a dual vegetarian/nonvegetarian dish, prepare the recipe with the following changes. For the ham portion, after stirring the beets and seasonings into the borscht, transfer half of the mixture to a medium saucepan. Stir in 6 ounces cubed cooked ham. Bring to a boil and proceed as directed.

# Honey-Melon Soup

IN A BLENDER OR FOOD PROCESSOR, combine the honeydew melon, cantaloupe, kiwifruit, fruit juice, yogurt, honey, and ginger.

TRANSFER TO A BOWL. Cover and refrigerate for at least 1 hour before serving. Garnish with the mint.

**Makes 4 servings**

***Per serving:*** *169 calories, 4 g. protein, 38 g. carbohydrates, 1 g. fat, 4 mg. cholesterol, 61 mg. sodium, 2 g. dietary fiber*

- **½ honeydew melon, cubed**
- **¼ cantaloupe, cubed**
- **1 kiwifruit, peeled and quartered**
- **1 cup tropical-blend fruit juice**
- **1 container (8 ounces) reduced-fat lemon-lime or lemon yogurt**
- **2 teaspoons honey**
- **¼ teaspoon ground ginger**
- **¼ cup chopped fresh mint**

# Gazpacho with Avocado Salsa

**Gazpacho**

- **3½ cups spicy mixed-vegetable juice**
- **2 small tomatoes, chopped**
- **1 cucumber, peeled and chopped**
- **1 green bell pepper, chopped**
- **½ small red onion, chopped**
- **2 tablespoons lime juice**
- **1 teaspoon red wine vinegar**
- **1 teaspoon vegetarian Worcestershire sauce**

**Salsa**

- **1 avocado, peeled and cubed**
- **1 tomato, finely chopped**
- **2 scallions, chopped**
- **¼ cup parsley or chopped fresh cilantro**
- **2 tablespoons lemon juice**
- **¼ teaspoon ground black pepper**

*To make the gazpacho:*

IN A LARGE GLASS BOWL, combine the vegetable juice, tomatoes, cucumber, bell pepper, onion, lime juice, vinegar, and Worcestershire sauce. Cover and refrigerate for 30 minutes to blend flavors.

*To make the salsa:*

IN A MEDIUM BOWL, combine the avocado, tomato, scallions, parsley or cilantro, lemon juice, and black pepper.

SPOON THE SOUP into bowls. Top with the salsa.

**Makes 4 servings**

***Per serving:*** *148 calories, 5 g. protein, 20 g. carbohydrates, 7 g. fat, 0 mg. cholesterol, 713 mg. sodium, 8 g. dietary fiber*

**Tip:** Vegetarian Worcestershire sauce made without anchovies is available in health food stores. You can also use regular Worcestershire sauce.

# Rice, Pea, and Orzo Soup

- 1 teaspoon olive oil
- 3 ribs celery, chopped
- 2 carrots, thinly sliced
- ½ small onion, chopped
- 8 cups low-sodium vegetable broth
- 1 can (14½ ounces) Italian-style diced tomatoes
- 1 cup water
- ½ pound split peas, sorted, rinsed, and drained
- ½ cup rice
- 4 ounces (⅔ cup) orzo

WARM THE OIL IN A LARGE SAUCEPAN over medium heat. Add the celery, carrots, and onion. Cook, stirring frequently, for 4 to 5 minutes, or until tender.

STIR IN THE BROTH, tomatoes (with juice), and water. Bring to a boil. Reduce the heat to low. Stir in the peas. Cover and simmer for 25 minutes, or until the peas are almost tender. Stir in the rice and cook, covered, for 8 minutes. Stir in the orzo and cook, partially covered, for 10 to 12 minutes, or until the orzo is tender.

**Makes 4 servings**

***Per serving:*** *499 calories, 25 g. protein, 92 g. carbohydrates, 5 g. fat, 0 mg. cholesterol, 513 mg. sodium, 19 g. dietary fiber*

# Wonton Soup with Ginger

**Wontons**

- **¼ cup instant rice**
- **½ cup finely shredded green cabbage**
- **1 small scallion, finely chopped**
- **2 teaspoons sesame oil**
- **1 teaspoon chopped fresh ginger**
- **1 large egg white, lightly beaten**
- **12 wonton wrappers (3½" square)**

**Soup**

- **3 cups vegetable broth**
- **3 cups water**
- **½ cup drained canned baby corn, sliced 1" thick**
- **1 tablespoon soy sauce**
- **1 teaspoon chopped fresh ginger**

*To make the wontons:*

COOK THE RICE according to package directions.

IN A SMALL BOWL, combine the rice, cabbage, scallion, oil, ginger, and egg white. Place a scant tablespoonful in the center of a wonton wrapper. Using a finger dipped into cold water, moisten the edges of the wrapper. Bring up adjacent sides and fold over the filling, forming a triangle. Twist the ends into a point. Moisten the points with water, bring up, and pinch together to form a wonton. Place on a plate lined with waxed paper. Repeat with remaining wrappers and filling.

*To make the soup:*

IN A LARGE SAUCEPAN, combine the broth, water, corn, soy sauce, and ginger. Bring to a boil over medium-high heat. Reduce the heat to low. Simmer for 5 minutes. Gently drop the wontons into the soup. Bring to a gentle boil. Reduce the heat to low. Cover and simmer for 5 minutes.

**Makes 4 servings**

***Per serving:*** *199 calories, 9 g. protein, 34 g. carbohydrates, 5 g. fat, 2 mg. cholesterol, 1,249 mg. sodium, 6 g. dietary fiber*

**Tip:** The filled wontons and soup can be frozen separately for up to 1 month. To use, thaw the soup overnight in the refrigerator. Bring to a boil on the stove top. Add the wontons and simmer for 5 to 10 minutes, or until cooked through and hot.

## Quick Conversion

**Wonton Soup with Ginger and Beef:** For a dual vegetarian/nonvegetarian dish, prepare the recipe with the following changes. Replace half of the cabbage with ¼ cup cooked ground beef. Divide the wonton-filling ingredients between 2 bowls, mixing the cabbage into one bowl and the beef into another. For the beef portion, fill half of the wrappers with the beef filling. Make the soup and pour half into another saucepan. Cook the vegetarian wontons in one saucepan and the beef wontons in the other.

# Sweet-and-Sour Soup

WARM THE OIL IN A LARGE SAUCEPAN over medium heat. Add the onion, celery, and snow peas. Cook, stirring frequently, for 4 to 5 minutes, or until tender. Stir in the tomatoes (with juice), water, vinegar, and brown sugar. Bring to a boil. Reduce the heat to low. Cover and simmer for 30 minutes, stirring frequently.

STIR IN THE BROTH, cabbage, water chestnuts, and bamboo shoots. Bring to a boil. Reduce the heat to low. Cover and simmer for 20 to 25 minutes, or until the cabbage is tender.

**Makes 4 servings**

***Per serving:*** *175 calories, 8 g. protein, 33 g. carbohydrates, 4 g. fat, 0 mg. cholesterol, 277 mg. sodium, 9 g. dietary fiber*

- **2 teaspoons canola oil**
- **1 small onion, chopped**
- **1 rib celery, chopped**
- **¼ pound snow peas, cut into thin strips**
- **1 can (16 ounces) low-sodium diced tomatoes**
- **1 cup water**
- **¼ cup cider vinegar**
- **1 tablespoon packed brown sugar**
- **5 cups low-sodium vegetable broth**
- **1 small head green cabbage, shredded**
- **½ cup drained sliced canned water chestnuts**
- **¼ cup drained canned bamboo shoots**

## Quick Conversion

**Sweet-and-Sour Soup with Pork:** For a dual vegetarian/nonvegetarian dish, prepare the recipe with the following changes. For the pork portion, after adding the bamboo shoots, transfer half of the soup to a medium saucepan. Stir in 6 ounces cooked pork cut into thin strips. Proceed as directed.

# Lentil and Dried-Tomato Soup

- **1 teaspoon olive oil**
- **2 carrots, thinly sliced**
- **3 ribs celery, chopped**
- **5 cups low-sodium vegetable broth**
- **1 cup lentils, sorted, rinsed, and drained**
- **2 cups low-sodium spicy mixed-vegetable juice**
- **2 cups low-sodium chopped canned tomatoes**
- **¼ cup sun-dried tomato bits**
- **1 tablespoon lime juice**
- **½ teaspoon ground cumin**
- **½ cup chopped jarred roasted red peppers**
- **2 tablespoons parsley**

WARM THE OIL IN A LARGE SAUCEPAN over medium heat. Add the carrots and celery. Cook, stirring frequently, for 4 to 5 minutes, or until tender. Add the broth and lentils. Bring to a boil. Reduce the heat to low, partially cover, and simmer for 10 to 15 minutes. Stir in the vegetable juice, tomatoes (with juice), sun-dried tomatoes, lime juice, and cumin. Bring to a boil over high heat. Reduce the heat to low, partially cover, and simmer for 20 to 25 minutes, or until the lentils are tender.

TOP WITH THE PEPPERS and parsley.

**Makes 4 servings**

***Per serving:*** *282 calories, 19 g. protein, 49 g. carbohydrates, 3 g. fat, 0 mg. cholesterol, 409 mg. sodium, 20 g. dietary fiber*

**Tip:** This soup can be frozen for up to 1 month without the peppers and parsley. To use, thaw overnight in the refrigerator. Reheat on the stove top or in the microwave oven at high power until hot and bubbly. Top with the peppers and parsley.

## Quick Conversion

**Lentil and Dried-Tomato Soup with Sausage:** For a dual vegetarian/nonvegetarian dish, prepare the recipe with the following changes. For the sausage portion, warm 1 teaspoon olive oil in a medium saucepan. Cut 10 ounces Italian turkey sausage into 1" pieces. Add to the saucepan and cook for 5 to 10 minutes, or until no longer pink. Stir in half of the completed soup. Cook for 10 minutes to blend flavors.

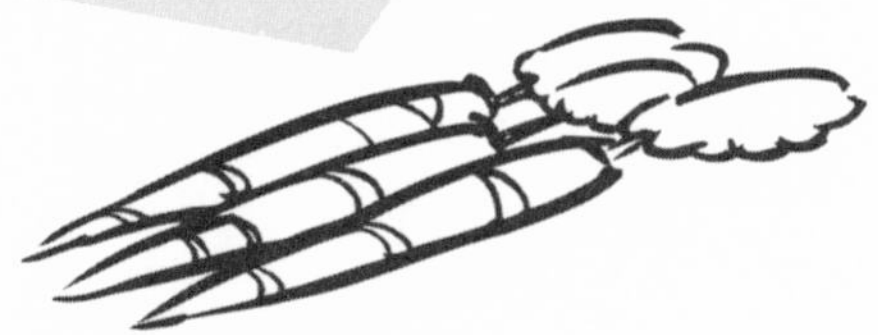

## Two 10-Minute Soups

A hot meal doesn't have to be fussy or time-consuming. I turn to these sensible soups when hunger pangs hit and time is short. Add some bread to soak up the broth. Leftovers can be refrigerated for up to 3 days.

### Quick Tortellini Soup

- **4 cups low-sodium vegetable broth**
- **1 cup low-sodium mixed-vegetable juice**
- **1 can (16 ounces) chickpeas, rinsed and drained**
- **1½ cups (6 ounces) cheese tortellini (thawed if frozen)**
- **1 cup frozen mixed vegetables**
- **1 tablespoon prepared pesto**
- **1 tablespoon (¼ ounce) grated Parmesan cheese**

In a large saucepan, bring the broth and vegetable juice to a boil. Add the chickpeas, tortellini, and vegetables. Reduce the heat to low and simmer for 8 minutes, or until the tortellini is tender. Stir in the pesto and sprinkle with the cheese.

Makes 4 servings

***Per serving:*** *296 calories, 14 g. protein, 47 g. carbohydrates, 7 g. fat, 9 mg. cholesterol, 642 mg. sodium, 7 g. dietary fiber*

### Quick Noodle Soup

- **1 teaspoon olive oil**
- **1 onion, chopped**
- **1 carrot, thinly sliced**
- **1 small rib celery, chopped**
- **5 cups low-sodium vegetable broth**
- **1 tomato, chopped**
- **½ teaspoon dried thyme**
- **3 ounces thin no-yolk egg noodles**

Warm the oil in a large saucepan over medium heat. Add the onion, carrot, and celery. Cook for 2 minutes, stirring frequently. Stir in the broth, tomato, and thyme. Bring to a boil. Add the noodles and cook for 8 minutes, or until tender.

Makes 4 servings

***Per serving:*** *146 calories, 6 g. protein, 27 g. carbohydrates, 3 g. fat, 0 mg. cholesterol, 201 mg. sodium, 2 g. dietary fiber*

# Summer Vegetable Stew

- **2 teaspoons olive oil**
- **1 green bell pepper, chopped**
- **1 small onion, chopped**
- **2 cloves garlic, minced**
- **2 zucchini, thinly sliced**
- **1 small eggplant, cubed**
- **2 tomatoes, chopped**
- **1 can (28 ounces) crushed tomatoes**
- **1 cup vegetable broth**
- **¼ cup tomato paste**
- **¼ cup chopped fresh basil or parsley**
- **1 tablespoon balsamic vinegar**

Warm the oil in a large saucepan over medium heat. Add the pepper, onion, and garlic. Cook, stirring frequently, for 4 to 5 minutes, or until tender. Stir in the zucchini, eggplant, and fresh tomatoes. Cook for 6 to 8 minutes, or until the vegetables are tender.

Stir in the crushed tomatoes (with juice), broth, tomato paste, basil or parsley, and vinegar. Bring to a boil. Reduce the heat to low. Partially cover and simmer for 20 to 25 minutes, or until thickened.

**Makes 4 servings**

***Per serving:*** *201 calories, 8 g. protein, 37 g. carbohydrates, 4 g. fat, 0 mg. cholesterol, 768 mg. sodium, 10 g. dietary fiber*

**Tip:** This soup can be frozen for up to 3 weeks. To use, thaw overnight in the refrigerator. Reheat on the stove top or in the microwave oven at high power just until hot and bubbly.

## Quick Conversion

**Summer Vegetable Stew with Smoked Ham:** For a dual vegetarian/nonvegetarian dish, prepare the recipe with the following changes. Divide the stew between 2 saucepans. Keep the vegetarian portion warm. For the ham portion, stir in ½ pound cubed cooked smoked ham. Simmer for 10 minutes to blend flavors.

# Eggplant-Couscous Stew

- 1 teaspoon olive oil
- 1 onion, chopped
- 1 red bell pepper, finely chopped
- 2 cloves garlic, minced
- 1 large eggplant, cubed
- 1 can (14½ ounces) stewed tomatoes
- 1 can (16 ounces) chickpeas, rinsed and drained
- 1 cup frozen corn, thawed
- 2 cups vegetable broth
- 1 cup couscous

WARM THE OIL IN A LARGE SAUCEPAN over medium heat. Add the onion, pepper, and garlic. Cook, stirring frequently, for 4 minutes. Add the eggplant. Cook for 6 to 8 minutes, or until the eggplant is tender.

STIR IN THE TOMATOES (with juice), chickpeas, corn, and broth. Bring to a boil. Reduce the heat to low. Simmer for 10 minutes. Remove from the heat.

SPRINKLE THE COUSCOUS over the vegetables, tilting the pan as necessary to moisten the couscous. Cover and let stand for 5 minutes, or until most of the liquid has been absorbed and the couscous is tender.

**Makes 4 servings**

***Per serving:*** *496 calories, 21 g. protein, 96 g. carbohydrates, 6 g. fat, 0 mg. cholesterol, 824 mg. sodium, 18 g. dietary fiber*

## Quick Conversion

**Eggplant-Couscous Stew with Beef:** For a dual vegetarian/nonvegetarian dish, prepare the recipe with the following changes. Divide the ingredients in half. To make the vegetarian portion, use half the ingredients in a medium saucepan. For the beef portion, cook the remaining half of the onion, pepper, and garlic in another medium saucepan. Add 6 ounces lean ground beef. Cook, stirring frequently, for 5 to 10 minutes, or until no longer pink. Stir in the remaining half of the eggplant. Cook and stir in the remaining half of the tomatoes, chickpeas, corn, broth, and couscous.

# Little Shells and Beans Stew

- 2 teaspoons olive oil
- 2 leeks, white part only, chopped
- 2 carrots, thinly sliced
- 3 ribs celery, chopped
- 5 cups low-sodium vegetable broth
- 1 cup water
- 1 cup red lentils, sorted, rinsed, and drained
- ½ pound green beans, sliced into 1" pieces, or green soybeans
- 1 can (14½ ounces) low-sodium stewed tomatoes
- ¼ cup parsley
- ¼ teaspoon ground black pepper
- 3 ounces (1 cup) small shell pasta
- 2 tablespoons (½ ounce) grated Parmesan cheese

Warm the oil in a large saucepan over medium heat. Add the leeks, carrots, and celery. Cook, stirring frequently, for 4 to 5 minutes, or until tender. Add the broth, water, lentils, green beans or soybeans, tomatoes (with juice), parsley, and pepper. Bring to a boil. Reduce the heat to low. Cover and simmer for 20 minutes, stirring occasionally.

Stir in the pasta. Cook for 10 to 12 minutes, or until the pasta and lentils are tender. Sprinkle with the cheese.

**Makes 4 servings**

***Per serving:*** *589 calories, 33 g. protein, 97 g. carbohydrates, 10 g. fat, 2 mg. cholesterol, 306 mg. sodium, 21 g. dietary fiber*

# Tomatillo-Bean Chili

- **2** **teaspoons olive oil**
- **1** **onion, chopped**
- **1** **green bell pepper, chopped**
- **2** **cloves garlic, minced**
- **1** **tablespoon chili powder**
- **1** **can (28 ounces) Mexican-style tomatoes**
- **1** **can (14½ ounces) chopped tomatoes**
- **2** **teaspoons cider vinegar**
- **1** **bay leaf**
- **¼** **teaspoon salt**
- **1** **can (16 ounces) cannellini beans, rinsed and drained**
- **1** **can (14 ounces) chickpeas, rinsed and drained**
- **1** **can (11 ounces) tomatillos, rinsed and drained**
- **½** **cup (2 ounces) shredded reduced-fat Monterey Jack cheese**

Warm the oil in a large saucepan over medium heat. Add the onion, pepper, and garlic. Cook, stirring frequently, for 4 to 5 minutes, or until tender. Stir in the chili powder. Cook for 1 minute, stirring constantly.

Stir in the Mexican-style tomatoes (with juice), chopped tomatoes (with juice), vinegar, bay leaf, and salt. Bring to a boil. Reduce the heat to low. Stir in the cannellini beans, chickpeas, and tomatillos. Cover and simmer for 20 to 25 minutes, or until thickened. Remove and discard the bay leaf. Sprinkle with the cheese.

**Makes 4 servings**

***Per serving:*** *504 calories, 27 g. protein, 79 g. carbohydrates, 11 g. fat, 9 mg. cholesterol, 1,000 mg. sodium, 21 g. dietary fiber*

**Tip:** This chili can be frozen for up to 1 month without the cheese. To use, thaw overnight in the refrigerator. Reheat on the stove top or in the microwave oven at high power until hot and bubbly. Top with the cheese.

## Quick Conversion

**Tomatillo-Bean Chili with Turkey:** For a dual vegetarian/nonvegetarian dish, prepare the recipe with the following changes. For the turkey portion, warm 1 teaspoon olive oil in a medium saucepan. Add ½ pound ground turkey breast and cook for 8 minutes, or until no longer pink, breaking up the meat with a spoon. After adding the tomatillos to the chili, transfer half of the mixture to the saucepan with the turkey. Add a bay leaf so that there is one in each saucepan. Stir and proceed with the recipe as directed.

# Bean Chili over Grilled Polenta

- **3 cups water**
- **¼ teaspoon salt**
- **¾ cup instant polenta**
- **3 tablespoons (½ ounce) grated Parmesan cheese**
- **2 teaspoons olive oil**
- **1 onion, chopped**
- **1 green bell pepper, chopped**
- **1 tablespoon chili seasoning mix**
- **1 can (14 ounces) black beans, rinsed and drained**
- **1 can (14 ounces) red kidney beans, rinsed and drained**
- **1 can (14 ounces) great Northern beans, rinsed and drained**
- **1 can (14½ ounces) chopped tomatoes**
- **2 tablespoons chopped fresh cilantro or parsley**
- **2 tablespoons reduced-fat sour cream**

BRING THE WATER TO A BOIL in a large saucepan over high heat. Add the salt. Reduce the heat to medium and slowly stir in the polenta. Cook, stirring constantly, for 20 to 25 minutes, or until the mixture pulls away from the sides of the pan. Remove from the heat and stir in the cheese.

COAT A 9" × 9" BAKING DISH with nonstick spray. Spoon the polenta into the dish, pressing to smooth the top. Cover and refrigerate until completely cool, at least 30 minutes.

MEANWHILE, WARM THE OIL in a large saucepan over medium heat. Add the onion and pepper. Cook, stirring frequently, for 4 to 5 minutes, or until tender. Stir in the seasoning mix. Cook for 1 minute. Add the black beans, kidney beans, great Northern beans, and tomatoes (with juice), stirring to mix. Bring to a boil. Reduce the heat to low. Cook for 10 minutes, stirring frequently, to blend flavors.

TURN OUT THE POLENTA onto a cutting board. Cut into 4 squares. Coat an indoor ridged grill pan or a broiler pan with nonstick spray. Grill or broil the polenta for 5 minutes on each side, or until golden.

DIVIDE THE POLENTA among 4 shallow bowls. Top with the bean mixture, cilantro or parsley, and sour cream.

**Makes 4 servings**

***Per serving:*** *588 calories, 33 g. protein, 99 g. carbohydrates, 8 g. fat, 8 mg. cholesterol, 954 mg. sodium, 27 g. dietary fiber*

## Quick Conversion

**Bean Chili over Grilled Polenta with Turkey:** For a dual vegetarian/nonvegetarian dish, prepare the recipe with the following changes. Divide the completed polenta among 4 bowls. Divide the completed bean-tomato mixture between 2 medium saucepans. For the turkey portion, stir ½ pound cubed cooked turkey into one of the saucepans. Top half of the polenta with the bean chili. Top the remaining half with the turkey-bean chili.

# Greens and Beans Stew

- 1 cup rinsed and drained canned cannellini beans
- 1 cup rinsed and drained canned red kidney beans
- 4 cups low-sodium vegetable broth
- 1 cup low-sodium mixed-vegetable juice
- 2 large carrots, thinly sliced
- 2 large ribs celery, sliced
- 1 onion, chopped
- 1 bay leaf
- 1 pound assorted greens (spinach, kale, broccoli raab), tough ends trimmed
- 1 loaf (6 ounces) dry sourdough bread, cubed
- 1 tablespoon olive oil
- 2 cloves garlic, crushed

IN A LARGE SAUCEPAN, combine the cannellini beans, kidney beans, broth, vegetable juice, carrots, celery, onion, and bay leaf. Bring to a boil. Reduce the heat to low. Cover and simmer for 20 minutes, or until the carrots are tender.

STIR IN THE GREENS. Simmer for 4 to 5 minutes, or until the greens are tender.

MEANWHILE, place the bread in a blender or food processor. Blend or process until reduced to coarse crumbs. Warm the oil in a small nonstick skillet over low heat. Add the garlic. Cook, stirring constantly, for 1 minute. Add the bread. Cook, stirring frequently, for 2 to 3 minutes, or until golden.

REMOVE and discard the bay leaf. Top each serving with the bread crumbs.

**Makes 4 servings**

***Per serving:*** *399 calories, 22 g. protein, 68 g. carbohydrates, 7 g. fat, 0 mg. cholesterol, 628 mg. sodium, 17 g. dietary fiber*

**Tips:** This stew can be frozen for up to 2 months. To use, thaw in the refrigerator overnight. Reheat on the stove top or in the microwave oven at high power until hot and bubbly.

If you can't find broccoli raab, use regular broccoli instead.

## Quick Conversion

**Greens and Beans Stew with Sausage:** For a dual vegetarian/nonvegetarian dish, prepare the recipe with the following changes. For the sausage portion, warm 1 teaspoon olive oil in a medium saucepan. Add 4 ounces of thinly sliced cooked kielbasa sausage. Brown over medium-high heat. Pour in half of the cooked bean-carrot mixture. Stir in half of the greens. Proceed as directed.

# Fennel and Bean Cassoulet

- **4 teaspoons olive oil**
- **½ teaspoon paprika**
- **½ teaspoon dried Italian seasoning**
- **4 slices white or whole wheat bread, trimmed and cubed**
- **2 carrots, thinly sliced**
- **1 small fennel bulb, thinly sliced**
- **1 onion, chopped**
- **1 garlic clove, minced**
- **3 cups vegetable broth**
- **1 can (16 ounces) red kidney beans, rinsed and drained**
- **1 can (16 ounces) white beans, rinsed and drained**
- **2 tomatoes, chopped**
- **½ teaspoon dried sage**
- **½ teaspoon dried thyme**
- **1 tablespoon cornstarch**

PREHEAT THE OVEN TO 350°F. Coat an 11" × 7" baking dish with nonstick spray.

WARM 2 TEASPOONS OF THE OIL in a large nonstick skillet over medium heat. Stir in the paprika and Italian seasoning. Cook for 1 minute. Add the bread cubes. Cook, stirring frequently, for 3 to 5 minutes, or until golden. Remove and set aside.

WARM THE REMAINING 2 TEASPOONS OIL in the same skillet over medium heat. Add the carrots, fennel, onion, and garlic. Cook, stirring frequently, for 8 minutes, or until tender. Stir in 2½ cups broth, the kidney beans, white beans, tomatoes, sage, and thyme. In a cup, combine the cornstarch and the remaining ½ cup broth. Stir into the vegetables. Cover and simmer for 10 to 15 minutes, or until the mixture thickens slightly.

SPOON THE FENNEL MIXTURE into the baking dish. Top with the bread cubes.

BAKE FOR 20 TO 25 MINUTES, or until the mixture is bubbly and the bread is browned.

**Makes 4 servings**

***Per serving:*** *441 calories, 25 g. protein, 77 g. carbohydrates, 7 g. fat, 3 mg. cholesterol, 918 mg. sodium, 22 g. dietary fiber*

**Tip:** This stew can be frozen for up to 1 month without the bread cubes. To use, thaw in the refrigerator overnight. Top with the bread cubes, and bake for 25 to 30 minutes, or until the mixture is bubbly and the bread is browned.

## Quick Conversion

**Fennel and Bean Cassoulet with Sausage:** For a dual vegetarian/nonvegetarian dish, prepare the recipe with the following changes. Coat two 8" × 8" baking dishes with nonstick spray. Divide the vegetable-bean mixture between the baking dishes. To make the sausage portion, remove the casings from ½ pound of sausage. Cook in the same skillet used for the vegetables for 5 to 8 minutes, or until no longer pink, stirring frequently to crumble. Stir into one of the baking dishes. Place the bread cubes over both portions. Bake for 15 to 20 minutes, or until the mixtures are bubbly and the cubes are browned.

# Tofu Ragout with Root Vegetables

- ¼ cup all-purpose flour
- ½ teaspoon paprika
- ¼ teaspoon garlic salt
- 8 ounces extra-firm tofu, drained, squeezed dry, and cubed
- 2 teaspoons olive oil
- 1 small onion, chopped
- 2 cloves garlic, minced
- 3 ribs celery, chopped
- ½ butternut or acorn squash, peeled and cubed
- 2 sweet potatoes, cubed
- 2 parsnips, thinly sliced
- 1 cup vegetable broth
- ¼ cup dry red wine or nonalcoholic wine
- ½ teaspoon dried thyme

In a large food-storage bag, combine the flour, paprika, and garlic salt. Add the tofu. Shake to coat.

Warm 1 teaspoon of the oil in a large saucepan over medium heat. Add the tofu, shaking off excess flour. Cook, stirring frequently, for 4 to 5 minutes, or until golden. Transfer to a bowl. Cover to keep warm.

Add the remaining 1 teaspoon oil to the saucepan. Stir in the onion, garlic, and celery. Cook, stirring frequently, for 4 minutes. Add the squash, potatoes, parsnips, and ½ cup of the broth. Cook over medium heat for 6 to 8 minutes, or just until the vegetables are tender. Stir in the wine, thyme, and remaining ½ cup broth. Bring to a boil. Reduce the heat to low, cover, and simmer for 10 minutes.

Mash some of the vegetables in the pan with the back of a spoon to thicken. Stir in the tofu. Cook for 8 to 10 minutes, or until the mixture is thick and the vegetables are tender.

**Makes 4 servings**

***Per serving:*** *241 calories, 8 g. protein, 40 g. carbohydrates, 6 g. fat, 0 mg. cholesterol, 356 mg. sodium, 6 g. dietary fiber*

## Quick Conversion

**Tofu Ragout with Root Vegetables and Ham:** For a dual vegetarian/non-vegetarian dish, prepare the recipe with the following changes. Before adding the tofu, divide the stew between 2 saucepans. For the ham portion, stir in ½ pound cubed cooked lean ham. Cook both portions for 8 to 10 minutes, or until thick and the vegetables are tender.

# Squash and Corn Stew

- 2 teaspoons olive oil
- 1 onion, chopped
- 1 green bell pepper, chopped
- 2 cloves garlic, minced
- ½ teaspoon ground cumin
- 1 small winter squash, peeled and cubed
- 2 Idaho potatoes, peeled and cubed
- 2½ cups vegetable broth
- 1 can (14½ ounces) chopped tomatoes
- 1 cup 1% buttermilk
- 1 cup frozen corn, thawed
- 2 tablespoons parsley

WARM THE OIL IN A LARGE SAUCEPAN over medium heat. Add the onion, pepper, and garlic. Cook, stirring frequently, for 4 to 5 minutes, or until tender. Stir in the cumin. Cook for 1 minute. Stir in the squash and potatoes. Cook for 2 minutes.

ADD THE BROTH AND TOMATOES (with juice). Bring to a boil. Reduce the heat to low. Simmer for 20 to 30 minutes, or until the vegetables are tender.

STIR IN THE BUTTERMILK, corn, and parsley. Cook for 5 minutes to blend flavors.

**Makes 4 servings**

***Per serving:*** *218 calories, 8 g. protein, 40 g. carbohydrates, 5 g. fat, 2 mg. cholesterol, 1,105 mg. sodium, 3 g. dietary fiber*

**Tip:** This stew can be frozen for up to 2 months. To use, thaw in the refrigerator overnight. Reheat on the stove top or in the microwave oven at high power until hot and bubbly.

## Quick Conversion

**Squash and Corn Stew with Chicken:** For a dual vegetarian/nonvegetarian dish, prepare the recipe with the following changes. Pour half of the completed soup into a medium saucepan. For the chicken portion, stir in ½ pound cubed cooked chicken. Simmer for 5 minutes to blend flavors.

# Substantial Salads and Vegetable Dishes

*"If Elvis Presley had eaten green vegetables, he'd still be alive."*

—Ian Dury, British musician

# Substantial Salads and Vegetable Dishes

VEGETABLES HAVE COME into their own. They no longer play second fiddle to the meat on the plate. Now, they can be the soloist! Vegetable-Tortilla Bake, for example, is a meal in itself. It's chock-full of vegetables, beans, cheese, and tortilla chips. And Lemon-Marinated Vegetable Kabobs make a vibrant main dish for the summertime grill.

Of course, vegetables are perfect side dishes, too. Roasted Red and Sweet Potatoes pair well with any cool-weather meal. Or if you're planning a light spring dinner, Artichokes with Creamy Horseradish Dip makes a wonderful first course.

## Recipes

● Kid-Friendly Recipe

● Freezable Recipe

● Microwaveable Recipe

# Spicy Asian Slaw

- ½ **cup rice wine vinegar**
- 2 **tablespoons sesame oil**
- 1 **teaspoon soy sauce**
- 1 **teaspoon sugar**
- ¼ **teaspoon dried red-pepper flakes**
- ½ **small head red cabbage, thinly sliced**
- ½ **small head napa or green cabbage, thinly sliced**
- ½ **cup rinsed and drained sliced canned water chestnuts**
- 2 **scallions, chopped**
- 1 **carrot, shredded**
- 2 **tablespoons chopped fresh cilantro or parsley**
- ¼ **cup unsalted dry-roasted peanuts**

IN A LARGE BOWL, combine the vinegar, oil, soy sauce, sugar, and red-pepper flakes. Add the red cabbage, napa or green cabbage, water chestnuts, scallions, carrot, and cilantro or parsley. Toss to mix. Sprinkle with the peanuts.

**Makes 4 servings**

***Per serving:*** *168 calories, 4 g. protein, 12 g. carbohydrates, 12 g. fat, 0 mg. cholesterol, 104 mg. sodium, 4 g. dietary fiber*

## Quick Conversion

**Spicy Asian Slaw with Chicken:** For a dual vegetarian/nonvegetarian dish, prepare the recipe with the following changes. Divide the salad between 2 serving bowls. For the chicken portion, add ½ pound cubed cooked chicken breast to one of the bowls.

# Crispy Caesar Salad

- **10** ounces green beans, steamed
- **½** cup (4 ounces) reduced-fat plain yogurt
- **¼** cup (2 ounces) reduced-fat sour cream
- **2** tablespoons lemon juice
- **1** tablespoon Dijon mustard
- **1** teaspoon vegetarian Worcestershire sauce
- **2** cloves garlic, crushed
- **1** head romaine lettuce, torn
- **1** cup rinsed and drained canned cannellini beans
- **1** teaspoon olive oil
- **4** slices pumpernickel bread, cubed
- **1** tablespoon (¼ ounce) grated Parmesan cheese

PLACE THE GREEN BEANS IN A STEAMER BASKET over simmering water. Steam for 7 minutes, or until tender. Let cool to room temperature.

MEANWHILE, IN A LARGE BOWL, combine the yogurt, sour cream, lemon juice, mustard, Worcestershire sauce, and garlic. Add the green beans, lettuce, and cannellini beans. Toss to mix.

WARM THE OIL in a large nonstick skillet over medium heat. Add the bread cubes. Cook for 4 to 5 minutes, or until crisp. Remove from the heat and stir in the cheese. Add to the lettuce-bean mixture. Toss to mix.

**Makes 4 servings**

***Per serving:*** *244 calories, 12 g. protein, 40 g. carbohydrates, 5 g. fat, 8 mg. cholesterol, 295 mg. sodium, 8 g. dietary fiber*

**Tip:** Vegetarian Worcestershire sauce made without anchovies is available in health food stores. You can also use regular Worcestershire sauce.

## Quick Conversion

**Crispy Caesar Salad with Chicken:** For a dual vegetarian/nonvegetarian dish, prepare the recipe with the following changes. Divide the salad between 2 serving bowls. Season 12 ounces chicken tenders with ¼ teaspoon garlic salt and ¼ teaspoon ground black pepper. Grill or broil for 5 to 10 minutes, or until a thermometer inserted in a tender registers 160°F and the juices run clear when pierced. Add to one of the bowls.

# Lentil-Pea Salad

- 3½ cups vegetable broth
- 1 cup brown lentils, sorted, rinsed, and drained
- 2 cloves garlic
- 3 tablespoons red wine vinegar
- 2 teaspoons dried dillweed or 2 tablespoons chopped fresh dill
- ¼ teaspoon salt
- ¼ teaspoon ground black pepper
- 2 teaspoons olive oil
- 2 scallions, chopped
- 2 cups frozen peas, thawed
- 2 tomatoes, chopped

IN A 2-QUART SAUCEPAN over high heat, combine 3 cups of the broth and the lentils. Bring to a boil. Reduce the heat to low. Partially cover and simmer for 30 to 40 minutes, or until the lentils are tender.

MEANWHILE, MASH THE GARLIC in a large serving bowl. Mix in the vinegar, dill, salt, pepper, and remaining ½ cup broth.

WARM THE OIL in a medium nonstick skillet over medium-high heat. Add the scallions and cook for 2 minutes. Stir in the peas and tomatoes. Cook, stirring frequently, 6 to 8 minutes, or until the tomatoes are tender. Transfer to the serving bowl.

DRAIN THE LENTILS and add to the serving bowl. Toss to mix.

**Makes 4 servings**

***Per serving:*** *281 calories, 20 g. protein, 43 g. carbohydrates, 5 g. fat, 0 mg. cholesterol, 1,112 mg. sodium, 19 g. dietary fiber*

**Tip:** This dish can be frozen for up to 2 weeks. To use, thaw overnight in the refrigerator and serve cold. To serve warm, reheat in the microwave oven at high power. You can also use this filling to stuff steamed bell pepper halves.

## Quick Conversion

**Lentil-Pea Salad with Ham:** For a dual vegetarian/nonvegetarian dish, prepare the recipe with the following changes. Divide the salad between 2 serving bowls. For the ham portion, add ½ pound cubed cooked lean ham to one of the bowls.

# Tangy Potato Salad

- **1 pound red potatoes, quartered**
- **1 head broccoli, separated into florets**
- **1 teaspoon butter**
- **1 bunch scallions, chopped**
- **1 tablespoon all-purpose flour**
- **½ cup cider vinegar**
- **¼ cup vegetable broth**
- **2 teaspoons honey**
- **¼ teaspoon celery seeds**
- **2 tablespoons (½ ounce) crumbled blue cheese**

PLACE THE POTATOES AND BROCCOLI in a steamer basket over simmering water. Steam for 10 to 12 minutes, or until tender.

MEANWHILE, MELT THE BUTTER in a small saucepan over medium heat. Add the scallions. Cook for 2 to 4 minutes, or until tender. Remove from the heat. Whisk in the flour (a whisk will make a smoother sauce than a spoon will). Return to the heat. Cook for 1 minute, whisking constantly. Add the vinegar, broth, honey, and celery seeds. Bring to a boil. Reduce the heat to low. Cook, whisking constantly, for 2 to 3 minutes, or until the sauce thickens slightly.

PLACE THE POTATOES and broccoli in a large serving bowl. Pour on the vinegar mixture and toss to mix. Sprinkle with the cheese.

**Makes 4 servings**

***Per serving:*** *146 calories, 5 g. protein, 27 g. carbohydrates, 3 g. fat, 6 mg. cholesterol, 88 mg. sodium, 4 g. dietary fiber*

## Quick Conversion

**Tangy Potato Salad with Ham:** For a dual vegetarian/nonvegetarian dish, prepare the recipe with the following changes. Divide the salad between 2 bowls. For the ham portion, add ½ pound cubed baked ham to one of the bowls. You can also use 1 can (6 ounces) water-packed white tuna in place of the ham.

# Macaroni-Bean Salad

- **1 cup (about 5 ounces) elbow macaroni**
- **⅓ cup reduced-fat mayonnaise**
- **¼ cup (2 ounces) reduced-fat sour cream**
- **⅓ cup (1⅓ ounces) crumbled herb-flavored feta cheese**
- **2 tablespoons 1% milk**
- **1 teaspoon cider vinegar**
- **¼ teaspoon ground black pepper**
- **1 can (14½ ounces) chickpeas, rinsed and drained**
- **1 carrot, shredded**
- **2 ribs celery, chopped**
- **¼ cup pimiento-stuffed olives**
- **1 small red bell pepper, chopped (optional)**
- **¼ teaspoon salt**

COOK THE MACARONI according to package directions. Drain well.

IN A LARGE BOWL, mix the mayonnaise, sour cream, cheese, milk, vinegar, and black pepper. Add the cooked macaroni, chickpeas, carrot, celery, olives, bell pepper (if using), and salt. Toss to mix.

**Makes 4 servings**

***Per serving:*** *350 calories, 11 g. protein, 53 g. carbohydrates, 11 g. fat, 19 mg. cholesterol, 947 mg. sodium, 7 g. dietary fiber*

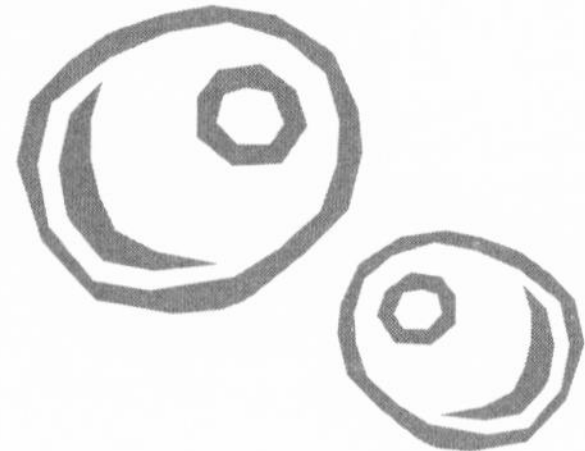

## Quick Conversion

**Macaroni-Bean Salad with Pastrami:** For a dual vegetarian/nonvegetarian dish, prepare the recipe with the following changes. Divide the salad between 2 bowls. For the pastrami portion, add ¼ pound cubed cooked pastrami to one of the bowls. I sometimes use ½ pound peeled and deveined cooked medium shrimp instead of pastrami.

# Watercress-Apple Salad

- ½ cup (4 ounces) reduced-fat plain yogurt
- ½ small red onion, minced
- 1 garlic clove, minced
- 1 teaspoon Dijon mustard
- 1 teaspoon cider vinegar
- ¼ teaspoon ground black pepper
- 2 bunches watercress, stems removed
- 2 large leaves red-leaf lettuce, torn
- 1 Granny Smith apple, thinly sliced
- ¼ cup (1 ounce) crumbled blue cheese

IN A LARGE BOWL, combine the yogurt, onion, garlic, mustard, vinegar, and pepper. Add the watercress, lettuce, apple, and cheese. Toss to mix.

**Makes 4 servings**

***Per serving:*** *79 calories, 4 g. protein, 10 g. carbohydrates, 3 g. fat, 8 mg. cholesterol, 151 mg. sodium, 1 g. dietary fiber*

**Tip:** Arugula makes a nice addition to or substitute for the watercress.

## Quick Conversion

**Watercress-Apple Salad with Chicken:** For a dual vegetarian/nonvegetarian dish, prepare the recipe with the following changes. Divide the salad between 2 serving bowls. For the chicken portion, add ½ pound cubed cooked chicken breast to one of the bowls.

# Mango-Black Bean Salad

- 2 tablespoons olive oil
- 1 tablespoon lime juice
- 1 tablespoon honey
- 1 teaspoon ground cumin
- ½ teaspoon mustard powder
- ¼ teaspoon ground black pepper
- 1 can (16 ounces) black beans, rinsed and drained
- 2 tomatoes, chopped
- 1½ mangoes, cubed, or 2 mandarin oranges, separated into sections
- ½ avocado, cubed
- 2 scallions, chopped

In a large bowl, combine the oil, lime juice, honey, cumin, mustard, and pepper. Add the beans, tomatoes, mangoes or oranges, avocado, and scallions. Toss to mix.

Let stand at room temperature for 15 minutes to blend flavors.

**Makes 4 servings**

***Per serving:*** *341 calories, 13 g. protein, 49 g. carbohydrates, 12 g. fat, 0 mg. cholesterol, 13 mg. sodium, 15 g. dietary fiber*

## Quick Conversion

**Mango-Black Bean Salad with Chicken:** For a dual vegetarian/nonvegetarian dish, prepare the recipe with the following changes. Divide the salad between 2 serving bowls. For the chicken portion, add ½ pound cubed cooked chicken to one of the bowls.

# Tabbouleh-Artichoke Salad

- 1¼ cups vegetable broth
- 1 cup bulgur
- ¼ cup dry-pack sun-dried tomatoes
- 1 cup coarsely chopped marinated artichoke hearts
- 1 bunch arugula or ¼ pound spinach, finely chopped
- 2 scallions, chopped
- ¼ cup sliced black olives
- 2 tablespoons parsley
- ½ cup reduced-fat Italian salad dressing
- ¼ cup (1 ounce) crumbled feta cheese
- 2 tablespoons slivered almonds (optional)

BRING THE BROTH TO A BOIL in a medium saucepan over high heat. Remove from the heat. Stir in the bulgur. Cover and let stand for 15 to 20 minutes, or until the bulgur is soft.

MEANWHILE, SOAK THE TOMATOES in hot water to cover for 10 minutes, or until soft. Drain well and chop.

IN A LARGE SERVING BOWL, combine the artichokes, arugula or spinach, scallions, olives, parsley, and tomatoes. Stir in the bulgur. Add the dressing and toss to mix. Sprinkle with the cheese and almonds, if using.

**Makes 4 servings**

***Per serving:*** *382 calories, 9 g. protein, 49 g. carbohydrates, 17 g. fat, 8 mg. cholesterol, 1,028 mg. sodium, 12 g. dietary fiber*

## Quick Conversion

**Tabbouleh-Artichoke Salad with Prosciutto:** For a dual vegetarian/nonvegetarian dish, prepare the recipe with the following changes. Divide the salad between 2 serving bowls. For the prosciutto portion, add 3 ounces finely chopped prosciutto to one of the bowls.

# Cauliflower with Citrus Vinaigrette

- 2 tablespoons olive oil
- 1 red onion, thinly sliced and separated into rings
- 2 cloves garlic, crushed
- ¼ cup orange juice
- ¼ cup pink grapefruit juice
- 1 tablespoon balsamic vinegar
- 2 tablespoons honey
- 1 small head cauliflower, separated into florets
- ¼ cup pitted kalamata olives
- 1 navel orange, separated into sections

WARM THE OIL in a large nonstick skillet over medium heat. Add the onion and garlic. Cook for 4 minutes, or until soft. Add the orange juice, grapefruit juice, vinegar, honey, cauliflower, and olives. Cover and simmer for 6 to 8 minutes, or until the cauliflower is crisp-tender. Stir in the orange sections.

**Makes 4 servings**

***Per serving:*** *181 calories, 6 g. protein, 26 g. carbohydrates, 8 g. fat, 0 mg. cholesterol, 105 mg. sodium, 7 g. dietary fiber*

## Quick Conversion

**Cauliflower and Scallops with Citrus Vinaigrette:** For a dual vegetarian/nonvegetarian dish, prepare the recipe with the following changes. Divide the salad between 2 serving bowls. For the scallop portion, brush ½ pound sea scallops with 2 tablespoons grapefruit juice and 2 teaspoons olive oil. Broil for 4 to 8 minutes, or until opaque and cooked through. Add to one of the bowls.

# Creamed Spinach 

- **1½ pounds spinach, stems removed**
- **2 teaspoons butter**
- **1 small onion, chopped**
- **1 tablespoon all-purpose flour**
- **¾ cup 1% milk**
- **2 tablespoons reduced-fat sour cream**
- **¼ teaspoon ground nutmeg**
- **¼ teaspoon salt**
- **⅛ teaspoon ground black pepper**

RINSE THE SPINACH, leaving water still on the leaves. Place in a large saucepan. Cover and cook over medium heat for 3 to 4 minutes, or until wilted. Drain and keep warm.

MEANWHILE, MELT THE BUTTER in a small saucepan over medium heat. Add the onion. Cook for 2 to 3 minutes, or until tender. Whisk in the flour (a whisk will make a smoother sauce than a spoon will). Cook for 1 minute, whisking constantly. Whisk in the milk. Bring to a boil. Reduce the heat to low. Cook, whisking constantly, for 4 to 5 minutes, or until the sauce thickens. Remove from the heat. Stir in the sour cream, nutmeg, salt, and pepper.

PLACE THE SPINACH in a large serving bowl. Pour on the sauce and toss to mix.

**Makes 4 servings**

***Per serving:*** *87 calories, 7 g. protein, 8 g. carbohydrates, 4 g. fat, 10 mg. cholesterol, 395 mg. sodium, 16 g. dietary fiber*

**Tip:** For variety, replace half of the spinach with kale, torn into large pieces.

# Brussels Sprouts with Roasted Red Peppers

- **1 pound brussels sprouts, halved**
- **1 tablespoon olive oil**
- **2 cloves garlic, minced**
- **1 package (10 ounces) frozen pearl onions, thawed**
- **1 cup chopped jarred roasted red peppers**
- **½ cup vegetable broth**
- **1 tablespoon white wine vinegar**
- **½ teaspoon dried thyme**

PLACE THE BRUSSELS SPROUTS in a steamer basket over simmering water. Steam for 10 minutes, or just until tender.

MEANWHILE, WARM THE OIL in a large nonstick skillet over medium heat. Add the garlic. Cook, stirring frequently, for 1 minute. Stir in the onions and peppers. Cook for 4 to 5 minutes, or until the onions are tender.

ADD THE BRUSSELS SPROUTS, broth, vinegar, and thyme. Bring to a boil over high heat. Reduce the heat to medium. Cook for 2 to 3 minutes, or until the liquid reduces slightly.

**Makes 4 servings**

***Per serving:*** *130 calories, 5 g. protein, 20 g. carbohydrates, 4 g. fat, 0 mg. cholesterol, 344 mg. sodium, 6 g. dietary fiber*

## Quick Conversion

**Brussels Sprouts with Roasted Red Peppers and Bacon:** For a dual vegetarian/nonvegetarian dish, prepare the recipe with the following changes. For the bacon portion, cook 3 pieces of bacon in a medium nonstick skillet over medium heat until crisp. Transfer to a plate lined with paper towels. Crumble over half of the brussels sprouts.

# Southwest Succotash

- ½ cup ranch salad dressing
- 2 tablespoons lime juice
- 2 tablespoons chopped fresh cilantro or parsley
- ½ teaspoon chili powder
- 1 package (10 ounces) frozen lima beans, thawed
- 1 package (10 ounces) frozen corn, thawed
- 1 red bell pepper, chopped
- 4 scallions, chopped
- 1 avocado, cubed (optional)

IN A LARGE BOWL, combine the dressing, lime juice, cilantro or parsley, and chili powder. Add the beans, corn, pepper, scallions, and avocado, if using. Toss to mix.

**Makes 4 servings**

***Per serving:*** *293 calories, 8 g. protein, 35 g. carbohydrates, 16 g. fat, 1 mg. cholesterol, 228 mg. sodium, 9 g. dietary fiber*

## Quick Conversion

**Southwest Succotash with Shrimp:** For a dual vegetarian/nonvegetarian dish, prepare the recipe with the following changes. Divide the salad between 2 bowls. For the shrimp portion, stir 1 pound peeled and deveined cooked medium shrimp into one of the bowls.

# Carrot-Apple Pudding

- **1 tablespoon butter**
- **1 tablespoon sugar**
- **1 pound carrots, thinly sliced**
- **¼ cup all-purpose flour**
- **½ teaspoon baking powder**
- **½ teaspoon pumpkin pie spice**
- **¼ cup finely chopped dried apples**
- **¼ cup (1 ounce) reduced-fat Cheddar cheese**
- **¼ cup chopped dried apricots (optional)**
- **¼ cup golden raisins (optional)**
- **2 large egg whites**

PREHEAT THE OVEN TO 475°F. Rub the butter over the bottom and sides of a 1½-quart baking dish. Sprinkle with the sugar.

PLACE THE CARROTS in a medium saucepan. Cover with water. Bring to a boil over high heat. Reduce the heat to medium-low, partially cover, and simmer for 10 to 12 minutes, or until tender. Drain and place in a medium bowl. In a blender or food processor or with a spoon, blend or process or mash the carrots until almost smooth.

IN A LARGE BOWL, combine the flour, baking powder, and pumpkin pie spice. Stir in the carrots, apples, cheese, apricots (if using), and raisins (if using).

IN A MEDIUM BOWL, with a mixer set at high speed, beat the egg whites until stiff peaks form. Gently fold into the carrot mixture. Spoon into the baking dish.

BAKE FOR 10 MINUTES. Reduce the heat to 350°F and bake for 45 to 50 minutes, or until set and golden brown.

**Makes 4 servings**

***Per serving:*** *207 calories, 6 g. protein, 36 g. carbohydrates, 5 g. fat, 13 mg. cholesterol, 215 mg. sodium, 5 g. dietary fiber*

**Tip:** This dish can be frozen for up to 3 weeks. To use, thaw overnight in the refrigerator. Reheat in the oven at 350°F or in the microwave oven at medium power just until warm. You can also use 1½ boxes frozen butternut squash (15 ounces total) in place of the carrots.

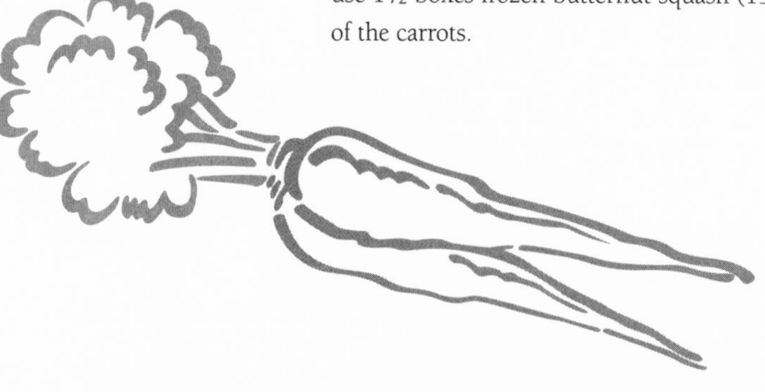

# Artichokes with Creamy Horseradish Dip

- **4** **artichokes**
- **½** **cup vegetable broth**
- **3** **tablespoons lemon juice**
- **½** **cup (4 ounces) reduced-fat plain yogurt**
- **2** **teaspoons dried chives or 2 tablespoons chopped fresh**
- **1** **tablespoon parsley**
- **1** **tablespoon prepared white horseradish**
- **2** **cloves garlic, crushed**

RINSE THE ARTICHOKES. With a sharp knife, cut off the stems and about 1" straight across the top. With kitchen scissors, trim off any thorny leaf tips. Pull off any loose leaves from around the bottoms.

PLACE THE ARTICHOKES, stem side down, in a deep nonstick saucepan that is just wide enough to hold them tightly in a single layer. Add the broth and 2 tablespoons of the lemon juice. Cover and bring to a boil over medium-high heat. Reduce the heat to medium-low. Cook, covered, for 30 to 40 minutes, or until an outer leaf pulls off easily. If liquid evaporates during cooking, add a little water to the pan.

MEANWHILE, IN A SMALL BOWL, combine the remaining 1 tablespoon lemon juice, yogurt, chives, parsley, horseradish, and garlic.

TO SERVE, dip the leaves into the yogurt mixture and eat the tender underside of each leaf. Discard the fuzzy center (the choke). Cut the solid heart into chunks and dip into the yogurt mixture.

**Makes 4 servings**

***Per serving:*** *91 calories, 6 g. protein, 18 g. carbohydrates, 1 g. fat, 2 mg. cholesterol, 268 mg. sodium, 7 g. dietary fiber*

# Roasted Red and Sweet Potatoes

- **¾ pound sweet potatoes, sliced 2" thick**
- **¾ pound red potatoes, sliced 2" thick**
- **1 small fennel bulb, sliced**
- **1 leek, white part only, thinly sliced**
- **1 cup golden raisins**
- **¼ cup vegetable broth**
- **1 tablespoon balsamic vinegar**
- **1 tablespoon olive oil**
- **1 teaspoon dried tarragon or 1 tablespoon chopped fresh**
- **2 cloves garlic, minced**

PREHEAT THE OVEN TO 400°F. Coat a large roasting pan with nonstick spray.

PLACE THE SWEET POTATOES, red potatoes, fennel, leek, raisins, broth, vinegar, and oil in the pan. Toss to mix. Roast for 20 to 25 minutes, or just until tender.

STIR IN THE TARRAGON and garlic. Roast for 10 minutes.

**Makes 4 servings**

***Per serving:*** *347 calories, 6 g. protein, 76 g. carbohydrates, 4 g. fat, 0 mg. cholesterol, 117 mg. sodium, 8 g. dietary fiber*

## Best Seasonal Vegetables

Eating seasonally means getting the freshest, best-tasting, least expensive produce available. Here are my top 20 vegetables to use year-round. Look for these on your next trip to the store.

**Winter:** Brussels sprouts, cauliflower, fennel, parsnips, rutabagas

**Spring:** Artichokes, asparagus, beets, green beans, peas

**Summer:** Corn, jícama, snow peas, tomatoes, zucchini

**Fall:** Endive, leeks, pumpkin, sweet potatoes, winter squash

# Braised Winter Vegetables

- 1 red onion, chopped
- ½ acorn squash, peeled and cubed
- 2 parsnips, sliced
- 2 carrots, sliced
- ¼ small head red cabbage, shredded
- ½ cup golden raisins
- ½ cup vegetable broth
- 1 tablespoon packed brown sugar
- 2 teaspoons Dijon mustard
- ½ teaspoon dried thyme
- 1 tablespoon vegetable-protein bacon bits

COAT A LARGE NONSTICK SKILLET with nonstick cooking spray and warm over medium heat. Add the onion and cook, stirring frequently, for 2 minutes. Add the squash, parsnips, and carrots. Cook for 5 minutes, or just until the vegetables are tender. Stir in the cabbage and raisins. Cook for 2 to 4 minutes, or until the cabbage begins to wilt.

STIR IN THE BROTH, brown sugar, mustard, and thyme. Bring to a boil over medium-high heat. Reduce the heat to medium-low. Cover and simmer for 5 minutes. Sprinkle with the bacon bits.

**Makes 4 servings**

***Per serving:*** *169 calories, 3 g. protein, 39 g. carbohydrates, 1 g. fat, 0 mg. cholesterol, 134 mg. sodium, 7 g. dietary fiber*

**Tip:** Most brands of bacon bits are made from vegetable protein.

## Quick Conversion

**Braised Winter Vegetables with Bacon:** For a dual vegetarian/nonvegetarian dish, prepare the recipe with the following changes. Divide the vegetables between 2 bowls. Use only half the vegetable-protein bacon bits and sprinkle them over the vegetarian portion. For the bacon portion, cook 3 strips of bacon in a medium nonstick skillet over medium heat until crisp. Transfer to a plate lined with paper towels. Crumble over the other portion.

# Stuffed Acorn Squash

- 2 acorn squash, halved and seeded
- Juice of ½ lemon
- ½ cup vegetable broth
- 1 cup coarsely chopped mixed dried fruit
- 1 small pear, chopped
- ¼ cup pine nuts
- 1 tablespoon packed brown sugar
- ¼ teaspoon ground cinnamon
- ¼ cup maple syrup

PREHEAT THE OVEN TO 400°F. Place the squash, cut side up, in a 13" × 9" baking dish.

IN A MEDIUM BOWL, combine the lemon juice, broth, dried fruit, pear, pine nuts, brown sugar, and cinnamon. Spoon into the squash, drizzling any remaining liquid onto the cut side of the squash. Drizzle with the maple syrup.

COVER WITH FOIL and bake for 30 to 35 minutes, or until the squash is tender, basting occasionally with the juices.

**Makes 4 servings**

***Per serving:*** *329 calories, 6 g. protein, 74 g. carbohydrates, 5 g. fat, 0 mg. cholesterol, 137 mg. sodium, 8 g. dietary fiber*

## 8 Tips on Picking Produce

Look for the best fruits and vegetables you can find. Fresh produce tastes better and lasts longer. Knowing exactly what to look for also cuts down on shopping time. Here are the basics.

1. Buy loose produce by the pound. It always has better flavor than prepackaged produce.
2. Pick fruits and vegetables that look alive. They should be firm and plump with vivid color and no bruising.
3. Shop for produce that is in season. It's the most flavorful, least expensive, and easiest to prepare.
4. Pick leafy vegetables that are brightly colored and not wilted. Avoid lettuces with browned edges.
5. Look for summer fruits and vegetables that feel heavy for their size and have no spots or scars (includes avocados, cucumbers, eggplants, summer squash, and tomatoes).
6. Fresh root vegetables will be firm and heavy with no bruises, soft spots, or sprouting (such as eyes on potatoes).
7. Cabbages, broccoli, and cauliflower should have firm, compact heads with no browning or yellowing on the leaves or florets. Brussels sprouts should be free of yellowing leaves.
8. Fresh onions, garlic, scallions, and shallots will feel tight, firm, and somewhat heavy but never damp or soft.

# Lemon-Marinated Vegetable Kabobs 

- ¼ cup (2 ounces) reduced-fat plain yogurt
- 2 tablespoons mayonnaise
- 2 tablespoons lemon juice
- 1 tablespoon chopped fresh rosemary or 1 teaspoon dried
- ¼ teaspoon salt
- ¼ teaspoon ground black pepper
- 1 small eggplant, cubed
- 1 zucchini, sliced 1" thick
- 2 yellow bell peppers, chopped
- 1 pint cherry tomatoes

COAT A BROILER PAN OR GRILL RACK with nonstick spray. Preheat the broiler or grill according to the manufacturer's directions.

IN A LARGE GLASS BOWL, combine the yogurt, mayonnaise, lemon juice, rosemary, salt, and black pepper. Add the eggplant, zucchini, bell peppers, and tomatoes. Toss to mix. Let stand for 20 minutes or up to 2 hours to blend flavors.

THREAD ONTO 8 METAL SKEWERS. Broil or grill about 5" from the heat for 4 to 6 minutes, or until the vegetables are just tender, basting with any remaining marinade. Turn and cook for 4 to 6 minutes longer, or until the eggplant is tender but the tomatoes are still intact.

**Makes 4 servings**

***Per serving:*** *145 calories, 4 g. protein, 21 g. carbohydrates, 7 g. fat, 5 mg. cholesterol, 209 mg. sodium, 6 g. dietary fiber*

## Quick Conversion

**Lemon-Marinated Vegetable and Shrimp Kabobs:** For a dual vegetarian/nonvegetarian dish, prepare the recipe with the following changes. Use half the ingredients for the vegetarian portion. For the shrimp portion, add 3 peeled and deveined medium shrimp to each skewer. Broil or grill until the shrimp are cooked through and pink. I sometimes use 3 ounces cubed boneless, skinless chicken breast instead of or in addition to the shrimp.

# Eggplant Casserole

- **1 large eggplant, peeled and cubed**
- **½ cup Italian-flavored dry bread crumbs**
- **2 scallions, chopped**
- **¼ cup chopped fresh basil leaves**
- **⅛ teaspoon ground black pepper**
- **2 large eggs**
- **6 plum tomatoes, thinly sliced**
- **1 small zucchini or yellow summer squash, thinly sliced**
- **½ cup (2 ounces) shredded reduced-fat mozzarella cheese**
- **2 tablespoons (½ ounce) grated Parmesan cheese**

PREHEAT THE OVEN TO 350°F.

COAT AN 11" × 7" BAKING DISH with nonstick spray. Add the eggplant and coat with spray. Bake, stirring occasionally, for 20 to 25 minutes, or until very soft.

MEANWHILE, IN A LARGE BOWL, combine the bread crumbs, scallions, basil, and pepper. Stir in the cooked eggplant and eggs.

SPOON INTO THE BAKING DISH. Top with the tomatoes, zucchini or yellow squash, mozzarella, and Parmesan.

BAKE FOR 20 TO 25 MINUTES, or until the cheese melts and the zucchini or yellow squash is tender.

**Makes 4 servings**

***Per serving:*** *222 calories, 13 g. protein, 30 g. carbohydrates, 7 g. fat, 116 mg. cholesterol, 283 mg. sodium, 7 g. dietary fiber*

**Tip:** This dish can be frozen for up to 1 month. To use, thaw overnight in the refrigerator. Bake, covered, at 350°F until hot throughout.

## Quick Conversion

**Eggplant Casserole with Beef:** For a dual vegetarian/nonvegetarian dish, prepare the recipe with the following changes. Bake the eggplant in two 8" × 8" baking dishes. Divide the eggplant-egg mixture between the dishes. For the beef portion, warm a medium nonstick skillet over medium heat. Place 8 ounces beef in the skillet. Cook, stirring frequently, for 5 to 10 minutes, or until no longer pink. Stir into 1 of the baking dishes. Top both mixtures with the remaining ingredients. Bake both portions for 15 to 20 minutes, or until the zucchini or yellow squash is tender.

# Vegetable-Tortilla Bake

- **1** **zucchini, thinly sliced**
- **1** **can (16 ounces) red kidney beans, rinsed and drained**
- **1** **cup frozen corn, thawed**
- **¼** **cup chopped canned green chiles**
- **1¼** **cups (5 ounces) reduced-fat Cheddar cheese**
- **1½** **cups salsa**
- **1** **cup coarsely crushed baked tortilla chips**
- **½** **cup (4 ounces) reduced-fat sour cream**
- **1** **tomato, chopped**

PREHEAT THE OVEN TO 350°F.

COAT AN 11" × 7" BAKING DISH with nonstick spray. Add the zucchini, beans, corn, and chiles. Stir to mix. Sprinkle with ½ cup of the cheese. Spread the salsa over the cheese. Sprinkle with the chips and top with the remaining ¾ cup cheese.

BAKE FOR 20 TO 25 MINUTES, or until the cheese melts and the zucchini is tender. Serve with the sour cream and tomato.

**Makes 4 servings**

***Per serving:*** *522 calories, 26 g. protein, 83 g. carbohydrates, 13 g. fat, 37 mg. cholesterol, 843 mg. sodium, 14 g. dietary fiber*

**Tip:** This dish can be frozen for up to 1 month. To use, thaw overnight in the refrigerator. Reheat, covered, in the oven at 350°F or in the microwave oven on medium power until hot throughout.

## Quick Conversion

**Vegetable-Tortilla Bake with Chicken:** For a dual vegetarian/nonvegetarian dish, prepare the recipe with the following changes. Divide the zucchini mixture between two 8" × 8" baking dishes. For the chicken portion, stir ½ pound cubed cooked chicken breast into one of the baking dishes. Top with the cheese and salsa as directed. Bake both portions for 15 to 20 minutes, or until the cheese melts and the zucchini is tender.

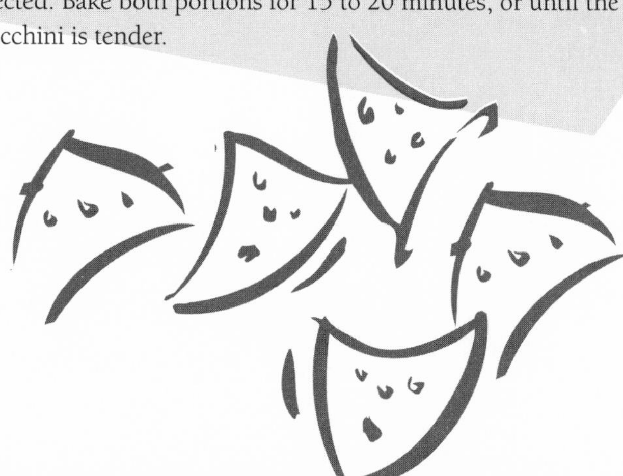

# Pizza, Tacos, and Sandwiches

*"I'm not deprived; I can eat whatever I want."*

—Alicia Silverstone, U.S. actress, on being vegetarian

# *Pizza, Tacos, and Sandwiches*

THIS IS MY FAVORITE CHAPTER. Bread-based dishes like pizza and sandwiches have universal appeal. And they're loved equally by youngsters and adults. I can't imagine anyone of any age not liking a Grilled Tomato and Mozzarella Sandwich or Peanut Butter and Raisin Spirals. Maybe it's because eating bread foods is so informal. "Fingers were made before forks," as the old saying goes.

## Recipes

● Kid-Friendly Recipe

● Freezable Recipe

● Microwaveable Recipe

# Master Pizza Dough

- **3 cups all-purpose flour**
- **1 package (¼ ounce) quick-rising yeast**
- **½ teaspoon salt**
- **1⅓ cups warm water (105°–115°F)**
- **2 teaspoons olive oil**
- **All-purpose flour**

IN A FOOD PROCESSOR OR LARGE BOWL, combine the flour, yeast, and salt.

IN A LARGE MEASURING CUP, combine the water and oil. Slowly pour into the flour mixture, with the food processor running or stirring constantly. Process or stir until the mixture forms a ball.

LIGHTLY FLOUR A WORK SURFACE. Turn the dough out onto the work surface. Knead for 1 minute to form a smooth ball.

COAT A LARGE CLEAN BOWL with nonstick spray. Add the dough and turn to coat all sides with the spray. Cover with a kitchen towel and set in a warm, draft-free place for 30 minutes, or until the dough doubles in bulk.

PUNCH DOWN and divide into 4 pieces. On a lightly floured work surface, roll each piece into an 8" circle, keeping the other pieces covered with a towel as you work. Top with your favorite ingredients and bake 12 to 15 minutes, or until the crust is golden.

**Makes 4 pizza shells (8" diameter each)**

***Per serving:*** *374 calories, 10 g. protein, 72 g. carbohydrates, 4 g. fat, 0 mg. cholesterol, 295 mg. sodium, 3 g. dietary fiber*

**Tips:** All or part of the completed unrolled pizza dough can be frozen for up to 3 months. Place in a freezer bag, seal, and freeze.

For a whole wheat crust, substitute 1 cup whole wheat flour for 1 cup of the all-purpose flour.

For an herb crust, add ¼ cup chopped fresh basil or parsley along with the flour, yeast, and salt.

For a tomato-flavored crust, substitute ⅓ cup tomato juice for ⅓ cup of the water.

# Baked Ziti Pizza 

- **1** **cup (about 2 ounces) ziti**
- **1** **cup prepared spaghetti sauce**
- **1** **cup (8 ounces) reduced-fat ricotta cheese**
- **½** **cup (2 ounces) shredded reduced-fat mozzarella cheese**
- **1** **teaspoon dried Italian seasoning**
- **1** **tablespoon yellow cornmeal**
- **1** **tube (10 ounces) refrigerated pizza dough or ½ recipe Master Pizza Dough (opposite page)**
- **2** **plum tomatoes, thinly sliced**
- **2** **tablespoons (½ ounce) grated Parmesan cheese**

PREHEAT THE OVEN TO 425°F.

COOK THE PASTA according to package directions. Drain well.

IN A MEDIUM BOWL, combine the ziti, ¾ cup of the spaghetti sauce, the ricotta, mozzarella, and Italian seasoning.

SPRINKLE THE CORNMEAL over a 12" pizza pan or stone. Unroll the dough and stretch it to fit the pan.

SPREAD THE REMAINING ¼ CUP SPAGHETTI SAUCE over the dough. Top with the tomato slices. Spread the ziti mixture evenly over the dough, leaving a 1" border. Sprinkle with the Parmesan.

BAKE FOR 12 TO 15 MINUTES, or until the crust is golden and the ziti is heated through. Let stand for 5 minutes before slicing.

**Makes 4 servings**

***Per serving:*** *278 calories, 20 g. protein, 36 g. carbohydrates, 6 g. fat, 52 mg. cholesterol, 968 mg. sodium, 3 g. dietary fiber*

## Quick Conversion

**Baked Ziti Pizza with Sausage:** For a dual vegetarian/nonvegetarian dish, prepare the recipe with the following changes. Sprinkle half of the dough with 3 ounces cooked and crumbled Italian sausage.

# Caponata Pizza

- 4 teaspoons olive oil
- 1 eggplant, peeled and cut into small cubes (2–2½ cups)
- 1 zucchini, sliced
- 2 ribs celery, chopped
- 1 onion, chopped
- ¼ cup sliced pitted kalamata or black olives
- 2 tomatoes, chopped
- 2 tablespoons balsamic vinegar
- 1 tablespoon capers
- 1 teaspoon sugar
- 1 prepared pizza crust (12" diameter)
- ½ cup (2 ounces) crumbled feta cheese

PREHEAT THE OVEN TO 350°F.

WARM THE OIL in a large nonstick skillet over medium-high heat. Add the eggplant, zucchini, celery, and onion. Cook, stirring frequently, for 6 to 8 minutes, or until the eggplant is tender. Add the olives and tomatoes. Bring to a boil. Reduce the heat to low and stir in the vinegar, capers, and sugar. Simmer for 15 to 20 minutes, or until the liquid evaporates and the mixture is thick.

PLACE THE CRUST on a large ungreased baking sheet. Spread the eggplant mixture over the crust. Sprinkle with the cheese.

BAKE FOR 15 TO 20 MINUTES, or until the crust is golden and the cheese begins to melt. Let stand for 5 minutes before slicing.

**Makes 4 servings**

***Per serving:*** *289 calories, 9 g. protein, 49 g. carbohydrates, 8 g. fat, 8 mg. cholesterol, 1,097 mg. sodium, 7 g. dietary fiber*

**Tip:** Prepared and rolled pizza crusts are available in the refrigerated sections of most supermarkets.

## Quick Conversion

**Caponata Pizza with Tuna:** For a dual vegetarian/nonvegetarian dish, prepare the recipe with the following changes. Arrange 1 can (3½ ounces) rinsed, drained, and flaked water-packed white tuna over half of the caponata. Top with the cheese and bake as directed.

# Tossed Salad Pizza

- **1** tablespoon yellow cornmeal
- **1** tube (10 ounces) refrigerated pizza dough or ½ recipe Master Pizza Dough (page 118)
- **1** tablespoon olive oil
- **½** teaspoon dried Italian seasoning
- **4** ounces mesclun or mixed baby salad greens
- **1** onion, thinly sliced and separated into rings
- **1** tomato, chopped
- **1** green bell pepper, cut into strips
- **⅓** cup Italian salad dressing
- **2** tablespoons (½ ounce) grated Parmesan cheese

PREHEAT THE OVEN TO 375°F.

SPRINKLE THE CORNMEAL over a large pizza pan or stone. Unroll the dough and stretch into a 15" circle. Place on the pan or stone. Brush the oil over the dough. Sprinkle with the Italian seasoning. Bake for 10 to 15 minutes, or just until golden.

REDUCE THE HEAT to 350°F.

IN A MEDIUM BOWL, combine the mesclun or salad greens, onion, tomato, pepper, and dressing. Top the crust with the salad. Sprinkle with the cheese. Bake for 8 to 10 minutes, or until heated through and the crust is golden brown.

**Makes 4 servings**

***Per serving:*** *265 calories, 5 g. protein, 28 g. carbohydrates, 15 g. fat, 2 mg. cholesterol, 286 mg. sodium, 3 g. dietary fiber*

**Tip:** You may prefer to eat this pizza with a knife and a fork.

# Deep-Dish Spinach Pie

- **1 tube (10 ounces) refrigerated pizza dough or ½ recipe Master Pizza Dough (page 118)**
- **2 teaspoons olive oil**
- **6 ounces mushrooms, thinly sliced**
- **1 tomato, chopped**
- **1 onion, chopped**
- **4 cups coarsely chopped fresh spinach**
- **½ teaspoon dried basil**
- **¼ teaspoon salt**
- **1 container (15 ounces) reduced-fat ricotta cheese**
- **¼ cup (1 ounce) grated Parmesan cheese**
- **1 large egg, lightly beaten**
- **½ cup (2 ounces) shredded reduced-fat mozzarella cheese**

PREHEAT THE OVEN TO 375°F. Coat a 10" springform pan or deep-dish pie plate with nonstick spray. Press the dough into the bottom and up the sides of the pan.

WARM THE OIL in a large nonstick skillet over medium-high heat for 1 minute. Add the mushrooms, tomato, and onion. Cook, stirring frequently, for 4 to 5 minutes, or until the vegetables are tender. Add the spinach, basil, and salt. Cook for 2 to 4 minutes, or until the spinach is tender.

IN A MEDIUM BOWL, combine the ricotta, Parmesan, and egg. Spread over the dough. Top with the mushroom mixture and mozzarella. Fold any visible dough over the outer edge of the filling (dough will not completely cover the filling). Bake for 15 to 20 minutes, or until the crust is golden and the filling is heated through. Let stand for 5 minutes before removing the sides of the springform pan. Cut into wedges.

**Makes 4 servings**

***Per serving:*** *249 calories, 26 g. protein, 10 g. carbohydrates, 13 g. fat, 82 mg. cholesterol, 567 mg. sodium, 4 g. dietary fiber*

# No-Bake Mushroom Pizza



- **4** **ounces reduced-fat cream cheese**
- **¼** **cup (2 ounces) reduced-fat sour cream**
- **1** **tablespoon Dijon mustard**
- **1** **tablespoon parsley**
- **1** **teaspoon olive oil**
- **6** **ounces mushrooms, chopped**
- **1** **onion, chopped**
- **½** **teaspoon dried thyme**
- **¼** **teaspoon salt**
- **1** **prepared prebaked pizza crust (12" diameter)**
- **2** **cups coarsely chopped fresh spinach**

IN A SMALL BOWL, combine the cream cheese, sour cream, mustard, and parsley.

WARM THE OIL in a large nonstick skillet over medium-high heat. Add the mushrooms, onion, thyme, and salt. Cook, stirring frequently, for 4 to 5 minutes, or until the onion is tender.

SPREAD THE CREAM CHEESE MIXTURE over the crust to within ½" of the edge. Top with the mushroom mixture and spinach. Cut into wedges.

**Makes 4 servings**

***Per serving:*** *268 calories, 10 g. protein, 33 g. carbohydrates, 11 g. fat, 23 mg. cholesterol, 336 mg. sodium, 3 g. dietary fiber*

**Tips:** This makes a great appetizer for 8 when cut into small wedges.

Be sure to use a prebaked crust for this pizza (such as Boboli) because it is not cooked after the toppings are added.

# Mushroom and Artichoke French Bread Pizza

- **2** **teaspoons olive oil**
- **6** **ounces mushrooms, thinly sliced**
- **1** **bunch scallions, chopped**
- **½** **teaspoon dried oregano**
- **1** **large loaf French bread, split lengthwise**
- **1** **jar (4½ ounces) marinated artichoke hearts, drained and coarsely chopped**
- **1** **can (14½ ounces) diced Italian-style tomatoes, drained**
- **¼** **cup (1 ounce) grated Parmesan cheese**

PREHEAT THE OVEN TO 375°F.

WARM THE OIL in a large nonstick skillet over medium-high heat. Add the mushrooms, scallions, and oregano. Cook, stirring frequently, for 4 to 5 minutes, or until the mushrooms are tender.

PLACE THE BREAD HALVES on a large ungreased baking sheet. Top each with the mushroom mixture, artichokes, tomatoes, and cheese. Bake for 15 to 20 minutes, or until the cheese is melted and the pizza is heated through. Let stand for 5 minutes. Cut into 4 pieces.

**Makes 4 servings**

***Per serving:*** *258 calories, 10 g. protein, 36 g. carbohydrates, 10 g. fat, 5 mg. cholesterol, 1,028 mg. sodium, 4 g. dietary fiber*

## Quick Conversion

**Mushroom and Sausage French Bread Pizza:** For a dual vegetarian/non-vegetarian dish, prepare the recipe with the following changes. For the sausage portion, remove the casings from ½ pound Italian-style turkey sausage. Cook in a medium skillet over medium-high heat for 8 minutes, or until no longer pink, stirring frequently to crumble. Arrange on one half of the bread before topping with the cheese. Bake as directed.

# Oven-Fried Tomato Baguette

- **½ cup yellow cornmeal**
- **2 tablespoons (½ ounce) grated Parmesan cheese**
- **¼ teaspoon ground black pepper**
- **2 large egg whites, lightly beaten**
- **2 tomatoes, cut into ½"-thick slices**
- **2 teaspoons olive oil**
- **¼ cup reduced-fat mayonnaise**
- **1 tablespoon Dijon mustard**
- **1 teaspoon white wine vinegar or cider vinegar**
- **1 large sourdough or French baguette, split lengthwise**
- **1 cup packed fresh basil leaves**
- **½ green bell pepper, chopped (optional)**
- **½ cup (2 ounces) shredded reduced-fat mozzarella cheese**

PREHEAT THE OVEN TO 375°F. Coat a large baking sheet with nonstick spray.

ON A LARGE PIECE OF WAXED PAPER, combine the cornmeal, Parmesan, and black pepper. Place the egg whites in a small shallow bowl. Dip the tomatoes in the whites. Coat with the cornmeal mixture. Place on the prepared baking sheet. Drizzle the olive oil over the tomatoes. Bake for 5 to 6 minutes on each side, or until golden. Remove from the oven and set aside. Change the oven temperature to broil.

MEANWHILE, IN A SMALL BOWL, mix the mayonnaise, mustard, and vinegar. Spread over the cut sides of the baguette. Top with the basil, tomatoes, bell pepper (if using), and mozzarella. Place on the baking sheet. Broil for 2 to 3 minutes, or until the mozzarella melts. Cut into 4 pieces.

**Makes 4 servings**

***Per serving:*** *264 calories, 11 g. protein, 33 g. carbohydrates, 10 g. fat, 12 mg. cholesterol, 419 mg. sodium, 3 g. dietary fiber*

## Quick Conversion

**Oven-Fried Tomato Baguette with Sausage:** For a dual vegetarian/nonvegetarian dish, prepare the recipe with the following changes. For the sausage portion, cook 6 ounces loose sausage in a medium nonstick skillet over medium heat for 5 to 7 minutes, or until no longer pink, breaking up the meat with a spoon. Sprinkle over half of the baguette before topping with the cheese. Broil as directed.

# Mixed Olive and Goat Cheese Pita Pizza

- ½ cup dry-pack sun-dried tomatoes
- ½ cup pimiento-stuffed olives, coarsely chopped
- ¼ cup sliced pitted kalamata or black olives
- 1 tablespoon balsamic vinegar
- 2 large pitas, split through the side
- 1 cup (4 ounces) crumbled herb-flavored goat cheese

PREHEAT THE OVEN TO 425°F. In a small bowl, soak the tomatoes in hot water to cover for 10 minutes, or until soft. Drain well.

IN A MEDIUM BOWL, combine the tomatoes, pimiento-stuffed olives, kalamata or black olives, and vinegar.

PLACE THE 4 PITA ROUNDS on a large baking sheet or a pizza pan. Coat with nonstick spray. Arrange the olive mixture evenly over the pitas. Sprinkle with the cheese.

BAKE FOR 8 TO 10 MINUTES, or until the cheese is melted and the pitas are golden.

**Makes 4 servings**

***Per serving:*** *214 calories, 9 g. protein, 24 g. carbohydrates, 10 g. fat, 13 mg. cholesterol, 835 mg. sodium, 1 g. dietary fiber*

## Quick Conversion

**Mixed Olive and Goat Cheese Pita Pizza with Roasted Chicken:** For a dual vegetarian/nonvegetarian dish, prepare the recipe with the following changes. For the chicken portion, arrange 6 ounces roasted chicken cut into thin strips over half the pitas. Top with the remaining ingredients and bake as directed.

# Scrambled Egg Soft Tacos

- 8 flour tortillas (6" diameter)
- 2 teaspoons butter
- 4 scallions, chopped
- 1 cup chopped spinach (optional)
- ¼ cup chopped canned green chiles
- 6 eggs
- 2 ounces reduced-fat cream cheese
- ¼ teaspoon salt
- ¼ teaspoon ground black pepper
- ½ cup salsa

WARM THE TORTILLAS according to the package directions.

MEANWHILE, MELT THE BUTTER in a medium nonstick skillet over medium heat. Add the scallions, spinach (if using), and chiles. Cook, stirring frequently, for 2 minutes.

IN A MEDIUM BOWL, lightly beat the eggs, cream cheese, salt, and pepper. Pour into the skillet. Cook, stirring gently, for 2 to 3 minutes, or until the eggs are set. Spoon down the centers of the warmed tortillas. Top each with 1 tablespoon salsa. Roll up to enclose.

**Makes 4 servings**

***Per serving:*** *292 calories, 15 g. protein, 24 g. carbohydrates, 15 g. fat, 333 mg. cholesterol, 511 mg. sodium, 2 g. dietary fiber*

## Quick Conversion

**Scrambled Egg Soft Tacos with Bacon:** For a dual vegetarian/nonvegetarian dish, prepare the recipe with the following changes. For the bacon portion, cook 4 slices bacon in a medium nonstick skillet over medium-high heat until crisp. Transfer to a plate lined with paper towels. Crumble over half of the filled tortillas before rolling up.

# Grilled Vegetable Tacos

- **2 tablespoons olive oil**
- **2 tablespoons balsamic vinegar**
- **2 tablespoons chopped fresh rosemary or 1 teaspoon dried**
- **¼ teaspoon salt**
- **2 zucchini, cut lengthwise into ¼"-thick slices**
- **1 eggplant, cut into ½"-thick slices**
- **1 red bell pepper, cut into strips**
- **2 ounces portobello mushrooms, sliced**
- **4 flour tortillas (12" diameter)**
- **½ cup (2 ounces) crumbled goat cheese**
- **¼ cup chopped fresh basil**

COAT A GRILL RACK OR AN INDOOR GRILL PAN with nonstick spray. Preheat according to manufacturer's directions.

IN A LARGE SHALLOW DISH, combine the oil, vinegar, rosemary, and salt. Add the zucchini, eggplant, pepper, and mushrooms. Toss to coat and let stand for at least 15 minutes or up to 2 hours to blend the flavors. Grill for 10 to 12 minutes, or until tender, turning frequently and brushing with any remaining marinade.

MEANWHILE, HEAT THE TORTILLAS according to the package directions. Arrange the vegetable mixture down the centers of the warmed tortillas. Top with the cheese and basil. Roll up.

**Makes 4 servings**

***Per serving:*** *280 calories, 9 g. protein, 41 g. carbohydrates, 9 g. fat, 7 mg. cholesterol, 379 mg. sodium, 7 g. dietary fiber*

## Quick Conversion

**Grilled Vegetable and Chicken Tacos:** For a dual vegetarian/nonvegetarian dish, prepare the recipe with the following changes. Divide the marinade and vegetables between 2 dishes. For the chicken portion, add 6 ounces boneless, skinless chicken breast cut into strips to one of the dishes. Marinate as directed. Grill the vegetables as directed. Grill the chicken for 20 minutes, or until no longer pink and the juices run clear when pierced. Fill half of the tortillas with the chicken and vegetables. Fill the other half with the vegetables. Proceed as directed.

# Curried Vegetable Tacos

- **½ cup (4 ounces) reduced-fat plain yogurt**
- **1 tablespoon lime juice**
- **¼ teaspoon ground cumin**
- **Pinch of ground red pepper**
- **2 teaspoons olive oil**
- **2 red potatoes, cubed**
- **2 parsnips, sliced**
- **1 butternut squash, cubed**
- **1 green bell pepper, chopped**
- **¼ teaspoon ground black pepper**
- **½ cup vegetable broth**
- **¾ teaspoon curry powder**
- **1 tomato, chopped**
- **8 corn taco shells or pitas**
- **8 large romaine lettuce leaves**

In a medium bowl, combine the yogurt, lime juice, cumin, and red pepper.

Warm the oil in a large nonstick skillet over medium heat. Add the potatoes, parsnips, squash, bell pepper, and black pepper. Cook, stirring frequently, for 4 to 5 minutes, or just until tender.

In a small bowl, mix the broth and curry powder. Pour into the skillet. Bring to a boil over medium-high heat. Reduce the heat to low and simmer for 5 to 10 minutes, or until the liquid evaporates and the vegetables are tender.

Remove from the heat and stir in the tomato. Line the taco shells or pitas with the lettuce. Fill with the vegetable mixture. Top each with 1 tablespoon of the yogurt mixture.

**Makes 4 servings**

***Per serving:*** *305 calories, 7 g. protein, 54 g. carbohydrates, 9 g. fat, 1 mg. cholesterol, 250 mg. sodium, 8 g. dietary fiber*

# Mixed-Bean Tacos

- **2 teaspoons olive oil**
- **1 onion, chopped**
- **1 green bell pepper, chopped**
- **1 tablespoon chili powder**
- **1 can (16 ounces) black beans, rinsed and drained**
- **1 can (16 ounces) red kidney beans, rinsed and drained**
- **2 cans (8 ounces each) low-sodium tomato sauce**
- **2 tablespoons chopped fresh cilantro or parsley**
- **2 teaspoons red wine vinegar or lime juice**
- **12 corn taco shells**
- **1 cup shredded lettuce**
- **1 tomato, chopped**
- **½ cup (4 ounces) reduced-fat sour cream**

WARM THE OIL IN A LARGE NONSTICK SKILLET over medium-high heat. Add the onion and pepper. Cook, stirring frequently, for 4 to 5 minutes, or until the onion is tender. Stir in the chili powder and cook for 1 minute. Add the black beans, kidney beans, tomato sauce, and cilantro or parsley. Simmer for 6 to 8 minutes, or until slightly thickened. Stir in the vinegar or lime juice. Cook for 2 minutes to blend the flavors.

HEAT THE TACO SHELLS according to the package directions. Spoon the bean mixture into the shells. Top with the lettuce, tomato, and sour cream.

**Makes 4 servings**

***Per serving:*** *442 calories, 15 g. protein, 72 g. carbohydrates, 13 g. fat, 0 mg. cholesterol, 1,057 mg. sodium, 20 g. dietary fiber*

## Quick Conversion

**Mixed-Bean Tacos with Beef:** For a dual vegetarian/nonvegetarian dish, prepare the recipe with the following changes. Use 8-ounce cans of black beans and red kidney beans. For the beef portion, cook ½ pound lean ground beef and 1 teaspoon chili powder in a medium nonstick skillet over medium heat for 5 minutes, or until the beef is no longer pink. Add half of the completed bean mixture. Fill half of the taco shells with the beef mixture. Top with the remaining ingredients.

# Couscous-Stuffed Tacos

- **2 teaspoons olive oil**
- **4 scallions, chopped**
- **2 cloves garlic, minced**
- **1 cup mixed-vegetable juice**
- **1 cup water**
- **1½ cups couscous**
- **2 tomatoes, chopped**
- **½ cup golden raisins**
- **¼ cup coarsely chopped pimiento-stuffed olives**
- **2 tablespoons toasted pine nuts**
- **4 flour tortillas (12" diameter)**
- **¼ cup (2 ounces) fat-free sour cream**

WARM THE OIL IN A MEDIUM SAUCEPAN over medium-high heat. Add the scallions and garlic. Cook for 2 to 3 minutes, or until tender. Stir in the vegetable juice and water. Bring to a boil. Stir in the couscous, tomatoes, raisins, olives, and pine nuts. Remove from the heat. Cover and let stand for 5 minutes. Uncover and fluff with a fork.

MEANWHILE, WARM THE TORTILLAS according to the package directions. Spoon the couscous mixture down the centers of the tortillas. Top each with 1 tablespoon sour cream. Roll up.

**Makes 4 servings**

***Per serving:*** *546 calories, 15 g. protein, 99 g. carbohydrates, 11 g. fat, 6 mg. cholesterol, 574 mg. sodium, 7 g. dietary fiber*

**Tip:** To toast the pine nuts, place them in a dry skillet over medium heat and shake the pan for 2 minutes, or until fragrant and golden.

# Gorgonzola-Apple Melt

- **¼ cup prepared mango chutney**
- **8 slices whole wheat bread**
- **1 large Golden Delicious apple, peeled, cored, and thinly sliced**
- **1 cup (4 ounces) crumbled Gorgonzola cheese**
- **2 teaspoons butter**

SPREAD THE CHUTNEY EVENLY over 4 slices of the bread. Top with the apple slices, cheese, and remaining bread slices.

MELT THE BUTTER in a large nonstick skillet over medium heat. Add the sandwiches. Cook for 2 to 3 minutes on each side, or until golden and the cheese begins to melt.

**Makes 4 servings**

***Per serving:*** *290 calories, 11 g. protein, 35 g. carbohydrates, 13 g. fat, 36 mg. cholesterol, 482 mg. sodium, 5 g. dietary fiber*

**Tip:** I sometimes replace the apple with a pear.

# Grilled Portobello Sandwiches

- **4 portobello mushroom caps (about 1 pound)**
- **½ cup balsamic or red wine vinaigrette salad dressing**
- **¼ cup prepared roasted red-pepper sauce**
- **4 onion rolls, split**
- **4 slices provolone cheese**
- **2 cups fresh arugula or spinach leaves**

PLACE THE MUSHROOMS in a large shallow baking dish. Pour on the dressing, turning the mushrooms to coat all sides. Let stand for 15 minutes.

COAT A GRILL RACK or an indoor ridged grill pan with non-stick spray. Preheat according to manufacturer's directions. Grill the mushrooms for 5 minutes on each side, or until the centers are fork-tender, basting occasionally with any leftover marinade.

SPREAD 1 TABLESPOON RED-PEPPER SAUCE on the bottom of each roll. Top each with a mushroom, 1 slice of the cheese, arugula or spinach, and the remaining roll half.

**Makes 4 servings**

***Per serving:*** *301 calories, 15 g. protein, 34 g. carbohydrates, 11 g. fat, 34 mg. cholesterol, 432 mg. sodium, 6 g. dietary fiber*

**Tip:** To make your own roasted red-pepper sauce, place ¼ cup undrained jarred roasted red peppers in a blender or food processor. Blend or process until smooth.

## Quick Conversion

**Grilled Portobello and Chicken Sandwiches:** For a dual vegetarian/nonvegetarian dish, prepare the recipe with the following changes. Divide the mushrooms and marinade between 2 baking dishes. For the chicken portion, add a 3-ounce chicken breast cutlet to one of the dishes and marinate as directed. Grill the chicken for 6 to 8 minutes on each side, or until no longer pink and the juices run clear when pierced. Cut the chicken in half and add to 2 of the sandwiches.

# Grilled Tomato and Mozzarella Sandwich

- ¼ cup prepared pesto
- 8 slices Italian or sourdough bread, cut into ½"-thick slices
- 4 ounces mozzarella cheese, thinly sliced
- 1 large tomato, thinly sliced
- ¼ cup chopped fresh basil leaves
- 1 teaspoon butter

SPREAD THE PESTO EVENLY over 4 slices of the bread. Top with the cheese, tomato, basil, and remaining bread slices.

MELT THE BUTTER in a large nonstick skillet over medium heat. Add the sandwiches. Cook for 2 to 3 minutes on each side, or until golden brown and the cheese is melted.

**Makes 4 servings**

***Per serving:*** *302 calories, 13 g. protein, 30 g. carbohydrates, 15 g. fat, 21 mg. cholesterol, 548 mg. sodium, 2 g. dietary fiber*

## Quick Conversion

**Grilled Tomato and Mozzarella Sandwich with Turkey:** For a dual vegetarian/nonvegetarian dish, prepare the recipe with the following changes. For the turkey portion, add 2 ounces thinly sliced smoked turkey to half of the sandwiches before cooking.

# Alfalfa-Tofu Sandwich

- **¼ cup honey Dijon or plain Dijon mustard**
- **1 tablespoon cider vinegar**
- **1 teaspoon curry powder**
- **8 ounces firm tofu, drained, squeezed dry, and cubed**
- **3 ribs celery, chopped**
- **2 carrots, shredded**
- **1 bunch scallions, chopped**
- **4 large pitas, halved and split to form a pocket**
- **1 tomato, chopped**
- **1 cup alfalfa sprouts**
- **½ cup sliced sweet-and-sour pickles**

In a large bowl, combine the mustard, vinegar, and curry powder. Gently stir in the tofu, celery, carrots, and scallions. Let stand for 10 minutes.

Spoon into the pitas. Top with the tomato, sprouts, and pickles.

**Makes 4 servings**

***Per serving:*** *269 calories, 13 g. protein, 46 g. carbohydrates, 5 g. fat, 0 mg. cholesterol, 715 mg. sodium, 5 g. dietary fiber*

## Quick Conversion

**Alfalfa-Chicken Sandwich:** For a dual vegetarian/nonvegetarian dish, prepare the recipe with the following changes. Divide the mustard mixture, celery, carrots, and scallions between 2 bowls. Use only 4 ounces tofu and add to one of the bowls. For the chicken portion, add 4 ounces cubed cooked chicken to the other bowl. Proceed as directed, using the chicken mixture to prepare half of the sandwiches.

# Hummus-Pumpernickel Club

- 1 can (12 ounces) chickpeas, rinsed and drained
- ¼ cup (2 ounces) fat-free plain yogurt
- 2 scallions, minced
- 1 tablespoon lime or lemon juice
- 1 tablespoon tahini
- 2 teaspoons olive oil
- ¼ teaspoon ground cumin
- ⅛ teaspoon ground red pepper
- 8 slices pumpernickel bread
- ½ avocado, thinly sliced
- ½ red onion, thinly sliced and separated into rings
- 1 tomato, thinly sliced

PLACE THE CHICKPEAS in a food processor or blender. Process or blend until smooth, scraping down the sides of the container as necessary. Add the yogurt, scallions, lime or lemon juice, tahini, oil, cumin, and pepper. Process or blend until smooth and creamy.

SPREAD EQUAL AMOUNTS OF THE HUMMUS over 4 bread slices. Top with the avocado, onion, tomato, and remaining bread slices.

**Makes 4 servings**

***Per serving:*** *390 calories, 14 g. protein, 57 g. carbohydrates, 13 g. fat, 1 mg. cholesterol, 715 mg. sodium, 10 g. dietary fiber*

**Tip:** Tahini (sesame paste) is available in the international aisle of most supermarkets. If the hummus is too thick, thin it with a small amount of water.

# Crunchy Egg-Stuffed Pitas

- **3 red potatoes, finely chopped**
- **½ teaspoon salt**
- **4 large eggs**
- **½ cup reduced-fat mayonnaise**
- **2 tablespoons 1% milk**
- **1 tablespoon honey Dijon mustard**
- **2 teaspoons sweet pickle relish**
- **2 ribs celery, chopped**
- **1 carrot, shredded**
- **1 small red bell pepper, chopped**
- **4 large whole wheat pitas, halved and split to form a pocket**
- **1 cup chopped fresh arugula or spinach**
- **¼ cup coarsely chopped toasted walnuts (optional)**

PLACE THE POTATOES IN A MEDIUM SAUCEPAN with water to cover. Add the salt. Bring to a boil over high heat. Reduce the heat to low, cover, and simmer for 15 to 20 minutes, or until tender. Drain and let cool.

MEANWHILE, PLACE THE EGGS in a medium saucepan. Pour in water to cover. Bring to a boil over high heat. Reduce the heat to low and simmer for 15 minutes. Drain and let cool. Peel and chop.

IN A LARGE BOWL, combine the mayonnaise, milk, mustard, and relish. Stir in the potatoes, eggs, celery, carrot, and pepper.

LINE THE PITAS with the arugula or spinach. Stuff with the egg mixture. Top with the walnuts, if using.

**Makes 4 servings**

***Per serving:*** *426 calories, 15 g. protein, 64 g. carbohydrates, 12 g. fat, 221 mg. cholesterol, 620 mg. sodium, 5 g. dietary fiber*

**Tip:** To toast the walnuts, place them in a dry skillet over medium heat and shake the pan for 2 minutes, or until fragrant and golden.

## Quick Conversion

**Crunchy Egg-Stuffed Pitas with Shrimp:** For a dual vegetarian/nonvegetarian dish, prepare the recipe with the following changes. Use half the potatoes and eggs. Divide the prepared mayonnaise-potato mixture in half. For the shrimp portion, add ½ pound chopped peeled and deveined cooked medium shrimp to half of the mixture. Line the pitas as directed. Stuff half the pitas with the shrimp mixture and drizzle with 1 tablespoon lemon juice. Top with the walnuts, if using.

# Fruit and Nut Sandwiches

- 4 ounces reduced-fat cream cheese
- ¼ cup chopped pitted dates
- ¼ cup chopped dried apricots
- 2 tablespoons finely chopped walnuts
- 2 tablespoons 1% milk
- 1 tablespoon lemon juice
- 1 teaspoon grated lemon peel
- 8 slices raisin bread or date and nut bread
- 4 large romaine lettuce leaves

IN A SMALL BOWL, combine the cream cheese, dates, apricots, walnuts, milk, lemon juice, and lemon peel. Spread over 4 slices of the bread. Top with the lettuce and remaining bread slices.

**Makes 4 servings**

***Per serving:*** *350 calories, 10 g. protein, 45 g. carbohydrates, 15 g. fat, 17 mg. cholesterol, 298 mg. sodium, 4 g. dietary fiber*

## Quick Conversion

**Fruit and Nut Sandwiches with Smoked Turkey:** For a dual vegetarian/non-vegetarian dish, prepare the recipe with the following changes. For each turkey portion, top the cream cheese mixture with 1 ounce thinly sliced smoked turkey. Top with the lettuce and remaining bread slices.

# Peanut Butter and Raisin Spirals

- ½ cup natural peanut butter
- ¼ cup (2 ounces) fat-free plain yogurt
- 1 tablespoon honey
- ¼ teaspoon ground cinnamon
- 4 flour tortillas (8" diameter)
- ¼ cup golden raisins
- 2 tablespoons honey-flavored wheat germ

IN A SMALL BOWL, combine the peanut butter, yogurt, honey, and cinnamon.

SPREAD OVER THE TORTILLAS, coming to within ½" of the edges. Sprinkle with the raisins and wheat germ. Roll up and cut into 2" pieces.

**Makes 4 servings**

***Per serving:*** *376 calories, 13 g. protein, 42 g. carbohydrates, 19 g. fat, 1 mg. cholesterol, 329 mg. sodium, 4 g. dietary fiber*

# Southwestern Wrap

- 1 can (16 ounces) black beans, rinsed and drained
- 1 cup (4 ounces) crumbled feta cheese
- ½ cup salsa
- 2 tablespoons chopped fresh cilantro or parsley
- 1 can (12 ounces) cannellini beans, rinsed and drained
- 2 tablespoons reduced-fat cream cheese
- 1 tablespoon lime juice
- 4 flour tortillas (12" diameter)
- 1 cup (4 ounces) shredded reduced-fat Monterey Jack or Cheddar cheese

IN A MEDIUM BOWL, combine the black beans, feta, salsa, and cilantro or parsley.

IN A FOOD PROCESSOR or blender, combine the cannellini beans, cream cheese, and lime juice. Process or blend until smooth and spread over the tortillas. Top with the black bean mixture. Sprinkle each with ¼ cup Monterey Jack or Cheddar and roll up.

**Makes 4 servings**

***Per serving:*** *567 calories, 34 g. protein, 71 g. carbohydrates, 17 g. fat, 48 mg. cholesterol, 738 mg. sodium, 17 g. dietary fiber*

# Roasted Eggplant Wrap

- ½ cup dry-pack sun-dried tomatoes
- 1 eggplant, cubed
- 1 red bell pepper, cut into strips
- 1 red onion, thinly sliced and separated into rings
- ½ cup reduced-fat Caesar salad dressing
- 2 teaspoons olive oil
- 2 cups torn fresh spinach
- 1 cup (4 ounces) cubed smoked mozzarella cheese
- 4 flour tortillas or vegetable-flavored wraps (12" diameter)

PREHEAT THE OVEN TO 425°F.

IN A SMALL BOWL, soak the tomatoes in hot water to cover for 10 minutes, or until soft. Drain, reserving the liquid.

IN A LARGE ROASTING PAN, combine the tomatoes, eggplant, pepper, and onion. Pour in the dressing, oil, and reserved tomato liquid. Toss to coat. Bake, stirring occasionally, for 20 to 25 minutes, or until the vegetables are tender. Stir in the spinach and cheese.

SPOON THE EGGPLANT MIXTURE down the centers of the tortillas or wraps. Roll up to enclose.

**Makes 4 servings**

***Per serving:*** *291 calories, 13 g. protein, 36 g. carbohydrates, 11 g. fat, 16 mg. cholesterol, 853 mg. sodium, 7 g. dietary fiber*

# Cabbage Stir-Fry Wrap

- **2 ounces Chinese wheat noodles or spaghetti**
- **¼ cup natural peanut butter**
- **2 tablespoons fat-free plain yogurt**
- **Pinch of ground red pepper**
- **2 teaspoons sesame oil**
- **1 package (16 ounces) cole-slaw mix**
- **1 red bell pepper, cut into strips**
- **1 tablespoon chopped fresh ginger**
- **4 flour tortillas (12" diameter)**

COOK THE NOODLES OR SPAGHETTI according to package directions. Drain well.

MEANWHILE, IN A SMALL BOWL, combine the peanut butter, yogurt, and ground red pepper.

WARM THE OIL in a large wok or nonstick skillet over medium-high heat. Add the slaw mix, bell pepper, and ginger. Stir-fry for 5 to 7 minutes, or until the vegetables are just tender. Remove from the heat. Stir in the noodles or spaghetti.

SPOON THE VEGETABLE-PASTA MIXTURE down the centers of the tortillas. Roll up and serve with the peanut sauce.

**Makes 4 servings**

***Per serving:*** *333 calories, 11 g. protein, 42 g. carbohydrates, 15 g. fat, 0 mg. cholesterol, 271 mg. sodium, 6 g. dietary fiber*

## Quick Conversion

**Cabbage Stir-Fry Wrap with Shrimp:** For a dual vegetarian/nonvegetarian dish, prepare the recipe with the following changes. Transfer half of the completed cabbage mixture to a bowl and keep warm. To the remaining cabbage mixture in the wok or skillet, add 4 ounces peeled and deveined medium shrimp. Stir-fry for 4 minutes, or until the shrimp are opaque. Divide the noodles or spaghetti between both mixtures. Fill half the tortillas with the slaw filling and half with the shrimp filling. Sometimes I use 4 ounces bay scallops instead of the shrimp.

## Mix and Match a Sandwich

Deli meats are such popular sandwich fillings, you may think there's no such thing as a vegetarian sandwich. Here are a few ideas. Make a batch of the Balsamic Vinaigrette below and keep it in the refrigerator to drizzle over any of the sandwich fillings listed. Pick your favorite bread and additions to go with the filling. I often make a grain salad sandwich with the Tabbouleh-Artichoke Salad on page 103. For a pasta salad sandwich, try the Macaroni-Bean Salad on page 100.

| Fillers | Breads | Additions |
|---|---|---|
| Tomato, basil, and mozzarella | Baguettes | Arugula leaves |
| Grilled vegetables | Onion rolls | Spinach leaves |
| Egg and tofu salad | Multigrain bread | Roasted red peppers |
| Pasta salads | Large pitas | Sliced pickles |
| Grain salads | Large tortillas | Chopped walnuts |

### Balsamic Vinaigrette

- **3 tablespoons balsamic vinegar**
- **¼ teaspoon salt**
- **⅛ teaspoon ground black pepper**
- **½ cup olive oil**
- **2 tablespoons reduced-fat mayonnaise**
- **1 tablespoon Dijon mustard**

In a small bowl or glass bottle, combine the vinegar, salt, and pepper. Add the oil, mayonnaise, and mustard. Whisk or shake until well mixed. Refrigerate in a sealed container for up to 1 week.

Makes about ¾ cup

***Per tablespoon:*** *120 calories, 0 g. protein, 8 g. carbohydrates, 9 g. fat, 0 mg. cholesterol, 84 mg. sodium, 0 g. dietary fiber*

*"I am a vegetarian because it is a really good idea. It has to do with compassion and it is healthier too."*

—Paul McCartney, British musician

# Fast Five-Ingredient Main Dishes

FEELING PINCHED FOR TIME? You're not alone. Many cooks today say they have so little time they only want quick-cooking recipes with 8 to 10 ingredients.

Things are so hectic in my house that I created a slew of recipes with just 5 ingredients. It was a challenge, but the results are fantastic. Every recipe is fast. And much of the actual cooking is unattended, so you can read the mail, play with the kids, or just relax while dinner cooks itself.

## Recipes

● Kid-Friendly Recipe

● Freezable Recipe

● Microwaveable Recipe

# Lemon-Pepper Penne with Broccoli Raab

- **12** **ounces lemon-pepper penne**
- **2** **teaspoons olive oil**
- **4** **cloves garlic, minced**
- **1** **small bunch broccoli raab, tough stems removed**
- **½** **cup (2 ounces) crumbled feta cheese**

COOK THE PASTA according to package directions. Drain well and place in a large serving bowl.

MEANWHILE, WARM THE OIL in a large nonstick skillet over medium heat. Add the garlic and cook, stirring frequently, for 2 minutes. Add the broccoli raab and ⅛ teaspoon ground black pepper or lemon-pepper seasoning. Cook, stirring frequently, for 5 to 7 minutes, or until tender.

ADD THE BROCCOLI RAAB and cheese to the pasta. Toss to mix well.

**Makes 4 servings**

***Per serving:*** *434 calories, 16 g. protein, 67 g. carbohydrates, 11 g. fat, 25 mg. cholesterol, 333 mg. sodium, 3 g. dietary fiber*

**Tip:** For more zip, sprinkle with dried red-pepper flakes and Parmesan cheese.

## Quick Conversion

**Lemon-Pepper Penne with Broccoli Raab and Shrimp:** For a dual vegetarian/nonvegetarian dish, prepare the recipe with the following changes. Warm 1 teaspoon olive oil in the same skillet used to cook the broccoli raab. Add 1 teaspoon minced garlic and 14 peeled and deveined large shrimp. Cook for 5 minutes, or until opaque. Sprinkle with 1 teaspoon lemon juice and add to half of the pasta.

# Bow Ties with Pesto and Beans

**12** ounces bow-tie pasta
**1** onion, chopped
**1** red bell pepper, cut into short strips
**1** can (14 ounces) cannellini beans, rinsed and drained
**⅓** cup prepared pesto

COOK THE PASTA according to package directions. Drain well, reserving ½ cup cooking liquid.

MEANWHILE, COAT A LARGE NONSTICK SKILLET with nonstick spray. Warm over medium-high heat for 1 minute. Add the onion and bell pepper. Season with ¼ teaspoon salt and ⅛ teaspoon ground black pepper. Cook, stirring frequently, for 4 to 5 minutes, or until tender. Transfer to a large serving bowl.

ADD THE BEANS, pesto, and reserved cooking liquid. Toss to mix. Add the pasta and toss.

**Makes 4 servings**

***Per serving:*** *577 calories, 22 g. protein, 95 g. carbohydrates, 12 g. fat, 3 mg. cholesterol, 149 mg. sodium, 13 g. dietary fiber*

## Quick Conversion

**Bow Ties with Pesto, Beans, and Chicken:** For a dual vegetarian/nonvegetarian dish, prepare the recipe with the following changes. For the chicken portion, cut 4 ounces boneless, skinless chicken breasts into short strips. Coat the same skillet used to cook the onion and pepper with nonstick spray. Cook the chicken for 5 to 7 minutes over medium heat, or until no longer pink and the juices run clear when pierced. Add to half of the completed pasta.

# Rotelle with Artichoke Hearts

- **12** **ounces rotelle**
- **1** **jar (4½ ounces) marinated artichoke hearts, coarsely chopped**
- **½** **cup marinated sun-dried tomatoes, with liquid**
- **¼** **cup (1 ounce) crumbled goat cheese**
- **¼** **cup chopped fresh basil**

COOK THE PASTA according to package directions. Drain well.

MEANWHILE, IN A LARGE SERVING BOWL, combine the artichoke hearts, tomatoes, cheese, and basil. Add the pasta and toss to coat.

**Makes 4 servings**

***Per serving:*** *424 calories, 13 g. protein, 69 g. carbohydrates, 10 g. fat, 3 mg. cholesterol, 187 mg. sodium, 3 g. dietary fiber*

## Quick Conversion

**Rotelle with Artichoke Hearts and Tuna:** For a dual vegetarian/nonvegetarian dish, prepare the recipe with the following changes. Divide the complete dish between 2 bowls. For the tuna portion, add 1 can (6 ounces) flaked water-packed white tuna to one of the bowls.

## Salt, Pepper, and Water

In this chapter, three basic ingredients are not included in the 5-ingredient lineup: salt, pepper, and water. I excluded these because they are absolutely essential and extremely common in home kitchens. Amounts for these ingredients are specified in the directions rather than in the ingredient list for each recipe.

# Linguine with Lemon Cream Sauce

- **12 ounces linguine**
- **1 tablespoon cornstarch**
- **1 cup (8 ounces) reduced-fat lemon yogurt**
- **½ cup (2 ounces) grated Parmesan cheese**
- **¼ cup parsley**

COOK THE PASTA according to package directions. Drain and reserve ¼ cup cooking liquid.

MEANWHILE, IN A MEDIUM SAUCEPAN over low heat, combine the cornstarch and the reserved liquid. Stir until slightly thickened. Gradually stir in the yogurt and cheese. Stir in ¼ teaspoon ground black pepper or lemon-pepper seasoning. Add the pasta and toss to coat. Sprinkle with the parsley.

**Makes 4 servings**

***Per serving:*** *318 calories, 13 g. protein, 58 g. carbohydrates, 3 g. fat, 6 mg. cholesterol, 261 mg. sodium, 3 g. dietary fiber*

## Quick Conversion

**Linguine with Lemon Cream Sauce and Salmon:** For a dual vegetarian/non-vegetarian dish, prepare the recipe with the following changes. For the salmon portion, place 1 salmon steak (4 ounces) in a shallow baking dish. Pour ¼ cup Italian salad dressing over the salmon, turning to coat all sides. Let stand for 15 minutes. Coat a broiler pan with nonstick spray. Preheat the broiler. Broil the salmon for 5 to 7 minutes, or until opaque, occasionally basting with the marinade. Cut in half and serve over half of the pasta.

# Tortellini Lasagna

- **12** **ounces cheese tortellini**
- **1** **teaspoon olive oil**
- **1** **eggplant, cubed**
- **1½** **cups jarred vegetable-flavored spaghetti sauce**
- **½** **cup (2 ounces) shredded fontina or mozzarella cheese**

PREHEAT THE OVEN TO 350°F.

COOK THE PASTA according to package directions. Drain well.

MEANWHILE, WARM THE OIL in a large nonstick skillet over medium heat. Add the eggplant and cook, stirring frequently, for 6 to 8 minutes, or until tender.

SPREAD ½ CUP OF THE SAUCE in the bottom of a 1½-quart casserole. Top with half of the pasta, half of the eggplant, and another ½ cup sauce. Repeat layering, ending with the remaining ½ cup sauce. Top with the cheese.

COVER AND BAKE for 20 minutes. Uncover and bake for 10 minutes, or until bubbly.

**Makes 4 servings**

***Per serving:*** *348 calories, 15 g. protein, 49 g. carbohydrates, 11 g. fat, 30 mg. cholesterol, 742 mg. sodium, 8 g. dietary fiber*

**Tip:** For a chunkier mixture, add 1 chopped zucchini and 1 chopped onion to the eggplant when sautéing.

## Quick Conversion

**Tortellini Lasagna with Sausage:** For a dual vegetarian/nonvegetarian dish, prepare the recipe with the following changes. Place 6 ounces loose sausage in the skillet used to cook the eggplant. Cook over medium heat for 5 to 7 minutes, or until no longer pink. Sprinkle over half of the casserole before topping with the cheese. Bake as directed.

# Roquefort Focaccia

- 1 tube (10 ounces) refrigerated pizza dough or ½ recipe Master Pizza Dough (page 118)
- 1 large red onion, thinly sliced and separated into rings
- 1 small bunch arugula, stems removed and coarsely chopped
- 1 container (15 ounces) reduced-fat ricotta cheese
- ½ cup (2 ounces) crumbled Roquefort cheese

PREHEAT THE OVEN TO 375°F. Coat a 15½" jelly-roll pan with nonstick spray. Stretch the dough to fit the pan. Mist with olive-oil nonstick spray. Season with ⅛ teaspoon ground black pepper.

COAT A LARGE NONSTICK SKILLET with olive-oil nonstick spray. Add the onion and cook for 5 to 7 minutes, or until tender. Stir in the arugula and cook for 1 minute, or until wilted.

SPREAD THE RICOTTA over the dough. Top with the onion mixture and Roquefort. Bake for 25 to 30 minutes, or until the crust is golden.

**Makes 8 servings**

***Per serving:*** *110 calories, 10 g. protein, 8 g. carbohydrates, 4 g. fat, 16 mg. cholesterol, 230 mg. sodium, 0 g. dietary fiber*

# French Bread Pesto Pizza

- 4 long crusty rolls (4 ounces each), split
- ½ cup prepared pesto
- 2 tomatoes, thinly sliced
- 1 jarred roasted red pepper, cut into strips
- 1 cup (4 ounces) shredded reduced-fat mozzarella cheese

PREHEAT THE OVEN TO 375°F. Coat a large baking sheet with nonstick spray.

PLACE THE ROLLS on the baking sheet. Spread the pesto evenly over the cut sides of the rolls. Top evenly with the tomatoes, pepper strips, and cheese.

BAKE FOR 15 TO 20 MINUTES, or until the cheese melts and the bread begins to brown.

**Makes 4 servings**

***Per serving:*** *557 calories, 21 g. protein, 67 g. carbohydrates, 23 g. fat, 21 mg. cholesterol, 1,406 mg. sodium, 5 g. dietary fiber*

## Quick Conversion

**French Bread Pesto Pizza with Pepperoni:** For a dual vegetarian/nonvegetarian dish, prepare the recipe with the following changes. Add 2 ounces thinly sliced pepperoni to half of the rolls before topping with the cheese. Bake as directed.

# Smoked Mozzarella Pizza

- **4 ounces portobello or shiitake mushrooms, sliced**
- **1 red onion, thinly sliced and separated into rings**
- **1 prebaked cheese-flavored pizza shell (15" diameter)**
- **2 cups thinly sliced plum tomatoes**
- **½ cup (2 ounces) shredded smoked mozzarella cheese**

PREHEAT THE OVEN TO 350°F.

COAT A LARGE NONSTICK SKILLET with nonstick spray. Warm over medium-high heat for 1 minute. Add the mushrooms and onion. Cook, stirring frequently, for 5 to 7 minutes, or until tender.

PLACE THE PIZZA SHELL on a large pizza stone or ungreased baking sheet. Top with the tomatoes, mushroom mixture, and cheese.

BAKE FOR 15 TO 20 MINUTES, or until the bread is golden and the cheese is melted.

**Makes 4 servings**

***Per serving:*** *280 calories, 7 g. protein, 39 g. carbohydrates, 11 g. fat, 8 mg. cholesterol, 276 mg. sodium, 5 g. dietary fiber*

**Tip:** For more flavor, season the mushrooms with dried oregano and add Parmesan cheese along with the mozzarella.

## Quick Conversion

**Smoked Mozzarella Pizza with Sausage:** For a dual vegetarian/nonvegetarian dish, prepare the recipe with the following changes. For the sausage portion, cook 6 ounces loose sausage in a nonstick skillet over medium heat for 5 minutes, or until no longer pink. Sprinkle over half of the pizza before topping with the cheese. Bake as directed.

# Vegetable-Cheese Stacks

- ½ **cup canned bean dip**
- ½ **cup reduced-fat sour cream**
- 8 **flour tortillas (6" diameter)**
- 1 **tomato, chopped**
- 1 **cup (4 ounces) shredded reduced-fat Cheddar cheese**

PREHEAT THE OVEN TO 350°F. Coat a large baking sheet with nonstick spray.

SPREAD THE BEAN DIP and sour cream over 4 of the tortillas. Top with the tomato, cheese, and remaining 4 tortillas.

PLACE THE STACKS on the prepared baking sheet and coat them with nonstick spray. Bake for 5 minutes. Flip and bake 5 to 7 minutes longer, or until heated through.

**Makes 4**

***Per stack:*** *374 calories, 16 g. protein, 47 g. carbohydrates, 14 g. fat, 32 mg. cholesterol, 640 mg. sodium, 4 g. dietary fiber*

## Quick Conversion

**Vegetable-Cheese Stacks with Beef:** For a dual vegetarian/nonvegetarian dish, prepare the recipe with the following changes. For the beef portion, brown 6 ounces lean ground beef in a nonstick skillet over medium heat for 6 to 8 minutes, or until no longer pink. Sprinkle over half of the vegetable-cheese stacks before topping with the tortillas. Bake as directed.

# Avocado Wraps

- **1 avocado, chopped**
- **1 tomato, chopped**
- **1 can (14½ ounces) cannellini beans, rinsed and drained**
- **¼ cup Caesar salad dressing**
- **4 flour tortillas (12" diameter)**

IN A MEDIUM BOWL, combine the avocado, tomato, and beans. Add the dressing and toss gently to coat.

SPOON DOWN THE CENTER of the tortillas. Roll up.

**Makes 4 servings**

***Per serving:*** *419 calories, 14 g. protein, 50 g. carbohydrates, 19 g. fat, 0 mg. cholesterol, 343 mg. sodium, 10 g. dietary fiber*

## Quick Conversion

**Avocado Wraps with Chicken:** For a dual vegetarian/nonvegetarian dish, prepare the recipe with the following changes. Add 4 ounces cubed cooked smoked chicken to half of the tortillas before rolling up.

# Chili Sloppy Joes

- 1 onion, chopped
- 2 cups frozen vegetable-protein crumbles, thawed
- 1½ cups rinsed and drained canned red kidney beans
- 1 cup barbecue sauce
- ¼ cup chili sauce

COAT A LARGE NONSTICK SKILLET with nonstick spray. Warm over medium-high heat for 1 minute. Add the onion and cook, stirring frequently, for 2 to 3 minutes, or until tender. Stir in the protein crumbles, beans, barbecue sauce, and chili sauce. Add ½ cup water. Simmer for 8 to 10 minutes, or until the mixture thickens slightly.

**Makes 4 servings**

***Per serving:*** *379 calories, 31 g. protein, 60 g. carbohydrates, 1 g. fat, 0 mg. cholesterol, 103 mg. sodium, 9 g. dietary fiber*

**Tip:** Serve on lettuce-lined sandwich buns, over rice, or atop a baked potato.

## Quick Conversion

**Chili Sloppy Joes with Beef:** For a dual vegetarian/nonvegetarian dish, prepare the recipe with the following changes. Divide the onion between 2 separate skillets. For the vegetarian portion, use only 1 cup protein crumbles and half of the remaining ingredients in 1 skillet. For the beef portion, add 8 ounces lean ground beef to the onion in the other skillet. Cook over medium heat for 6 to 8 minutes, or until no longer pink, stirring frequently to crumble. Add the remaining ingredients and cook as directed.

# Lentil-Stuffed Tacos

- **1½ cups lentils, sorted, rinsed, and drained**
- **1 onion, chopped**
- **1 package (1.25 ounces) taco seasoning mix**
- **8 corn taco shells**
- **2 tomatoes, chopped**

BRING 4 CUPS WATER TO A BOIL in a 2- or 3-quart saucepan over high heat. Reduce the heat to low. Stir in the lentils, cover, and cook for 30 minutes, or until tender. Drain well.

MEANWHILE, COAT A LARGE NONSTICK SKILLET with nonstick spray. Warm over medium-high heat for 1 minute. Add the onion and cook, stirring frequently, for 4 to 5 minutes, or until tender. Add the seasoning mix and cook for 1 minute. Stir in ¾ cup water and bring to a boil.

STIR IN THE LENTILS. Reduce the heat to low. Simmer for 6 to 8 minutes, or until the mixture thickens slightly.

MEANWHILE, WARM THE SHELLS according to package directions.

SPOON THE LENTIL mixture into the shells. Top with the tomatoes.

**Makes 4 servings**

***Per serving:*** *256 calories, 10 g. protein, 41 g. carbohydrates, 6 g. fat, 0 mg. cholesterol, 685 mg. sodium, 10 g. dietary fiber*

**Tip:** Serve topped with shredded lettuce, chopped avocado, and sour cream.

## Quick Conversion

**Lentil-Stuffed Tacos with Beef:** For a dual vegetarian/nonvegetarian dish, prepare the recipe with the following changes. Use only ¾ cup lentils and cook in 2 cups water. For the beef portion, brown 8 ounces lean ground beef in a nonstick skillet over medium heat for 6 to 8 minutes, or until no longer pink, stirring frequently to crumble. Add half of the cooked lentil mixture and cook for 2 minutes, or until heated through. Fill half of the shells with the beef mixture. Top with the tomatoes.

# Black-Eyed Pea Sauté

- 6 small red potatoes, quartered
- 1 small head broccoli, separated into florets
- 1 onion, chopped
- 1 can (16 ounces) black-eyed peas
- ½ cup balsamic or red wine vinegar salad dressing

COAT A LARGE NONSTICK SKILLET with nonstick spray and warm over medium heat. Add the potatoes, broccoli, and onion. Season with ½ teaspoon salt and ⅛ teaspoon ground black pepper. Cook, stirring frequently, for 8 to 10 minutes, or until tender. Add ½ cup water and cook for 5 minutes.

DRAIN THE BLACK-EYED PEAS, reserving ¼ cup liquid. Rinse and drain the beans. Stir the beans, reserved liquid, and dressing into the skillet. Simmer for 10 minutes.

**Makes 4 servings**

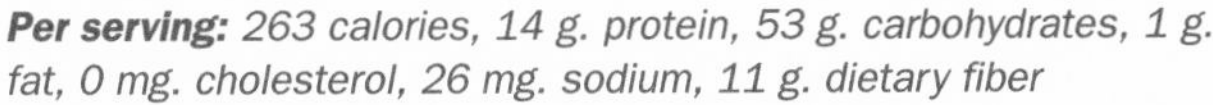

***Per serving:*** *263 calories, 14 g. protein, 53 g. carbohydrates, 1 g. fat, 0 mg. cholesterol, 26 mg. sodium, 11 g. dietary fiber*

**Tip:** This dish can be frozen for up to 1 month. To use, thaw in the refrigerator overnight. Reheat on the stove top or in the microwave oven on high power until heated through. Serve over rice, if desired.

## Quick Conversion

**Black-Eyed Pea Sauté with Ham:** For a dual vegetarian/nonvegetarian dish, prepare the recipe with the following changes. After stirring in the black-eyed peas, reserved liquid, and dressing, transfer half of the mixture to another skillet. For the ham portion, stir 4 ounces cubed cooked ham into one of the skillets. Simmer as directed.

# Skillet Rice and Beans

- **1 can (16 ounces) black beans, rinsed and drained**
- **1 can (14½ ounces) Mexican-style tomatoes**
- **2 cups Mexican-style frozen vegetables**
- **½ cup salsa**
- **2 cups long-grain rice**

IN A LARGE NONSTICK SKILLET, combine the beans, tomatoes (with juice), vegetables, and salsa. Add 1 cup water. Bring to a boil. Stir in the rice. Reduce the heat to low, cover, and simmer for 20 to 25 minutes, or until the rice is tender and the liquid has been absorbed. Fluff with a fork before serving.

**Makes 4 servings**

***Per serving:*** *581 calories, 18 g. protein, 121 g. carbohydrates, 2 g. fat, 0 mg. cholesterol, 688 mg. sodium, 13 g. dietary fiber*

**Tips:** This dish can be frozen for up to 1 month. To use, thaw in the refrigerator overnight. Reheat on the stove top or in the microwave oven at high power until heated through.

Serve topped with shredded Cheddar or Monterey Jack cheese and chopped scallions.

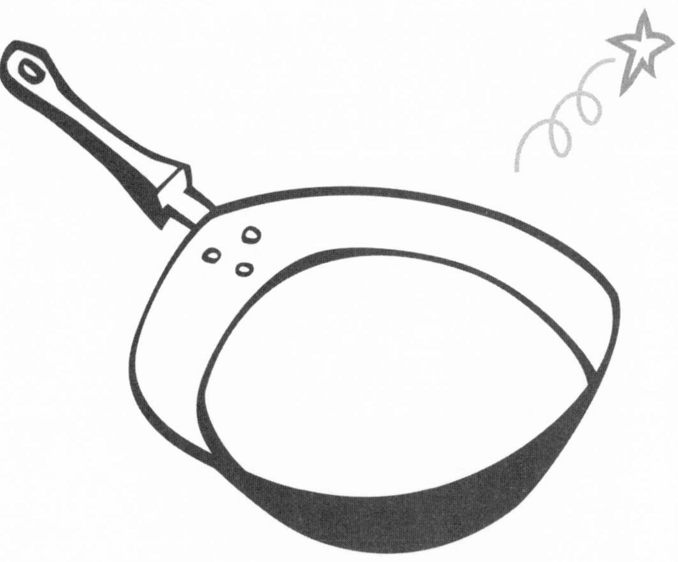

# Black Bean Pie

PREHEAT THE OVEN TO 375°F. Line a 9" pie plate with the pie crust. Fold in and crimp the edges.

PLACE THE BEANS in a large bowl and mash with a potato masher or fork, leaving some chunky pieces. Stir in the salsa. Spread the bean mixture over the pie crust. Top with the tomatoes, spreading them to within ½" of the edge. Top with the cheese.

BAKE FOR 30 TO 35 MINUTES, or until the crust is golden, the cheese melts, and the filling is heated through.

**Makes 4 servings**

- **1 pie crust (9" diameter)**
- **1 can (16 ounces) black beans, rinsed and drained**
- **1 cup salsa**
- **1 can (14½ ounces) Mexican-style stewed tomatoes, drained**
- **½ cup (2 ounces) shredded Mexican-style cheese**

***Per serving:*** *458 calories, 16 g. protein, 58 g. carbohydrates, 18 g. fat, 10 mg. cholesterol, 773 mg. sodium, 12 g. dietary fiber*

## Quick Conversion

**Black Bean Pie with Beef:** For a dual vegetarian/nonvegetarian dish, prepare the recipe with the following changes. Brown 6 ounces lean ground beef in a nonstick skillet over medium heat for 6 to 8 minutes, or until no longer pink. For the beef portion, arrange the cooked beef over half of the tomatoes. Top with the cheese and bake as directed.

# Roasted Tofu and Vegetables

- **1 pound extra-firm tofu, drained and squeezed dry**
- **1 head broccoli, separated into florets**
- **1 large red bell pepper, sliced**
- **1 large onion, thinly sliced and separated into rings**
- **½ cup prepared stir-fry sauce**

PREHEAT THE OVEN TO 425°F. Coat a 15½" × 10½" jelly-roll pan with nonstick spray.

CUT THE TOFU in quarters through the side to make 4 thin cutlets. Arrange the tofu, broccoli, pepper, and onion on the pan in a single layer. Drizzle evenly with the stir-fry sauce. Roast for 25 to 30 minutes, or until the vegetables are tender.

ARRANGE THE TOFU on plates and top with the vegetable mixture.

**Makes 4 servings**

***Per serving:*** *146 calories, 12 g. protein, 16 g. carbohydrates, 5 g. fat, 0 mg. cholesterol, 1,081 mg. sodium, 2 g. dietary fiber*

# Baked Tofu Cutlets with Mozzarella

- 1 pound extra-firm tofu, drained and squeezed dry
- 1 egg, beaten
- ½ cup seasoned dry bread crumbs
- 1 can (14½ ounces) stewed tomatoes
- ½ cup (2 ounces) shredded reduced-fat mozzarella cheese

PREHEAT THE OVEN TO 350°F. Coat a 9" × 9" baking dish with nonstick spray.

CUT THE TOFU in quarters through the side to make 4 thin cutlets. Place the egg in a shallow bowl. Place the bread crumbs on waxed paper. Dip each cutlet into the egg, then coat with the bread crumbs.

ARRANGE IN THE PREPARED BAKING DISH. Spoon in the tomatoes (with juice), evenly covering the tofu. Top with the cheese.

BAKE FOR 20 TO 25 MINUTES, or until the tofu is heated through and the cheese is melted.

**Makes 4 servings**

***Per serving:*** *225 calories, 17 g. protein, 21 g. carbohydrates, 9 g. fat, 61 mg. cholesterol, 791 mg. sodium, 2 g. dietary fiber*

**Tip:** I sometimes top the tofu with jarred roasted red peppers, add white beans, or serve the cutlets over rice or pasta.

## Surprising Sources of Protein

Does a vegetarian diet really provide enough protein? According to the American Dietetic Association, the answer is yes. Just make sure you eat a varied, balanced diet including plenty of beans, grains, fruits, and vegetables. If you do that, it would be nearly impossible *not* to get the required amount of protein. Just in case you're wondering where the protein is, take a peek at the following sources.

| Food | Amount | Protein (g) |
|---|---|---|
| Vegetable lasagna | 1 serving | 21 |
| Cottage cheese (2%) | ½ cup | 15 |
| Yogurt (nonfat plain) | 1 cup | 14 |
| Quinoa | ½ cup cooked | 11 |
| Buttermilk (2%) | 1 cup | 10 |
| French toast | 2 slices | 10 |
| Grilled cheese sandwich | 1 | 10 |
| Tofu | 4 ounces | 9 |
| White beans | ½ cup cooked | 9 |
| Black beans | ½ cup cooked | 8 |
| Cheese pizza | 1 slice | 8 |
| Granola | ½ cup | 8 |
| Peanuts | 1 ounce | 7 |
| Soy milk | 1 cup | 7 |
| Eggs | 1 | 6 |
| Sunflower seeds | 1 ounce | 6 |
| Sweetened condensed milk | ¼ cup | 6 |
| Waffles | 1 | 6 |
| Almonds | 1 ounce | 5 |
| Split-pea soup | ½ cup | 5 |
| Onion soup (canned) | ½ cup | 4 |
| Pasta (fresh, made with eggs) | ½ cup cooked | 4 |
| Cream cheese (low-fat) | 2 tablespoons | 3 |
| Cream of tomato soup | ½ cup | 3 |
| Pasta (dry) | ½ cup cooked | 3 |

# Tofu-Garlic Kabobs

- 1 pound extra-firm tofu, drained and squeezed dry
- 1 eggplant, peeled and cubed
- 24 cherry tomatoes
- 1 large red onion, cut into 12 wedges
- ¾ cup creamy roasted garlic salad dressing

COAT A BROILER RACK OR GRILL RACK with nonstick spray. Preheat the broiler or an outdoor grill according to the manufacturer's directions. Soak 12 bamboo skewers in water to cover for 20 minutes. (You can also use metal skewers without soaking them.)

CUT THE TOFU into 1" cubes and place in a large bowl. Add the eggplant, tomatoes, onion, and ½ cup of the dressing. Toss to mix and let stand for 15 minutes to blend flavors.

THREAD THE TOFU and vegetables onto separate skewers. Broil or grill for 10 to 15 minutes, or until the tofu is browned and the vegetables are tender, turning and brushing with the remaining ¼ cup dressing every 2 minutes.

**Makes 4 servings**

***Per serving:*** *317 calories, 16 g. protein, 33 g. carbohydrates, 16 g. fat, 0 mg. cholesterol, 508 mg. sodium, 9 g. dietary fiber*

## Quick Conversion

**Chicken-Garlic Kabobs:** For a dual vegetarian/nonvegetarian dish, prepare the recipe with the following changes. Use only ½ pound tofu. Divide the vegetables and marinade between 2 bowls. Add the tofu to one of the bowls. For the chicken portion, add ½ pound cubed boneless, skinless chicken breast to the other bowl. Marinate as directed. Thread the tofu and chicken portions onto separate skewers. Grill or broil as directed, or until the chicken is no longer pink and the juices run clear when pierced.

# Creamy Bean-Stuffed Potatoes

- **4** **large russet potatoes, baked**
- **1** **can (16 ounces) black beans or red kidney beans, rinsed and drained**
- **1** **cup salsa**
- **¼** **cup (2 ounces) reduced-fat sour cream**
- **½** **cup (2 ounces) shredded reduced-fat Cheddar cheese**

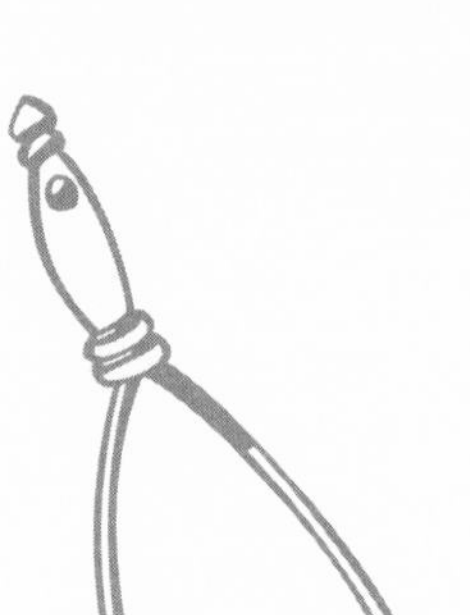

PREHEAT THE OVEN TO 425°F. Coat a large baking sheet with nonstick spray.

QUARTER THE POTATOES and scoop out the pulp, leaving a ¼" shell. Set aside the pulp. Arrange the skins on a baking sheet. Bake for 8 to 10 minutes, or just until crisp.

MEANWHILE, IN A FOOD PROCESSOR or medium bowl, process or mash the reserved pulp, beans, salsa, and sour cream until combined but still chunky.

FILL THE POTATO SHELLS with the potato-bean mixture. Sprinkle with the cheese.

BAKE FOR 5 TO 7 MINUTES, or until heated through and the cheese is melted.

**Makes 4 servings**

***Per serving:*** *377 calories, 16 g. protein, 69 g. carbohydrates, 5 g. fat, 16 mg. cholesterol, 580 mg. sodium, 11 g. dietary fiber*

**Tip:** The potatoes can be baked in a microwave oven. Microwave the filled potatoes on high power for 2 to 3 minutes, or until heated through and the cheese is melted.

# Mexican Spaghetti Squash 

1 **large spaghetti squash**
1 **cup salsa**
1 **can (16 ounces) red kidney beans, rinsed and drained**
1 **zucchini, shredded**
2 **tablespoons chopped canned green chiles**

PLACE THE SQUASH IN A LARGE SAUCEPAN and add water to cover. Bring to a boil. Reduce the heat to medium. Cover and cook for 35 to 40 minutes, or until easily pierced with a fork.

HALVE LENGTHWISE. Scoop out and discard the seeds. With a fork, separate the flesh into strands and place in a large bowl. Add the salsa, beans, zucchini, and chiles. Toss gently to mix well.

**Makes 4 servings**

***Per serving:*** *270 calories, 14 g. protein, 53 g. carbohydrates, 2 g. fat, 0 mg. cholesterol, 230 mg. sodium, 15 g. dietary fiber*

**Tips:** The squash can be cooked in a microwave oven. Halve lengthwise and place cut side down on a microwaveable plate. Cook on high power for 10 to 15 minutes, or until fork-tender.

For variety, sprinkle shredded Monterey Jack cheese over the finished dish.

# Couscous-Stuffed Peppers

- **1 package (5.9 ounces) broccoli-flavored couscous**
- **4 red, green, and/or yellow bell peppers**
- **1 tomato, chopped**
- **¼ cup chopped pitted kalamata or black olives**
- **½ cup vegetable broth**

PREHEAT THE OVEN TO 375°F. Coat a 9" × 9" baking dish with nonstick spray.

PREPARE THE COUSCOUS according to package directions.

MEANWHILE, SLICE THE TOPS off the peppers. Remove and discard the membranes and seeds. Stand the peppers in the prepared baking dish, cutting off a very thin slice from the bottoms to make the peppers stable, if necessary.

STIR THE TOMATO, olives, and ⅛ teaspoon ground black pepper into the couscous. Spoon into the peppers. Pour the broth evenly over the tops.

COVER AND BAKE FOR 20 TO 25 MINUTES, or until heated through.

**Makes 4 servings**

***Per serving:*** *100 calories, 3 g. protein, 19 g. carbohydrates, 2 g. fat, 0 mg. cholesterol, 293 mg. sodium, 3 g. dietary fiber*

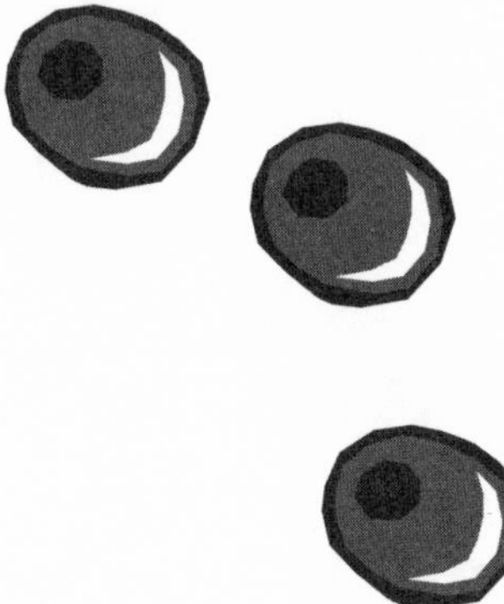

# Curried Couscous with Chickpeas



- **1** **bunch scallions, chopped**
- **1** **teaspoon curry powder**
- **1¼** **cups spicy mixed-vegetable juice**
- **1** **can (16 ounces) chickpeas, rinsed and drained**
- **1** **package (5.9 ounces) broccoli-flavored couscous**

COAT A LARGE NONSTICK SKILLET WITH NONSTICK SPRAY and warm over medium-high heat. Add the scallions and cook, stirring frequently, for 2 to 3 minutes, or until tender. Stir in the curry powder and cook for 1 minute. Stir in 2 tablespoons water and cook for 1 to 2 minutes, or until the water evaporates.

ADD THE VEGETABLE JUICE and chickpeas. Bring to a boil. Remove from the heat and stir in the couscous. Cover and let stand for 5 minutes, or until the couscous is tender and most of the liquid is absorbed. Fluff with a fork before serving.

**Makes 4 servings**

***Per serving:*** *204 calories, 8 g. protein, 40 g. carbohydrates, 2 g. fat, 0 mg. cholesterol, 490 mg. sodium, 7 g. dietary fiber*

# Spinach-Phyllo Rolls

**4 sheets thawed phyllo dough**

**8 slices reduced-fat Swiss cheese**

**12 large fresh spinach leaves, stems removed**

**1 cup drained chopped jarred roasted red peppers**

**1 tablespoon sesame seeds**

PREHEAT THE OVEN TO 400°F. Coat a large baking sheet with butter-flavored nonstick spray.

UNFOLD THE PHYLLO and place 1 sheet on waxed paper. Coat with the nonstick spray. Top with the remaining sheets, misting each layer with nonstick spray.

ARRANGE THE CHEESE, spinach, and peppers on top of the phyllo. Sprinkle with the sesame seeds.

CUT CROSSWISE into 4 equal strips. Starting with a short edge, roll up each strip jelly-roll style. Place, seam side down, on the prepared baking sheet.

BAKE FOR 15 TO 20 MINUTES, or until golden brown. Let rest for 5 minutes. Cut each roll in half.

**Makes 4 servings (8 slices)**

***Per serving:*** *191 calories, 12 g. protein, 19 g. carbohydrates, 7 g. fat, 20 mg. cholesterol, 882 mg. sodium, 1 g. dietary fiber*

**Tip:** Serve with warmed roasted red pepper–flavored spaghetti sauce.

## Quick Conversion

**Spinach-Phyllo Rolls with Ham:** For a dual vegetarian/nonvegetarian dish, prepare the recipe with the following changes. For the ham portion, arrange 4 thin slices of cooked ham atop the cheese and vegetables on half of the filled phyllo. Cut, roll up, and bake as directed.

# Sweet-and-Sour Stir-Fry

- **12 ounces firm tofu, drained and squeezed dry**
- **3 cups frozen broccoli, cauliflower, and carrots, thawed**
- **¼ cup tomato paste**
- **1 tablespoon cider vinegar**
- **1 tablespoon packed brown sugar**

CUT THE TOFU INTO 1" CUBES. Coat a large nonstick skillet with nonstick spray and warm over medium heat. Add the tofu and stir-fry for 4 to 5 minutes, or until golden. Add the vegetables. Stir-fry for 2 minutes.

STIR IN 1 CUP WATER, the tomato paste, vinegar, and brown sugar. Bring to a boil. Reduce the heat to low and simmer for 5 to 7 minutes.

**Makes 4 servings**

***Per serving:*** *160 calories, 11 g. protein, 23 g. carbohydrates, 4 g. fat, 0 mg. cholesterol, 72 mg. sodium, 5 g. dietary fiber*

## Quick Conversion

**Sweet-and-Sour Stir-Fry with Chicken:** For a dual vegetarian/nonvegetarian dish, prepare the recipe with the following changes. Use only half the tofu and cook as directed with half of the remaining ingredients. For the chicken portion, cook ½ pound cubed boneless, skinless chicken breasts in a medium skillet for 5 minutes, or until no longer pink and the juices run clear when pierced. Add the remaining half of the ingredients and cook as directed.

# Potato-Carrot Cakes

- **6 carrots, shredded**
- **3 potatoes, shredded**
- **1 onion, grated**
- **¼ cup parsley**
- **6 eggs**

IN A LARGE BOWL, combine the carrots, potatoes, onion, and parsley. Season with ½ teaspoon salt and ⅛ teaspoon ground black pepper. Stir in the eggs.

COAT A LARGE NONSTICK SKILLET with nonstick spray and warm over medium-high heat. Drop the carrot-potato mixture into the skillet by tablespoonfuls, spreading to form thin pancakes. Cook for 2 minutes per side, or until golden. Transfer to a platter and cover with foil to keep warm.

RECOAT THE SKILLET and repeat with the remaining batter.

**Makes 8 servings**

***Per serving:*** *123 calories, 7 g. protein, 16 g. carbohydrates, 4 g. fat, 159 mg. cholesterol, 69 mg. sodium, 3 g. dietary fiber*

**Tips:** These pancakes can be frozen for up to 1 month. To use, thaw in the refrigerator overnight. Reheat in a skillet or in the microwave oven at high power until heated through.

Serve these pancakes with apple sauce and sour cream.

# Spanish Omelettes

1 potato, finely chopped
1 small onion, chopped
1 small red bell pepper, finely chopped
¼ cup sliced pimiento-stuffed olives
8 eggs

PLACE THE POTATO IN A MEDIUM SAUCEPAN and add water to cover. Bring to a boil over high heat. Reduce the heat to medium-low, cover, and cook for 15 to 20 minutes, or until tender. Drain and let cool.

COAT A LARGE NONSTICK SKILLET with nonstick spray and warm over medium-high heat. Add the potato, onion, and bell pepper. Cook, stirring frequently, for 4 to 5 minutes, or until the pepper is tender. Remove from the heat and stir in the olives. Transfer to a small bowl.

IN A MEDIUM BOWL, beat the eggs with ½ teaspoon salt and ⅛ teaspoon ground black pepper.

COAT THE SAME SKILLET with nonstick spray and warm over medium heat. Pour in half of the egg mixture and cook for 2 minutes, carefully lifting the edges of the omelette with a spatula to allow the uncooked mixture to flow underneath. Cook for 3 minutes more. Flip the omelette. Spoon 1 cup of the vegetable mixture onto half of the omelette. Carefully loosen with a spatula and fold in half over the vegetables. Cook for 1 minute on each side. Slide onto a plate.

RECOAT THE SKILLET and repeat with the remaining eggs and vegetable mixture. Cut each omelette in half.

**Makes 4 servings**

***Per serving:*** *213 calories, 14 g. protein, 13 g. carbohydrates, 11 g. fat, 425 mg. cholesterol, 384 mg. sodium, 2 g. dietary fiber*

## Quick Conversion

**Spanish Omelettes with Bacon:** For a dual vegetarian/nonvegetarian dish, prepare the recipe with the following changes. For the bacon portion, cook 4 strips of bacon in a nonstick skillet over medium heat for 5 to 7 minutes, or until crisp. Transfer to paper towels to drain. Crumble the bacon over the vegetables in 1 of the omelettes before folding in half.

# Cheesy Eggs

- **4 large eggs**
- **4 ounces fresh spinach, coarsely chopped**
- **½ cup (2 ounces) shredded reduced-fat mozzarella cheese**
- **4 sandwich-size English muffins, split and toasted**
- **½ cup prepared spaghetti sauce, heated**

COAT A LARGE NONSTICK SKILLET with nonstick spray and warm over medium heat.

IN A SMALL BOWL, beat the eggs with ½ teaspoon salt and ⅛ teaspoon ground black pepper. Pour into the skillet and cook, stirring frequently, for 4 to 5 minutes, or until thickened but not set.

STIR IN THE SPINACH and cheese. Cooking, stirring, until the eggs are set.

SPREAD THE MUFFINS with the sauce. Top with the eggs.

**Makes 4 servings**

***Per serving:*** *259 calories, 16 g. protein, 29 g. carbohydrates, 9 g. fat, 219 mg. cholesterol, 623 mg. sodium, 2 g. dietary fiber*

# Grilled Tempeh with Sour Cream

- 1 pound tempeh, cut into 4 pieces
- ½ cup prepared fajita marinade or stir-fry sauce
- ½ cup (4 ounces) reduced-fat sour cream
- 2 tablespoons lime juice
- 2 tomatoes, chopped

PLACE THE TEMPEH in a shallow medium glass baking dish. Pour the marinade or stir-fry sauce over the tempeh. Let stand for at least 1 hour or up to 8 hours to blend flavors, turning occasionally.

COAT AN INDOOR GRILL RACK or broiler pan with nonstick spray. Preheat the grill or broiler according to the manufacturer's directions.

PLACE THE TEMPEH on the grill or in the broiler pan. Grill or broil for 4 to 6 minutes on a side, or until browned.

MEANWHILE, IN A SMALL BOWL, combine the sour cream, lime juice, and ¼ teaspoon ground black pepper.

ARRANGE THE TEMPEH on dinner plates. Serve with the sour cream mixture and tomatoes.

**Makes 4 servings**

***Per serving:*** *311 calories, 24 g. protein, 30 g. carbohydrates, 13 g. fat, 12 mg. cholesterol, 1,085 mg. sodium, 1 g. dietary fiber*

**Tip:** For more zip, stir dried red-pepper flakes into the sour cream mixture.

# Veggie Burgers

- **1 package (12 ounces) frozen vegetable-protein crumbles, thawed**
- **2 eggs**
- **¼ cup seasoned dry bread crumbs**
- **2 scallions, finely chopped**
- **½ teaspoon mustard powder**

PLACE THE CRUMBLES IN A MEDIUM BOWL and lightly mash with a fork. Add the eggs, bread crumbs, scallions, and mustard. Season with ½ teaspoon salt and ⅛ teaspoon ground black pepper. Mix well and shape into 6 patties.

COAT A LARGE RIDGED GRILL PAN or skillet with nonstick spray and warm over medium-high heat for 1 minute. Add the patties and cook for 5 minutes on each side, or until browned.

**Makes 6 servings**

***Per serving:*** *280 calories, 29 g. protein, 28 g. carbohydrates, 3 g. fat, 71 mg. cholesterol, 567 mg. sodium, 0 g. dietary fiber*

## Quick Conversion

**Beef Burgers:** For a dual vegetarian/nonvegetarian dish, prepare the recipe with the following changes. Combine ½ package (6 ounces) protein crumbles with half of the remaining ingredients. For the beef portion, combine 6 ounces lean ground beef with the remaining half of the ingredients. Shape into patties and arrange both portions on the grill pan or skillet. Cook the beef burgers for 6 to 8 minutes, or until a thermometer inserted in the center registers 160°F and the meat is no longer pink.

# Veggie Meatballs

PLACE THE CRUMBLES in a large bowl and lightly mash with a fork. Add the eggs, bread crumbs, cheese, and basil. Season with ½ teaspoon salt and ⅛ teaspoon ground black pepper. Mix well and shape into 24 balls.

COAT A LARGE SKILLET with nonstick spray and warm over medium-high heat for 1 minute. Add the veggie meatballs, cover, and cook for 10 minutes, or until lightly browned, turning frequently.

**Makes 6 servings**

- **1 package (12 ounces) frozen vegetable-protein crumbles, thawed**
- **2 eggs, beaten**
- **¼ cup seasoned dry bread crumbs**
- **3 tablespoons (¾ ounce) grated Parmesan cheese**
- **2 tablespoons chopped fresh basil**

***Per serving:*** *278 calories, 30 g. protein, 28 g. carbohydrates, 3 g. fat, 73 mg. cholesterol, 613 mg. sodium, 0 g. dietary fiber*

**Tip:** To make spaghetti and meatballs, simmer the cooked meatballs in prepared spaghetti sauce for 30 minutes. Serve over cooked spaghetti.

## Quick Conversion

**Beef Meatballs:** For a dual vegetarian/nonvegetarian dish, prepare the recipe with the following changes. Combine ½ package (6 ounces) protein crumbles with half of the remaining ingredients. For the beef portion, combine 6 ounces lean ground beef with the remaining half of the ingredients. Place both portions in separate skillets and cook as directed, or until a thermometer inserted in the center of the beef meatballs registers 160°F and the meat is no longer pink.

## Timesaving Ingredients

Most of the time spent cooking is actually spent preparing ingredients to be cooked. Luckily, food companies have wised up to the fact that most people don't want to spend hours chopping vegetables or adding lots of seasonings to dishes. Here are some of the prepared and preseasoned ingredients I use to help cut down on prep time and get dinner on the table fast.

1. **Precut fresh vegetables.** They can't be beat for busy nights, on-the-run snacks, and quick salads. I regularly use baby carrots, broccoli florets, and cut red peppers.
2. **Frozen vegetable mixes.** Look for ones without added sauce, like frozen pepper and onion mix or frozen broccoli, carrot, and pepper mix. These keep in the freezer for weeks and make great soups, stir-fries, and casseroles.
3. **Flavored canned tomatoes.** Why waste time adding garlic and other seasonings? To speed things up, I stock cans of Italian-style or Mexican-style chopped tomatoes, which have the seasonings already mixed in.
4. **Prepared sauces.** Pesto, alfredo, stir-fry, teriyaki . . . You can buy all these sauces in the refrigerated or international section of the supermarket instead of making them yourself. Most make good marinades, too. I also use prepared balsamic vinaigrette to marinate vegetables and Italian salad dressing to marinate chicken.
5. **Oven-ready pasta.** The days of handling hot, sticky lasagna noodles are over. Oven-ready lasagna noodles and manicotti shells skip the boiling step and cook in the oven instead. What a time-saver.

6. **Premarinated tofu.** Preseasoned tofu is ready to grill, bake, or use in stir-fries. Chinese 5-Spice is one of my favorite flavors. Cajun is another good one. Look for flavored tofu near the regular tofu in the refrigerated produce section of your supermarket.
7. **Refrigerated pizza dough.** For the best flavor, buy the kind sold in bags in the refrigerated or frozen section (often near the refrigerated tortillas or near the frozen pizza). In a real pinch, you can also use refrigerated pizza dough that comes in a tube.
8. **Flavored cheeses.** I often use Mexican-style cheese for tacos, burritos, and casseroles. It has the chili powder and other seasonings mixed right in. Hot-pepper Jack cheese also adds a spicy flavor without having to chop up a jalapeño chile pepper.
9. **Vegetable-flavored wraps.** Spinach-flavored and sun-dried tomato–flavored wraps taste better than plain tortillas and allow you to get less fancy with the fillings. I use these for simple sandwich wraps like grilled vegetables.
10. **Prepared salad greens.** Nothing has made salad easier than bagged salad greens. Just check the expiration date to make sure the greens are still fresh.
11. **Frozen onions.** When you're chopping onions or peppers for a meal and it calls for only half of what you have, chop the whole thing anyway and freeze the extras. You'll be glad you did the next time you need a chopped onion in a hurry.
12. **Frozen rice.** Cooked rice keeps for weeks frozen and reheats quickly in the microwave oven. When I cook rice, I always make extra to have on hand for quick stir-fries, soups, or casseroles.

# Savory Pies, Casseroles, and One-Dish Meals

*"If the purpose of flavor is to arouse a special kind of emotion, that flavor must emerge from genuine feelings about the materials you are handling. What you are, you cook."*

—Marcella Hazan, Italian cookbook author

# Savory Pies, Casseroles, and One-Dish Meals

WHAT COULD BE SIMPLER than a meal that's quickly tossed together, then baked for just 20 to 30 minutes? Add a beverage and voilà! Dinner is ready!

Potpie, stroganoff, frittata . . . these dishes are perfect for busy weeknights. I especially love the casseroles on cool nights. Baked in the oven, they radiate warmth and aromas throughout the entire house.

## Recipes

● Kid-Friendly Recipe

● Freezable Recipe

● Microwaveable Recipe

# Mixed Potato Gratin

- 1 teaspoon canola oil
- 1 onion, chopped
- 2 cloves garlic, minced
- ¼ cup all-purpose flour
- 2 tablespoons (½ ounce) grated Parmesan cheese
- 1 teaspoon paprika
- ½ teaspoon garlic salt
- ¼ teaspoon ground black pepper
- 1 pound red potatoes, peeled and sliced ¼" thick
- 1 pound Idaho potatoes, peeled and sliced ¼" thick
- ½ cup (2 ounces) shredded Gruyère cheese or Swiss cheese
- 1 tomato, chopped
- ½ cup 1% milk or vegetable broth

PREHEAT THE OVEN TO 350°F. Coat a 2-quart baking dish with nonstick spray.

WARM THE OIL in a large nonstick skillet over medium-high heat. Add the onion and garlic. Cook, stirring frequently, for 2 to 4 minutes, or until tender.

IN A LARGE FOOD-STORAGE BAG, combine the flour, Parmesan, paprika, garlic salt, and pepper. Shake to mix. Add the red potatoes and Idaho potatoes. Close and shake to coat. Arrange in the prepared baking dish.

SPRINKLE WITH THE GRUYÈRE or Swiss and tomato. Drizzle the milk or broth over the top. Cover with foil. Bake for 30 minutes. Uncover and bake 20 to 25 minutes longer, or until the potatoes are tender.

**Makes 8 servings**

***Per serving:*** *153 calories, 6 g. protein, 26 g. carbohydrates, 3 g. fat, 8 mg. cholesterol, 174 mg. sodium, 2 g. dietary fiber*

# Broccoli and Cheese Soufflé

- **1** **package (10 ounces) frozen chopped broccoli, thawed**
- **1** **cup thawed frozen corn**
- **1** **cup whole milk**
- **¾** **cup (3 ounces) shredded reduced-fat Cheddar cheese**
- **½** **cup 1% cottage cheese or cottage cheese with herbs**
- **½** **cup all-purpose flour**
- **4** **eggs, separated**
- **¼** **teaspoon salt**
- **⅛** **teaspoon ground red pepper**
- **½** **teaspoon cream of tartar**

PREHEAT THE OVEN TO 375°F. Coat a 2-quart baking dish with nonstick spray.

IN A FOOD PROCESSOR, combine half the broccoli, ½ cup corn, the milk, Cheddar, cottage cheese, flour, egg yolks, salt, and pepper. Process until blended, scraping the sides of the bowl as necessary. Transfer to a large bowl. Stir in the remaining broccoli and ½ cup corn.

IN A MEDIUM BOWL with an electric mixer at high speed, beat the egg whites and cream of tartar until stiff peaks form. Gently fold into the broccoli mixture. Spoon carefully into the prepared baking dish.

PLACE IN THE OVEN. Reduce the heat to 350°F and bake for 50 to 55 minutes, or until puffy and golden.

**Makes 4 servings**

***Per serving:*** *311 calories, 22 g. protein, 29 g. carbohydrates, 12 g. fat, 237 mg. cholesterol, 553 mg. sodium, 4 g. dietary fiber*

**Tip:** This dish works well with 1 package (10 ounces) frozen chopped spinach, thawed and squeezed dry, in place of the broccoli.

# Mushroom and Rice Frittata

- ½ cup long-grain rice
- 2 teaspoons butter
- 2 cups thinly sliced mushrooms
- 6 scallions, chopped
- ½ teaspoon dried thyme
- ¼ teaspoon salt
- ⅛ teaspoon ground black pepper
- 6 large egg whites
- 4 eggs
- ½ cup (2 ounces) shredded provolone cheese
- 3 tablespoons seasoned dry bread crumbs

COOK THE RICE ACCORDING TO PACKAGE DIRECTIONS.

MEANWHILE, MELT THE BUTTER in a large nonstick skillet over medium-high heat (use an ovenproof skillet if you have one). Add the mushrooms and scallions. Cook, stirring frequently, for 4 to 5 minutes, or until tender. Stir in the rice, thyme, salt, and pepper. Cook 1 minute longer.

IN A MEDIUM BOWL, beat the egg whites, eggs, cheese, and bread crumbs. Pour into the mushroom mixture and swirl to evenly distribute. Cook for 5 minutes, or until the eggs are set on the bottom but still moist on the top. Remove the skillet from the heat. (If the skillet is not ovenproof, wrap the handle in several layers of heavy-duty foil.)

BROIL 4" FROM THE HEAT for 1 minute, or until the top is golden. Cut into wedges.

**Makes 4 servings**

***Per serving:*** *301 calories, 19 g. protein, 29 g. carbohydrates, 12 g. fat, 227 mg. cholesterol, 628 mg. sodium, 3 g. dietary fiber*

## Quick Conversion

**Mushroom and Rice Frittata with Bacon:** For a dual vegetarian/nonvegetarian dish, prepare the recipe with the following changes. Use 2 medium skillets instead of 1 large one. For the bacon portion, cook 2 strips of bacon in one of the skillets over medium heat for 7 minutes, or until well-done. Drain and transfer to a plate lined with paper towels. Cook the mushroom-rice mixture in the other skillet. Transfer half of the completed mushroom-rice mixture to the skillet used to cook the bacon. Crumble the bacon over the mushroom-rice mixture. Divide the egg mixture between the skillets. Proceed with the recipe as directed.

# Zucchini and Tofu Skillet Supper

WARM THE OIL IN A LARGE NONSTICK SKILLET. Add the tofu and soy sauce. Cook, stirring frequently, for 2 to 4 minutes, or until the tofu begins to brown. Add the zucchini, pepper, and onions. Cook, stirring frequently, for 5 to 6 minutes, or until the vegetables are tender.

STIR IN THE STEWED TOMATOES (with juice) and tomato sauce. Bring to a boil. Reduce the heat to low and stir in the spinach or bok choy. Cook for 2 minutes longer, or the until spinach wilts.

PLACE IN A LARGE SERVING BOWL. Add the cheese and toss to mix.

**Makes 4 servings**

***Per serving:*** *207 calories, 15 g. protein, 18 g. carbohydrates, 10 g. fat, 13 mg. cholesterol, 538 mg. sodium, 4 g. dietary fiber*

- **1 teaspoon olive oil**
- **1 pound firm tofu, drained, squeezed dry, and cubed**
- **1 tablespoon soy sauce**
- **1 zucchini, thinly sliced**
- **1 red bell pepper, cut into strips**
- **½ cup chopped onions**
- **1 can (14½ ounces) stewed tomatoes**
- **¼ cup tomato sauce**
- **4 cups coarsely chopped fresh spinach or bok choy**
- **½ cup (2 ounces) crumbled herb-flavored or plain feta cheese**

# Couscous Parmesan

- **1¼ cups vegetable broth**
- **1 can (14 ounces) chickpeas, rinsed and drained**
- **1 cup thawed frozen peas**
- **½ cup dry-pack sun-dried tomatoes**
- **1 package (5.9 ounces) Parmesan cheese–flavored couscous**

IN A MEDIUM SAUCEPAN, combine the broth, chickpeas, peas, and tomatoes. Bring to a boil over medium-high heat. Remove from the heat and stir in the couscous. Cover and let stand for 5 minutes. Fluff with a fork before serving.

**Makes 4 servings**

***Per serving:*** *462 calories, 21 g. protein, 82 g. carbohydrates, 6 g. fat, 7 mg. cholesterol, 1,055 mg. sodium, 16 g. dietary fiber*

**Tip:** I sometimes sauté vegetables in the saucepan before adding the broth and other ingredients. Onions, garlic, carrots, and bell peppers work well.

## Quick Conversion

**Couscous Parmesan with Chicken:** For a dual vegetarian/nonvegetarian dish, prepare the recipe with the following changes. Divide the completed recipe in half. For the chicken portion, stir ½ pound chopped cooked smoked chicken into half of the recipe.

# Eggplant Lasagne

- 1 large eggplant (about 2 pounds), sliced ⅛" thick
- 2 teaspoons olive oil
- 1 container (16 ounces) reduced-fat ricotta cheese
- 1 package (10 ounces) frozen chopped spinach, thawed and squeezed dry
- 2 tablespoons (½ ounce) grated Parmesan cheese
- 1 large egg
- ½ teaspoon dried basil
- ¼ teaspoon garlic powder
- 2 cups marinara sauce
- 1½ cups (6 ounces) shredded reduced-fat mozzarella cheese
- 1 tomato, sliced ¼" thick

PREHEAT THE BROILER. Coat a large baking sheet with non-stick spray.

PLACE HALF THE EGGPLANT on the prepared baking sheet. Drizzle with 1 teaspoon of the olive oil. Broil for 5 minutes, or until tender, turning the slices once. Remove to a platter and cover with foil to keep warm. Repeat with the remaining eggplant.

CHANGE THE OVEN TEMPERATURE to 350°F.

IN A MEDIUM BOWL, combine the ricotta, spinach, Parmesan, egg, basil, and garlic powder.

SPREAD 1 CUP MARINARA SAUCE in a 13" × 9" baking dish. Arrange half of the eggplant in the dish, overlapping the slices as necessary. Layer with half the ricotta mixture, ½ cup mozzarella, and ½ cup marinara sauce. Top with the remaining eggplant and repeat with the remaining ricotta mixture, ½ cup mozzarella, and the remaining ½ cup sauce. Arrange the sliced tomato evenly over the top.

BAKE FOR 30 MINUTES. Sprinkle with the remaining ½ cup mozzarella. Bake for 10 minutes, or until the mozzarella melts.

**Makes 8 servings**

***Per serving:*** *248 calories, 17 g. protein, 19 g. carbohydrates, 13 g. fat, 57 mg. cholesterol, 654 mg. sodium, 4 g. dietary fiber*

# Chiles Rellenos Casserole

- **1 cup long-grain rice**
- **1 teaspoon olive oil**
- **1 cup chopped onions**
- **2 garlic cloves, minced**
- **1½ teaspoons ground cumin**
- **1½ teaspoons dried oregano**
- **1 can (16 ounces) vegetarian refried beans**
- **2 cans (4 ounces each) whole green chiles, drained and cut lengthwise into quarters**
- **1 cup (4 ounces) shredded reduced-fat Monterey Jack cheese**
- **¼ cup all-purpose flour**
- **¼ teaspoon ground black pepper**
- **1¼ cups 1% milk**
- **¼ cup seasoned dry bread crumbs**

PREHEAT THE OVEN TO 350°F. Coat an 11" × 7" baking dish with nonstick spray. Cook the rice according to package directions.

MEANWHILE, WARM THE OIL in a large nonstick skillet over medium-high heat. Add the onions and garlic. Cook, stirring frequently, for 2 to 3 minutes, or until tender. Remove from the heat. Stir in the rice, cumin, and oregano. Stir in the beans.

ARRANGE HALF THE CHILES in the prepared baking dish. Sprinkle with ½ cup cheese. Gently spread the bean mixture over the cheese, leaving a ½" border around the edge of the dish. Top with the remaining chiles and remaining ½ cup cheese.

IN A MEDIUM BOWL, combine the flour and pepper. Gradually pour in the milk. Mix well. Pour over the chiles and cheese. Sprinkle with the bread crumbs.

BAKE FOR 40 TO 50 MINUTES, or until heated through and bubbly. Let stand for 5 minutes before serving.

**Makes 8 servings**

***Per serving:*** *245 calories, 10 g. protein, 38 g. carbohydrates, 6 g. fat, 12 mg. cholesterol, 646 mg. sodium, 3 g. dietary fiber*

## Quick Conversion

**Chiles Rellenos Casserole with Beef:** For a dual vegetarian/nonvegetarian dish, prepare the recipe with the following changes. Use two 1-quart baking dishes instead of one 11" × 7" dish. Use 8 ounces refried beans instead of 16 ounces. Use 2 medium skillets instead of 1 large one. For the beef portion, cook ½ pound extra-lean ground beef in 1 of the skillets until no longer pink. Cook the onions and garlic in the other skillet. Add the rice, cumin, and oregano. Transfer half of the rice mixture to the skillet with the beef and mix well. Add the 8 ounces of beans to the other skillet. Proceed with the recipe, dividing the fillings and remaining ingredients between the 2 baking dishes. Bake both portions for 25 to 30 minutes, or until heated through and bubbly. Let stand for 5 minutes before serving.

# Tofu-and-Bean-Stuffed Manicotti

- **16** **manicotti shells**
- **1** **pound firm tofu, drained and squeezed dry**
- **2** **cans (15 ounces each) cannellini beans, rinsed and drained**
- **½** **cup drained jarred roasted red peppers**
- **½** **cup (2 ounces) shredded reduced-fat mozzarella cheese**
- **2** **cloves garlic**
- **1** **teaspoon dried basil**
- **2** **cups tomato sauce or prepared Alfredo sauce**
- **2** **tablespoons (½ ounce) grated Parmesan cheese**

PREHEAT THE OVEN TO 375°F.

COOK THE PASTA according to package directions. Drain.

PLACE THE TOFU in a food processor. Process until smooth. Add the beans, peppers, mozzarella, garlic, and basil. Process until the beans are coarsely chopped.

SPOON ¼ CUP OF THE TOFU mixture into each manicotti shell. Spread 1 cup tomato sauce or Alfredo sauce in a 13" × 9" baking dish. Arrange the shells in the dish. Pour the remaining 1 cup sauce over the shells. Sprinkle with the Parmesan.

BAKE FOR 30 TO 35 MINUTES, or until the tofu mixture is heated through and the sauce is bubbly.

**Makes 4 servings**

***Per serving:*** *490 calories, 29 g. protein, 72 g. carbohydrates, 10 g. fat, 11 mg. cholesterol, 803 mg. sodium, 12 g. dietary fiber*

**Tip:** Oven-ready manicotti shells are available in some stores. To use them, simply skip the step for boiling the shells. The baking time remains the same. To vary the flavor, I sometimes stir into the bean mixture 1 box (10 ounces) frozen chopped spinach, thawed and squeezed dry. Or you can use the same amount of frozen broccoli florets, thawed.

## 10 Ideas for Tofu

Tofu isn't as scary as you might think. It's been loved in Asia for centuries. Just remember the basics. Firm tofu (the kind sold in tubs of water) is best for marinating, grilling, baking, broiling, stir-frying, and sautéeing. Always drain and squeeze it dry first. Silken tofu (sold in aseptic boxes) is best pureed to make creamy dips, soups, sauces, or desserts—anywhere you might use yogurt or sour cream. Here are my favorite ways to prepare this simple food.

**Stir-fries:** Heat peanut oil and stir-fry cubed firm tofu until browned. Add fresh mixed vegetables. Stir in prepared stir-fry sauce and serve with steamed rice.

**Fillings:** Mix pureed firm tofu with ricotta cheese, jarred marinara sauce, chopped spinach, and dried Italian seasoning. Spoon into jumbo shells or manicotti shells or spread on lasagna noodles, then bake.

**Soups:** Cube firm or silken tofu and drop into broth-based soups like miso or noodle soups.

**Stews:** Simmer cubed firm tofu along with vegetables and/or meats. The tofu will stay firm and make a hearty dish. It works especially well with chilies.

**Dips:** Puree silken tofu with jarred roasted red peppers, cream cheese, scallions, and garlic. Serve with chips or fresh vegetables.

**Salads:** Toss cubed firm tofu with salad greens. Tofu's mild flavor complements bitter greens and vinaigrette dressings.

**Pilafs:** Stir chopped firm tofu into grain and vegetable pilafs.

**Burgers:** Mash firm tofu and combine with eggs, seasoned dry bread crumbs, cooked rice, Dijon mustard, and chopped onion. Pan-fry until browned.

**Grilled or broiled:** Marinate cubed firm tofu (and cut vegetables, if you wish) in stir-fry marinade or Italian salad dressing. Grill or broil on a vegetable grate. Works well with kabobs.

**Scrambled:** Cube firm tofu and use in place of eggs for scrambling. Wonderful cooked with cubed potatoes.

# Polenta Torte

- 1 tube (16 ounces) prepared polenta
- 2 tablespoons (½ ounce) grated Parmesan cheese
- 1 jar (4½ ounces) marinated artichoke hearts, coarsely chopped
- 1 jar (3 ounces) water-packed roasted red peppers, coarsely chopped
- 1 package (10 ounces) frozen spinach, thawed and squeezed dry
- 1¼ cups (10 ounces) reduced-fat ricotta cheese
- 1 tablespoon balsamic vinegar
- 3 large egg whites, lightly beaten
- 1 large egg, lightly beaten
- ½ teaspoon dried basil
- ½ teaspoon garlic powder
- ¼ teaspoon salt
- 1 tomato, sliced ¼" thick
- ½ cup (2 ounces) shredded reduced-fat mozzarella cheese

PREHEAT THE OVEN TO 350°F. Coat a 10" springform pan with nonstick spray.

PLACE THE POLENTA in a medium bowl and mash lightly. Stir in the Parmesan. Spoon into the prepared pan, pushing some of the polenta up the sides to create a shell.

IN THE SAME BOWL, combine the artichokes, peppers, spinach, ricotta, vinegar, egg whites, egg, basil, garlic powder, and salt. Spread over the polenta. Top with the tomato and mozzarella. Place the pan on a large baking sheet.

BAKE FOR 1 HOUR. Cool for 10 minutes before serving.

**Makes 8 servings**

***Per serving:*** *365 calories, 17 g. protein, 48 g. carbohydrates, 12 g. fat, 48 mg. cholesterol, 769 mg. sodium, 5 g. dietary fiber*

## Quick Conversion

**Polenta Torte with Pepperoni:** For a dual vegetarian/nonvegetarian dish, prepare the recipe with the following changes. Divide the polenta and spinach-ricotta mixture between two 8" springform pans. For the pepperoni portion, arrange 1 ounce thinly sliced pepperoni over the spinach-ricotta mixture in one of the pans. Divide the tomato and mozzarella between the pans. Place both portions on a baking sheet and bake for 45 minutes. (If you don't have two 8" pans, arrange the pepperoni over half of the spinach-ricotta mixture in the 10" pan.)

# Tortilla Casserole

- 1 teaspoon olive oil
- ½ cup chopped onions
- 2 cloves garlic, minced
- 1 tablespoon all-purpose flour
- ½ teaspoon ground cumin
- 1 can (14½ ounces) Mexican-style tomatoes
- 1 can (14½ ounces) black beans, rinsed and drained
- 1 cup corn
- ¼ cup chopped canned green chiles
- 6 corn tortillas (6" diameter), quartered
- ½ cup (2 ounces) shredded Monterey Jack cheese
- ¼ cup chopped fresh cilantro or parsley
- ¼ cup (2 ounces) reduced-fat sour cream
- 2 small scallions, chopped (optional)
- ¼ cup chopped avocado (optional)

PREHEAT THE OVEN TO 350°F. Warm the oil in a large skillet over medium-high heat (use an ovenproof skillet if you have one). Add the onions and garlic. Cook, stirring frequently, for 3 to 4 minutes, or until soft. Stir in the flour and cumin. Cook for 1 minute.

STIR IN THE TOMATOES (with juice), beans, corn, and chiles. Cook for 2 minutes. Remove all but ½ cup to a medium bowl. In the skillet, top the tomato-bean mixture with half of the tortilla quarters and half of the tomato-bean mixture from the medium bowl. Repeat layering with the remaining tortillas and tomato-bean mixture. Top with the cheese. (If the skillet is not ovenproof, wrap the handle in several layers of heavy-duty foil.)

BAKE FOR 30 TO 35 MINUTES, or until heated through. Top each serving with equal amounts of cilantro or parsley, sour cream, scallions (if using), and avocado (if using).

**Makes 4 servings**

***Per serving:*** *354 calories, 15 g. protein, 54 g. carbohydrates, 10 g. fat, 18 mg. cholesterol, 718 mg. sodium, 11 g. dietary fiber*

# Creamy Dijon Stroganoff

- **12** **ounces wide egg noodles**
- **1** **teaspoon olive oil**
- **2** **cups thinly sliced mushrooms**
- **1** **onion, chopped**
- **2** **cloves garlic, minced**
- **¼** **cup vegetable broth**
- **1** **package (10 ounces) frozen mixed vegetables, thawed**
- **9** **ounces frozen vegetable-protein crumbles**
- **2** **cups 1% milk**
- **3** **tablespoons all-purpose flour**
- **2** **tablespoons Dijon mustard**
- **¾** **cup (6 ounces) reduced-fat sour cream**
- **½** **teaspoon dried thyme**
- **¼** **teaspoon salt**
- **¼** **teaspoon ground black pepper**

COOK THE NOODLES according to package directions. Drain well.

WARM THE OIL in a large nonstick skillet over medium-high heat. Add the mushrooms, onion, and garlic. Cook, stirring frequently, for 4 to 5 minutes, or until tender. Stir in the broth, mixed vegetables, and vegetable-protein crumbles. Bring to a boil. Reduce the heat to low. Cover and simmer for 5 to 6 minutes, or until the vegetables are tender.

IN A SMALL BOWL, combine the milk, flour, and mustard. Stir into the skillet. Bring to a boil. Cook, stirring constantly, for 2 to 3 minutes, or until the sauce is thickened slightly. Reduce the heat to low and gradually stir in the sour cream, thyme, salt, and pepper. Cook for 2 minutes, or until heated through.

PLACE THE NOODLES in a large serving bowl. Add the vegetable mixture. Toss to combine.

**Makes 4 servings**

***Per serving:*** *621 calories, 33 g. protein, 90 g. carbohydrates, 16 g. fat, 103 mg. cholesterol, 697 mg. sodium, 8 g. dietary fiber*

# Sweet Potato Casserole

- **4 pounds sweet potatoes, peeled and sliced ¼" thick**
- **1 cup (4 ounces) shredded reduced-fat Jarlsberg or Swiss cheese**
- **2 tablespoons (½ ounce) grated Parmesan cheese**
- **1 can (14½ ounces) chickpeas, rinsed and drained**
- **1 cup golden raisins**
- **1 cup 1% milk**
- **½ teaspoon ground cinnamon**
- **⅛ teaspoon ground allspice**
- **3 tablespoons plain dry bread crumbs**
- **2 teaspoons unsalted butter, cut into small pieces**

PREHEAT THE OVEN TO 400°F. Coat a 2-quart baking dish with nonstick spray.

ARRANGE HALF OF THE POTATOES in a single layer in the baking dish, overlapping the slices slightly. Sprinkle with ½ cup Jarlsberg or Swiss and 1 tablespoon Parmesan. Top with the chickpeas and raisins. Arrange the remaining potatoes on top of the chickpeas and raisins. Sprinkle with the remaining ½ cup Jarlsberg or Swiss and 1 tablespoon Parmesan.

IN A SMALL BOWL, combine the milk, cinnamon, and allspice. Pour over the potato mixture. Top with the bread crumbs and dot with the butter.

COVER WITH FOIL. Bake for 30 minutes. Uncover and bake for 20 to 25 minutes, or until the potatoes are tender and the crumbs are golden.

**Makes 8 servings**

***Per serving:*** *426 calories, 12 g. protein, 83 g. carbohydrates, 6 g. fat, 13 mg. cholesterol, 255 mg. sodium, 8 g. dietary fiber*

**Tip:** To vary the flavor, I sometimes replace 2 pounds of the sweet potatoes with 2 pounds root vegetables such as turnips or parsnips.

# Rice and Cheese Casserole 

- **1½ cups long-grain rice**
- **½ cup dry-pack sun-dried tomatoes**
- **4 cups frozen mixed broccoli, cauliflower, and pepper blend, thawed**
- **1 cup (4 ounces) shredded reduced-fat mozzarella cheese**
- **3 ounces reduced-fat cream cheese, cubed**

COOK THE RICE according to package directions.

PREHEAT THE OVEN to 350°F. Coat a 1½-quart baking dish with nonstick spray. In a small bowl, soak the tomatoes in hot water to cover for 10 minutes, or until soft. Drain and coarsely chop.

COMBINE THE RICE, tomatoes, mixed vegetables, mozzarella, and cream cheese in the prepared baking dish. Toss to mix. Bake for 20 to 30 minutes, or until heated through and the cheese is melted.

**Makes 4 servings**

***Per serving:*** *503 calories, 21 g. protein, 83 g. carbohydrates, 11 g. fat, 28 mg. cholesterol, 835 mg. sodium, 11 g. dietary fiber*

## Quick Conversion

**Rice and Cheese Casserole with Ham:** For a dual vegetarian/nonvegetarian dish, prepare the recipe with the following changes. Use two 1-quart baking dishes instead of one 1½-quart baking dish. Divide the mixture between the 2 dishes. For the ham portion, add ½ pound cubed cooked ham to one of the dishes. Bake both portions for 15 to 20 minutes, or until heated through and the cheese is melted.

# Mexican-Style Baked Bean Casserole

- **2 cans (15 ounces each) vegetarian baked beans**
- **1 cup salsa**
- **2 tablespoons lime juice**
- **1½ cups crushed baked tortilla chips**
- **¼ cup chopped fresh cilantro or parsley**
- **½ cup (2 ounces) shredded reduced-fat Cheddar cheese**

PREHEAT THE OVEN TO 350°F. Coat a 1½-quart baking dish with nonstick spray.

IN THE PREPARED BAKING DISH, combine the beans, salsa, and lime juice. Mix well. Top with the chips and cilantro or parsley. Sprinkle with the cheese.

BAKE FOR 25 TO 30 MINUTES, or until heated through and the cheese is melted.

**Makes 4 servings**

***Per serving:*** *297 calories, 15 g. protein, 56 g. carbohydrates, 5 g. fat, 3 mg. cholesterol, 1,189 mg. sodium, 12 g. dietary fiber*

**Tip:** This dish can be frozen in a tightly covered container for up to a month. Thaw in the refrigerator before baking.

## Quick Conversion

**Mexican-Style Baked Bean Casserole with Bacon:** For a dual vegetarian/nonvegetarian dish, prepare the recipe with the following changes. Divide the bean-salsa mixture between two 1-quart baking dishes. For the bacon portion, cook 3 or 4 strips of bacon in a large skillet over medium heat until very crispy. Transfer to a plate lined with paper towels. Crumble and stir into the bean-salsa mixture in one of the baking dishes. Top both portions with the chips and cilantro or parsley. Sprinkle with the cheese. Bake for 20 to 25 minutes, or until heated through and the cheese is melted.

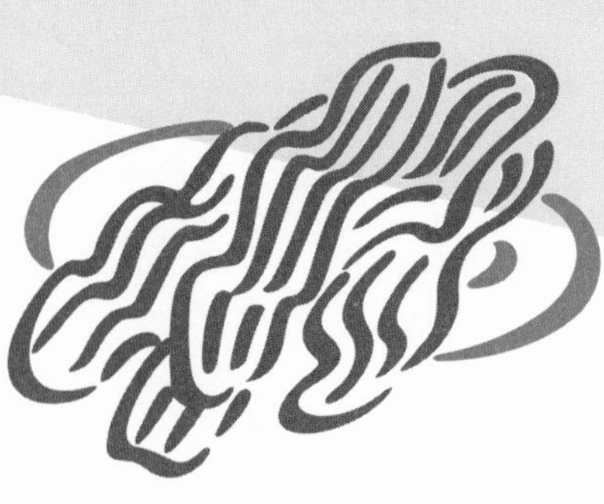

# Quick Cassoulet 

- 1 teaspoon olive oil
- 1 large carrot, chopped
- 1 cup chopped fennel or celery
- 1 onion, chopped
- 1 can (16 ounces) cannellini beans, rinsed and drained
- 1 can (16 ounces) red kidney beans, rinsed and drained
- 1 can (14½ ounces) stewed tomatoes
- ¼ cup vegetable broth
- ¼ teaspoon crushed dried rosemary
- 2 cups cubed French or Italian bread
- 1 tablespoon melted butter

PREHEAT THE OVEN to 425°F. Coat an 11" × 7" baking dish with nonstick spray.

WARM THE OIL in a large nonstick skillet over medium-high heat. Add the carrot, fennel or celery, and onion. Cook, stirring frequently, for 4 to 5 minutes.

SPOON INTO THE PREPARED BAKING DISH. Stir in the cannellini beans, kidney beans, tomatoes (with juice), broth, and rosemary. Top with the bread cubes.

COVER WITH FOIL and bake for 20 minutes. Uncover and drizzle the butter over the cubes. Bake, uncovered, for 8 to 10 minutes, or until the bread is golden.

**Makes 4 servings**

***Per serving:*** *395 calories, 17 g. protein, 69 g. carbohydrates, 6 g. fat, 8 mg. cholesterol, 788 mg. sodium, 18 g. dietary fiber*

**Tip:** This dish can be assembled and frozen in a tightly covered container for up to a month. Thaw in the refrigerator before baking. Drizzle with the butter during the second half of baking.

## Quick Conversion

**Quick Cassoulet with Prosciutto:** For a dual vegetarian/nonvegetarian dish, prepare the recipe with the following changes. Use two 1-quart baking dishes instead of one 11" × 7" baking dish. Divide the completed mixture between the 2 dishes. For the prosciutto portion, stir 2 ounces prosciutto into one of the dishes. Top each portion with the bread cubes. Bake both portions for 15 minutes. Drizzle with the butter and bake, uncovered, for 5 to 8 minutes, or until the bread is golden.

# Zucchini Casserole

- 3 cups cubed cornbread and herb stuffing or plain herb stuffing
- ¼ cup vegetable broth, warmed
- 1 can (10¾ ounces) cream of mushroom soup
- 1 small zucchini, shredded
- 1 small carrot, shredded
- 1 small red bell pepper, finely chopped
- ⅓ cup (about 3 ounces) reduced-fat sour cream
- ¼ cup (1 ounce) shredded reduced-fat Cheddar cheese
- ½ teaspoon dried thyme
- 1 tomato, chopped (optional)

PREHEAT THE OVEN TO 350°F. Coat a 2-quart baking dish with nonstick spray.

IN A MEDIUM BOWL, combine the stuffing and broth. Reserve ½ cup stuffing. Spoon the remainder into the prepared baking dish.

IN A SMALL BOWL, combine the soup, zucchini, carrot, pepper, sour cream, cheese, and thyme. Spread over the stuffing. Top with the reserved stuffing.

BAKE FOR 35 TO 40 MINUTES, or until hot and bubbly. Top with the tomato, if using.

**Makes 8 servings**

***Per serving:*** *198 calories, 6 g. protein, 24 g. carbohydrates, 9 g. fat, 4 mg. cholesterol, 669 mg. sodium, 3 g. dietary fiber*

# Greek Spinach and Olive Pie

**1** teaspoon olive oil

**1** onion, chopped

**1** red bell pepper, chopped

**1** package (10 ounces) frozen chopped spinach, thawed and squeezed dry

**1** cup (4 ounces) crumbled basil-flavored feta cheese or plain feta

**1** large egg white

**¼** cup chopped pitted kalamata or other black olives

**2** tablespoons chopped fresh dill or 2 teaspoons dried dillweed

**1** tablespoon lemon juice

**¼** teaspoon ground black pepper

**12** sheets frozen phyllo dough, thawed

PREHEAT THE OVEN TO 350°F. Coat a 9" tart pan with removable bottom with nonstick spray.

WARM THE OIL in a large nonstick skillet over medium-high heat. Add the onion and bell pepper. Cook, stirring frequently, for 4 to 5 minutes, or until tender. Remove from the heat. Let cool for 1 to 2 minutes. Stir in the spinach, cheese, egg white, olives, dill, lemon juice, and black pepper. Mix well.

PLACE A SHEET OF PHYLLO DOUGH on a flat work surface. Coat with nonstick spray. Lay another sheet on top at a 45° angle and coat with the spray. Repeat with 4 more sheets.

CAREFULLY LIFT THE STACK and press into the prepared pan. Spread the spinach-cheese mixture over the phyllo.

LAYER THE REMAINING 6 PHYLLO SHEETS on top of one another, coating each sheet with nonstick spray. With a knife, cut several slits near the center of the stack. Place on top of the spinach-cheese mixture. With kitchen scissors, trim the edges, leaving a 1½" overhang. Tuck into the pan.

BAKE FOR 45 TO 50 MINUTES, or until the crust is golden. Cool for 10 minutes before serving.

**Makes 8 servings**

***Per serving:*** *156 calories, 6 g. protein, 20 g. carbohydrates, 6 g. fat, 13 mg. cholesterol, 365 mg. sodium, 2 g. dietary fiber*

**Tips:** This dish can be assembled and frozen for up to a month. Thaw in the refrigerator before baking.

Cover the phyllo with a damp kitchen towel to keep it from drying out as you work.

# Macaroni and Cheese with Roasted Vegetables

- **2 tablespoons seasoned dry bread crumbs**
- **2 cups (10 ounces) elbow macaroni or ditalini pasta**
- **1 small eggplant, finely chopped**
- **2 cups broccoli florets**
- **3 tomatoes, coarsely chopped**
- **1 large red bell pepper, chopped**
- **2 cloves garlic**
- **$\frac{1}{2}$ cup reduced-fat Caesar salad dressing**
- **$\frac{1}{3}$ cup all-purpose flour**
- **$2\frac{1}{2}$ cups 1% milk**
- **1 cup (4 ounces) shredded reduced-fat sharp Cheddar cheese**
- **$\frac{1}{2}$ cup (2 ounces) grated Parmesan cheese**
- **$\frac{1}{8}$ teaspoon ground white or black pepper**

PREHEAT THE OVEN TO 450°F. Coat a $2\frac{1}{2}$-quart baking dish with nonstick spray. Sprinkle the bottom and sides with the bread crumbs.

COOK THE PASTA according to package directions. Drain well.

MEANWHILE, IN A SHALLOW ROASTING PAN, combine the eggplant, broccoli, tomatoes, bell pepper, and garlic. Add the dressing. Toss to coat. Bake the vegetables, stirring occasionally, for 20 to 30 minutes, or until tender. Reduce the heat to 375°F.

WHILE THE VEGETABLES are roasting, place the flour in a large saucepan. Gradually whisk in the milk. Cook, stirring constantly, over medium heat, for 6 to 8 minutes, or until the mixture thickens. Stir in the Cheddar, $\frac{1}{4}$ cup of the Parmesan, and the white or black pepper. Cook for 2 to 3 minutes, or until the cheeses melt.

REMOVE FROM THE HEAT and stir in the vegetables and pasta. Spoon into the prepared baking dish. Sprinkle with the remaining $\frac{1}{4}$ cup Parmesan. Bake for 20 to 25 minutes, or until bubbly.

**Makes 8 servings**

***Per serving:*** *264 calories, 15 g. protein, 36 g. carbohydrates, 7 g. fat, 19 mg. cholesterol, 526 mg. sodium, 2 g. dietary fiber*

## Quick Conversion

**Macaroni and Cheese with Roasted Vegetables and Pepperoni:** For a dual vegetarian/nonvegetarian dish, prepare the recipe with the following changes. Use two $1\frac{1}{2}$-quart baking dishes instead of one $2\frac{1}{2}$-quart baking dish. Divide the completed mixture between the 2 dishes. For the pepperoni portion, stir 6 ounces chopped pepperoni into one of the dishes. Sprinkle the remaining $\frac{1}{4}$ cup Parmesan over both dishes. Bake both dishes for 15 to 20 minutes, or until bubbly.

# Acorn Squash Rings

- 2 acorn squash (about 2 pounds), peeled, seeded, and cut into 1" slices
- 1 red onion, thinly sliced and separated into rings
- ⅓ cup vegetable broth
- 1 teaspoon olive oil
- 3 tomatoes, chopped
- ¼ cup parsley
- ½ cup (2 ounces) shredded reduced-fat Swiss cheese

PREHEAT THE OVEN TO 400°F.

PLACE THE SQUASH in an ungreased 13" × 9" baking dish. Arrange the onion over the squash. In a 1-cup measure, combine the broth and oil. Pour over the squash. Top with the tomatoes and parsley. Cover with foil.

BAKE FOR 30 MINUTES. Sprinkle with the cheese. Bake, uncovered, for 10 to 15 minutes, or until the cheese melts and the squash is tender.

**Makes 4 servings**

***Per serving:*** *146 calories, 7 g. protein, 28 g. carbohydrates, 2 g. fat, 5 mg. cholesterol, 158 mg. sodium, 4 g. dietary fiber*

**Tip:** On occasion, I make this dish with peeled and cubed butternut squash instead of acorn squash.

# Cabbage and Caraway Gratin

- 1 teaspoon canola oil
- 4 cups coarsely chopped green cabbage
- 1 onion, chopped
- 1 cup shredded carrots
- ¾ cup 1% milk
- 2 eggs
- ¼ cup vegetable broth
- ⅓ cup (1½ ounces) shredded reduced-fat Swiss cheese
- 1 tablespoon parsley
- ½ teaspoon caraway seeds

PREHEAT THE OVEN TO 350°F. Coat an 11" × 7" baking dish with nonstick spray.

WARM THE OIL in a large nonstick skillet over medium-high heat. Add the cabbage, onion, and carrots. Cook, stirring frequently, for 4 to 5 minutes, or until tender. Spoon into the prepared dish.

IN A SMALL BOWL, combine the milk, eggs, broth, cheese, parsley, and caraway seeds. Pour over the cabbage. Bake for 35 to 40 minutes, or until set and the top is golden. Let stand for 5 minutes before serving.

**Makes 4 servings**

***Per serving:*** *126 calories, 9 g. protein, 12 g. carbohydrates, 5 g. fat, 111 mg. cholesterol, 165 mg. sodium, 3 g. dietary fiber*

# Mediterranean Tofu

- **8 ounces wide egg noodles or 1 cup long-grain rice**
- **2 teaspoons olive oil**
- **1½ pounds firm tofu, drained, squeezed dry, and cubed**
- **2 large yellow squash, sliced**
- **2 cups sliced mushrooms**
- **3 scallions, thinly sliced**
- **1 tablespoon all-purpose flour**
- **3 tomatoes, chopped**
- **½ cup orange juice**
- **3 tablespoons chopped fresh oregano or 3 teaspoons dried**
- **1 tablespoon grated orange peel**
- **¼ teaspoon salt**
- **⅛ teaspoon ground black pepper**

Cook the noodles or rice according to package directions.

Meanwhile, warm the oil in a large nonstick skillet over medium heat. Add the tofu. Cook, stirring frequently, for 4 to 5 minutes, or until golden. Add the squash, mushrooms, and scallions. Cook, stirring frequently, for 3 to 4 minutes, or until tender. Stir in the flour. Cook for 1 minute.

Add the tomatoes, orange juice, oregano, orange peel, salt, and pepper. Simmer for 5 to 8 minutes, or until the sauce thickens slightly. Serve over the noodles or rice.

**Makes 4 servings**

***Per serving:*** *476 calories, 27 g. protein, 67 g. carbohydrates, 15 g. fat, 54 mg. cholesterol, 186 mg. sodium, 7 g. dietary fiber*

# Southwest Corn Casserole

- **1 can (16 ounces) cream-style corn**
- **2 large eggs**
- **1 can (16 ounces) corn, drained**
- **3 scallions, chopped**
- **1 small green bell pepper, chopped**
- **¼ cup chopped roasted red peppers**
- **¼ cup sliced pitted black olives**
- **¼ cup yellow cornmeal**
- **1 tablespoon Dijon mustard**
- **1 tablespoon chopped fresh cilantro**
- **½ cup coarsely crushed baked tortilla chips**
- **2 teaspoons olive oil**

Preheat the oven to 350°F. Coat a 2-quart baking dish with nonstick spray.

In a food processor, combine the cream-style corn and eggs. Process until smooth. Transfer to the prepared baking dish. Stir in the corn, scallions, bell pepper, roasted peppers, olives, cornmeal, mustard, and cilantro. Mix well.

Sprinkle with the tortilla chips. Drizzle with the oil. Bake for 40 to 45 minutes, or until set.

**Makes 8 servings**

***Per serving:*** *195 calories, 6 g. protein, 37 g. carbohydrates, 4 g. fat, 53 mg. cholesterol, 448 mg. sodium, 4 g. dietary fiber*

**Tip:** This dish can be assembled ahead and refrigerated until ready to bake. Sprinkle with the crushed tortilla chips right before baking.

# Baked Lentils

- ⅓ cup brown lentils
- 2 teaspoons butter
- 2 cups thinly sliced mushrooms
- 1 onion, chopped
- 1 green apple, peeled and finely chopped
- 1 tablespoon all-purpose flour
- 1 cup 1% milk
- 2⅓ cups vegetable broth
- ¼ cup long-grain rice
- ½ teaspoon dried thyme
- ¼ teaspoon salt
- ¼ teaspoon ground black pepper
- ¼ cup crushed reduced-fat butter-flavored crackers

PREHEAT THE OVEN TO 350°F.

RINSE AND PICK OVER the lentils, discarding any that are shriveled. Set aside.

MELT THE BUTTER in an ovenproof Dutch oven. Add the mushrooms and onion. Cook, stirring frequently, for 4 to 5 minutes over medium heat, or until tender. Stir in the apple. Cook for 5 minutes, or just until the apple is tender. Stir in the flour and cook for 1 minute. Add the milk and broth. Cook, stirring frequently, until slightly thickened. Remove from the heat and stir in the lentils, rice, thyme, salt, and pepper.

COVER AND BAKE for 45 minutes, or until the lentils and rice are tender and the liquid has been absorbed. Sprinkle with the cracker crumbs. Bake, uncovered, for 10 minutes, or until the crumbs are crisp.

**Makes 4 servings**

***Per serving:*** *220 calories, 11 g. protein, 36 g. carbohydrates, 5 g. fat, 8 mg. cholesterol, 820 mg. sodium, 7 g. dietary fiber*

## Quick Conversion

**Baked Lentils with Sausage:** For a dual vegetarian/nonvegetarian dish, prepare the recipe with the following changes. Divide the completed mixture between two 1½-quart baking dishes. For the sausage portion, cut ½ pound turkey sausage links into ½" pieces. Brown in the Dutch oven used to cook the mushrooms and onion. Stir into one of the baking dishes. Cover both dishes and bake as directed, reducing the initial baking time to 25 to 30 minutes.

## Spicing Up One-Dish Dinners

The best meals often emerge from the odds and ends in my pantry. But no matter what ingredients I start with, almost all casseroles and one-dish meals need extra seasoning at some point. Here's a chart of dried herbs and spices showing what goes with what. Stir in these seasonings early in the cooking process so that they have time to release their flavors.

| Herb/Spice | Flavor | Goes with . . . |
|---|---|---|
| Allspice | A blend of cinnamon, cloves, and nutmeg | Chili, curried dishes, sweet potatoes, winter squash |
| Basil | Sweet and aromatic with hints of mint, licorice, and pepper | Eggs, cheese, pasta, rice, tomatoes, most vegetables |
| Chili powder | Blend of spices such as cumin, oregano, and ground red pepper | Beans, rice, Mexican-style dishes |
| Cinnamon | Warm and sweet | Sweet potatoes, winter squash, Middle Eastern–style dishes |
| Coriander | Strong and aromatic with hints of citrus, sage, and caraway | Curried dishes, lentils, rice, Mediterranean-style dishes |
| Cumin | Aromatic, nutty, and earthy | Chili, Southwestern-style dishes, Middle Eastern–style dishes |
| Curry powder | A blend of spices such as turmeric, cumin, coriander, ginger, and ground red pepper | Indian-style dishes |
| Dill | Light and lemony with hints of caraway | Eggs, cheese, carrots, cucumbers, most vegetables |
| Fennel seeds | Mild licorice taste similar to anise | Pasta, cheese, tomatoes, cabbage |
| Oregano | Resinous pinelike taste similar to marjoram | Chili, most vegetables, Italian-style dishes, Mexican-style dishes |
| Paprika | Peppery, from sweet to hot | Potatoes, eggs, cheese |
| Rosemary | Strong and fragrant with an evergreen aroma | Eggs, potatoes, eggplant, mushrooms, most vegetables |
| Sage | Earthy and aromatic with hints of lemon | Eggs, pasta, rice, grains, beans, most vegetables |
| Tarragon | Licorice taste similar to anise | Eggs, beans, potatoes, tomatoes, most vegetables |
| Thyme | Earthy and slightly sweet with hints of mint and lemon | Eggs, cheese, beans, mushrooms, most vegetables |

# Vegetable Potpie

**1** baking potato, cubed
**2** cups broccoli florets
**2** large carrots, thinly sliced
**1** parsnip, thinly sliced
**1** can (10¾ ounces) cream of celery soup
**½** cup 1% milk
**2** tablespoons buttermilk biscuit baking mix
**½** teaspoon dried thyme
**⅛** teaspoon ground red pepper
**1** tube (4.5 ounces) refrigerated biscuit dough (6 biscuits)

Preheat the oven to 425°F. Coat a 2-quart baking dish with nonstick spray.

Bring a large saucepan of salted water to a boil. Add the potato, broccoli, carrots, and parsnip. Cook for 8 to 10 minutes, or until tender. Drain well and set aside.

In the same saucepan, combine the soup, milk, baking mix, thyme, and pepper. Stir in the cooked vegetables. Spoon into the prepared baking dish. Top with the biscuits.

Bake for 30 to 35 minutes, or until the biscuits are puffed and golden and the filling is bubbly.

**Makes 4 servings**

***Per serving:*** *284 calories, 8 g. protein, 48 g. carbohydrates, 8 g. fat, 4 mg. cholesterol, 807 mg. sodium, 6 g. dietary fiber*

## Quick Conversion

**Vegetable Potpie with Chicken:** For a dual vegetarian/nonvegetarian dish, prepare the recipe with the following changes. Use two 1-quart baking dishes instead of one 2-quart dish. Divide the completed mixture between the 2 dishes. For the chicken portion, stir ½ pound cubed cooked chicken into one of the dishes. Top each dish with 3 biscuits. Bake each for 20 to 25 minutes, or until the biscuits are puffed and golden and the filling is bubbly.

*"The closer you can live to being a vegetarian, the better."*

—Gary Player, professional golfer

# Plateful of Pasta

PEOPLE LOVE PASTA. You could say it's because pasta is healthy. One cup of cooked pasta has only 160 calories, virtually no fat, and plenty of complex carbohydrates for long-lasting energy. But I think the real reason that people love pasta is this: It's easy. Pasta dishes come together quickly. And it's extremely versatile. Pasta can be boiled, baked, and stuffed in countless ways. For my "mixed family," I simply start with the vegetarian recipe, then add a little beef, chicken, or sausage for the meat-lovers.

## Recipes

● Kid-Friendly Recipe

● Freezable Recipe

● Microwaveable Recipe

# Shells with Radicchio and Romano

- **12 ounces medium shell pasta**
- **1 tablespoon olive oil**
- **2 cloves garlic, minced**
- **1 cup vegetable broth**
- **2 tablespoons balsamic vinegar**
- **1 small bunch broccoli raab, tough stems removed**
- **1½ cups coarsely chopped radicchio**
- **¼ cup chopped fresh basil**
- **2 tablespoons (½ ounce) grated Romano cheese**

COOK THE PASTA according to package directions.

MEANWHILE, WARM THE OIL in a large nonstick skillet. Add the garlic. Cook, stirring frequently, for 2 to 3 minutes, or until tender. Stir in the broth and vinegar. Bring to a boil. Reduce the heat to medium-low. Stir in the broccoli raab, radicchio, and basil. Cook for 4 to 5 minutes, or until tender.

DRAIN THE PASTA and place in a large serving bowl. Add the broccoli rabe mixture. Toss to mix well. Sprinkle with the cheese before serving.

**Makes 4 servings**

***Per serving:*** *417 calories, 16 g. protein, 75 g. carbohydrates, 6 g. fat, 3 mg. cholesterol, 311 mg. sodium, 3 g. dietary fiber*

## Quick Conversion

**Shells with Radicchio, Romano, and Shrimp:** For a dual vegetarian/non-vegetarian dish, prepare the recipe with the following changes. Use 2 medium skillets instead of 1 large one. Prepare half of the broccoli raab mixture in each skillet, dividing the ingredients between the skillets. For the shrimp portion, add 6 peeled and deveined medium shrimp to one of the skillets along with the broccoli raab. Finish the mixture as directed, cooking until the shrimp are opaque. Toss each portion with half of the pasta.

# Wagon Wheels with Chunky Vegetable Sauce

- **12 ounces wagon wheel pasta**
- **2 teaspoons olive oil**
- **1 green bell pepper, chopped**
- **1 onion, chopped**
- **2 cloves garlic, minced**
- **1 tablespoon chili powder**
- **1 can (28 ounces) Mexican-style tomatoes**
- **1 cup drained Mexican-style canned corn**
- **1 tablespoon lime juice**
- **¼ cup (1 ounce) shredded reduced-fat Cheddar cheese**

COOK THE PASTA according to package directions.

MEANWHILE, WARM THE OIL in a large nonstick skillet. Add the pepper, onion, and garlic. Cook, stirring frequently, for 4 to 5 minutes, or just until the vegetables are tender. Stir in the chili powder. Cook for 1 minute.

STIR IN THE TOMATOES (with juice), corn, and lime juice. Bring to a boil. Reduce the heat to low. Cover partially and simmer for 15 to 20 minutes, or until slightly thickened.

DRAIN THE PASTA and place in a large serving bowl. Add the tomato mixture. Toss to mix well. Sprinkle with the cheese.

**Makes 4 servings**

***Per serving:*** *568 calories, 18 g. protein, 111 g. carbohydrates, 5 g. fat, 1 mg. cholesterol, 1,054 mg. sodium, 9 g. dietary fiber*

## Quick Conversion

**Wagon Wheels with Chunky Vegetable Sauce and Beef:** For a dual vegetarian/nonvegetarian dish, prepare the recipe with the following changes. For the beef portion, cook ½ pound ground beef in a medium skillet until the beef is no longer pink. After bringing the tomato mixture to a boil and reducing the heat, transfer half of the mixture to the skillet with the beef. Finish cooking both mixtures as directed. Toss each portion with half of the pasta. (I sometimes use spicy turkey sausage instead of beef. Remove the casings before using.) Sprinkle with the cheese.

# Bow Ties with Goat Cheese Sauce

- **8** **ounces bow-tie pasta**
- **1** **package (10 ounces) frozen peas, thawed**
- **½** **cup dry-pack sun-dried tomatoes (optional)**
- **1¼** **cups whole milk**
- **½** **cup vegetable broth**
- **½** **teaspoon dried thyme**
- **⅛** **teaspoon ground nutmeg**
- **1** **cup (4 ounces) crumbled herb-flavored goat cheese**
- **2** **tablespoons chopped fresh basil or parsley**

COOK THE BOW TIES in a large pot of boiling water over medium-high heat for 5 minutes. Add the peas and sun-dried tomatoes, if using. Cook for 5 to 6 minutes, or until the bow ties are tender.

MEANWHILE, IN A MEDIUM SAUCEPAN, bring the milk, broth, thyme, and nutmeg to a boil. Reduce the heat to low. Add the goat cheese. Cook and stir until melted.

DRAIN THE BOW TIES and peas. Place in a large serving bowl. Add the goat cheese sauce and toss to mix. Sprinkle with the basil or parsley.

**Makes 4 servings**

***Per serving:*** *268 calories, 15 g. protein, 31 g. carbohydrates, 10 g. fat, 36 mg. cholesterol, 374 mg. sodium, 6 g. dietary fiber*

**Tip:** Herb-flavored feta cheese can be used in place of goat cheese for this recipe.

# Roasted Peppers and Penne

- 6 ounces penne
- 3 red bell peppers, cut into strips
- 1 red onion, thinly sliced and separated into rings
- 2 ribs celery, chopped
- ¼ cup pitted and halved kalamata or other black olives
- 2 tablespoons balsamic vinegar
- 1 tablespoon orange juice
- 1 tablespoon olive oil
- 1 tablespoon finely grated orange peel
- ½ teaspoon crushed dried rosemary
- ¼ teaspoon salt

PREHEAT THE OVEN TO 400°F. Cook the pasta according to package directions. Drain and place in a large serving bowl.

MEANWHILE, IN A 13" × 9" BAKING DISH, combine the peppers, onion, celery, olives, vinegar, orange juice, oil, orange peel, rosemary, and salt. Toss to mix well. Bake for 20 minutes, stirring occasionally, or until the vegetables are tender.

REMOVE THE VEGETABLES from the oven and toss with the penne.

**Makes 4 servings**

***Per serving:*** *273 calories, 7 g. protein, 43 g. carbohydrates, 9 g. fat, 3 mg. cholesterol, 946 mg. sodium, 4 g. dietary fiber*

## Quick Conversion

**Roasted Peppers and Penne with Chicken:** For a dual vegetarian/nonvegetarian dish, prepare the recipe with the following changes. For the chicken portion, transfer half of the uncooked vegetable mixture to an 11" × 7" baking dish. In a medium bowl, combine ½ pound boneless, skinless chicken breast strips and 1 tablespoon reduced-fat Italian salad dressing. Toss to coat. Stir into the larger baking dish. Bake both portions for 15 to 20 minutes, stirring occasionally, or until the vegetables are tender and the chicken is no longer pink and the juices run clear when pierced. Toss each portion with half of the pasta.

# Mexican Pasta Toss

- **12** **ounces broken lasagna noodles**
- **1** **can (15 ounces) Mexican-style tomatoes**
- **1** **can (12 ounces) black beans, rinsed and drained**
- **1** **cup (8 ounces) reduced-fat sour cream**
- **½** **cup (2 ounces) shredded reduced-fat Cheddar cheese**
- **½** **cup drained canned corn**
- **¼** **cup sliced pitted black olives**
- **1** **tablespoon lime juice**
- **1** **tablespoon chopped fresh cilantro or 1 teaspoon dried**
- **⅛** **teaspoon ground red pepper**

COOK THE PASTA according to package directions.

IN A LARGE SERVING BOWL, combine the tomatoes (with juice), beans, sour cream, cheese, corn, olives, lime juice, cilantro, and pepper. Stir to combine.

DRAIN THE LASAGNA and add to the serving bowl. Toss to mix well.

**Makes 4 servings**

***Per serving:*** *337 calories, 13 g. protein, 53 g. carbohydrates, 9 g. fat, 20 mg. cholesterol, 629 mg. sodium, 7 g. dietary fiber*

# Rotelle Niçoise

- **12** **ounces rotelle**
- **1** **tablespoon olive oil**
- **1** **red onion, chopped**
- **2** **cloves garlic, minced**
- **4** **red potatoes, cubed**
- **2** **cups fresh green beans, cut into 2" pieces**
- **¼** **cup vegetable broth**
- **2** **tablespoons balsamic vinegar**
- **1** **tablespoon Dijon mustard**
- **1** **teaspoon dried oregano**
- **¼** **teaspoon freshly ground black pepper**
- **¼** **cup pitted kalamata or other black olives**

COOK THE PASTA according to package directions.

MEANWHILE, WARM 1 TEASPOON of the oil in a large nonstick skillet over medium-high heat. Add the onion and garlic. Cook, stirring frequently, for 2 minutes. Stir in the potatoes and beans. Cook, stirring frequently, for 5 minutes. Add the broth. Cook, covered, for 5 to 8 minutes, or until the potatoes are tender.

IN A SMALL BOWL, combine the vinegar, mustard, oregano, pepper, and the remaining 2 teaspoons olive oil. Mix well.

DRAIN THE ROTELLE and place in a large serving bowl. Add the potato mixture, olives, and vinegar mixture. Toss to combine.

**Makes 4 servings**

***Per serving:*** *543 calories, 16 g. protein, 101 g. carbohydrates, 9 g. fat, 0 mg. cholesterol, 389 mg. sodium, 7 g. dietary fiber*

## Quick Conversion

**Rotelle Niçoise with Tuna:** For a dual vegetarian/nonvegetarian dish, prepare the recipe with the following changes. Divide the completed recipe in half. For the tuna portion, stir in half of a 6½-ounce can drained and flaked water-packed tuna.

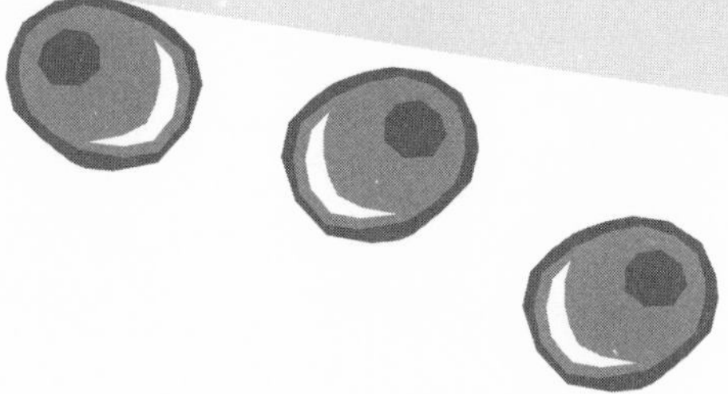

# Tortellini with Tomato Pesto

- **15 dry-pack sun-dried tomatoes**
- **¼ cup chopped fresh basil**
- **2 tablespoons parsley**
- **¼ cup walnut pieces**
- **1 tablespoon (¼ ounce) grated Parmesan cheese**
- **1 tablespoon red wine vinegar**
- **2 teaspoons olive oil**
- **12 ounces fresh cheese tortellini**

IN A SMALL BOWL, soak the tomatoes in hot water to cover for 10 minutes, or until soft. Drain, reserving 1 tablespoon of the soaking liquid.

IN A FOOD PROCESSOR, combine the tomatoes, basil, parsley, walnuts, and cheese. Process until coarsely chopped. Add the reserved soaking liquid, vinegar, and oil. Process until smooth.

COOK THE TORTELLINI in a large pot of boiling water for 5 to 7 minutes, or until tender. Drain well.

PLACE IN A LARGE SERVING BOWL. Add the tomato mixture. Toss to combine.

**Makes 4 servings**

***Per serving:*** *375 calories, 15 g. protein, 43 g. carbohydrates, 15 g. fat, 33 mg. cholesterol, 308 mg. sodium, 2 g. dietary fiber*

**Tip:** This tomato pesto (without the pasta) can be frozen in a tightly covered container for up to 3 months.

# Cavatelli with Asparagus

- **12 ounces cavatelli**
- **½ cup vegetable broth**
- **12 thin asparagus spears, trimmed and cut into 2" pieces**
- **2 teaspoons olive oil**
- **1 red bell pepper, cut into strips**
- **2 cloves garlic, minced**
- **1 can (12 ounces) cannellini beans, rinsed and drained**
- **1 tablespoon chopped fresh rosemary or 1 teaspoon dried**
- **2 tablespoons (½ ounce) grated Romano cheese**

COOK THE PASTA according to package directions.

MEANWHILE, BRING THE BROTH to a boil over high heat in a large nonstick skillet. Add the asparagus. Reduce the heat to low. Cover and simmer for 4 to 5 minutes, or until tender. Drain and reserve the broth. Transfer the asparagus to a platter and cover with foil to keep warm.

WARM THE OIL in the same skillet over medium-high heat. Add the pepper and garlic. Cook, stirring frequently, for 2 to 3 minutes, or until tender. Stir in the asparagus, beans, rosemary, and reserved broth. Cook for 2 minutes to blend flavors.

DRAIN THE CAVATELLI and place in a large serving bowl. Add the asparagus mixture. Toss to combine. Sprinkle with the cheese.

**Makes 4 servings**

***Per serving:*** *440 calories, 18 g. protein, 81 g. carbohydrates, 5 g. fat, 3 mg. cholesterol, 342 mg. sodium, 8 g. dietary fiber*

## Quick Conversion

**Cavatelli with Asparagus and Shrimp:** For a dual vegetarian/nonvegetarian dish, prepare the recipe with the following changes. After cooking the asparagus, divide the oil between the large skillet and another medium skillet. Cook half of the pepper and garlic in each skillet as directed. For the shrimp portion, add ½ pound peeled and deveined medium shrimp to one of the skillets. Cook until the shrimp are opaque. Divide the asparagus, beans, rosemary, and broth between the 2 skillets and cook as directed. Toss each portion with half of the pasta. Sprinkle the shrimp portion with 2 teaspoons lemon juice. (You can also use ½ pound boneless, skinless chicken breast in place of the shrimp. In that case, omit the lemon juice.) Sprinkle with the cheese.

# Mini Ravioli in Tomato Broth

- 1 can (14½ ounces) stewed tomatoes
- 1½ cups vegetable broth
- ¼ cup water
- 1 package (10 ounces) frozen green beans, thawed
- 12 ounces fresh mini cheese ravioli
- 4 slices toasted Italian bread (optional)
- 2 tablespoons chopped fresh basil
- 1 tablespoon (¼ ounce) grated Parmesan cheese

IN A LARGE, DEEP NONSTICK SKILLET, bring the tomatoes (with juice), broth, and water to a boil over medium-high heat. Reduce the heat to low. Add the green beans. Cover and cook for 2 minutes. Add the ravioli. Spooning the liquid over the ravioli occasionally, cook, partially covered, for 5 to 7 minutes, or until heated through.

PLACE 1 SLICE OF THE BREAD, if using, in each of 4 shallow bowls. Spoon in the ravioli mixture. Sprinkle with the basil and cheese.

**Makes 4 servings**

***Per serving:*** *246 calories, 9 g. protein, 48 g. carbohydrates, 3 g. fat, 4 mg. cholesterol, 1,045 mg. sodium, 5 g. dietary fiber*

# Hearty Vegetarian Bolognese

- **12** **ounces bow-tie pasta**
- **¼** **cup dry-pack sun-dried tomatoes**
- **1** **teaspoon olive oil**
- **1** **onion, chopped**
- **2** **ribs celery, chopped**
- **2** **cups sliced zucchini**
- **2** **cups sliced mushrooms**
- **1** **tomato, chopped**
- **¾** **cup vegetable broth**
- **½** **cup 1% milk**
- **½** **teaspoon dried Italian seasoning**
- **½** **cup frozen peas, thawed**

COOK THE PASTA according to package directions.

IN A SMALL BOWL, soak the sun-dried tomatoes in hot water to cover for 10 minutes, or until soft. Drain, reserving ¼ cup of the soaking liquid. Coarsely chop the tomatoes. Set aside.

WARM THE OIL in a large nonstick skillet over medium-high heat. Add the onion and celery. Cook, stirring frequently, for 2 to 3 minutes, or until tender. Stir in the zucchini, mushrooms, fresh tomato, sun-dried tomatoes, and reserved soaking liquid. Cook, stirring frequently, for 4 to 6 minutes, or until the liquid evaporates.

ADD THE BROTH, milk, and Italian seasoning. Bring to a simmer. Reduce the heat to low. Cook, stirring occasionally, for 10 to 15 minutes, or until the vegetables are tender. (Add another ¼ cup broth if the liquid evaporates before the vegetables are tender.) Stir in the peas. Cook for 5 minutes.

DRAIN THE PASTA and place in a large serving bowl. Add the vegetable mixture. Toss to combine.

**Makes 4 servings**

***Per serving:*** *411 calories, 17 g. protein, 80 g. carbohydrates, 4 g. fat, 1 mg. cholesterol, 340 mg. sodium, 6 g. dietary fiber*

# Linguine with Herbed Ricotta

- **12 ounces linguine**
- **1 container (16 ounces) reduced-fat ricotta cheese**
- **¼ cup packed fresh basil leaves**
- **2 tablespoons parsley**
- **2 tablespoons chopped fresh chives**
- **2 tablespoons 1% milk**
- **1 tablespoon grated lemon peel**
- **1 tablespoon softened butter**
- **¼ teaspoon ground black pepper**

COOK THE PASTA according to package directions.

MEANWHILE, IN A FOOD PROCESSOR, combine the cheese, basil, parsley, chives, milk, lemon peel, butter, and pepper. Process until smooth. Place in a large serving bowl.

DRAIN THE LINGUINE, reserving ¼ cup of the cooking liquid. Stir the reserved liquid into the cheese mixture. Add the linguine. Toss to combine.

**Makes 4 servings**

***Per serving:*** *504 calories, 24 g. protein, 70 g. carbohydrates, 13 g. fat, 43 mg. cholesterol, 179 mg. sodium, 2 g. dietary fiber*

## Pronto Pasta Sauces

Weeknights were made for pasta. Sometimes I get home and there's just no time to cook dinner. That's when I turn to these super-quick pasta sauces. Some require no cooking whatsoever. You can even make these in the morning, then pop them in the fridge until dinnertime. These recipes are scaled to sauce 12 ounces of uncooked pasta (about 4 to 6 cups cooked). When they're done, just toss with the hot pasta of your choice. I usually use these sauces for strand pastas like spaghetti and linguine.

**Roasted Red Pepper:** In a food processor, pulse 1 small jar roasted red peppers (drained), 1 can (16 ounces) Italian tomatoes (drained), ¼ cup chopped fresh basil, and ½ cup fat-free milk until finely chopped.

**Fresh Tomato and Spinach:** In a medium bowl, mix 2 chopped tomatoes, 1 cup finely chopped fresh spinach, 1 small red onion, chopped, ¼ cup chopped fresh basil, 2 tablespoons parsley, 1 tablespoon olive oil, and 1 tablespoon balsamic vinegar. Let stand at room temperature while pasta is cooking.

**Quick Cooked Tomato:** In a food processor, puree 4 tomatoes, 1 cup tomato puree, 1 cup vegetable broth, ¼ cup tomato paste, 1 tablespoon olive oil, 1 teaspoon dried basil, ½ teaspoon dried oregano, ¼ teaspoon salt, and ¼ teaspoon ground black pepper. Simmer in a saucepan until heated through.

**Pesto:** In a food processor, combine 2 cups fresh basil leaves, ¼ cup walnuts, and 2 cloves garlic until smooth. Add ¾ cup vegetable broth, 2 tablespoons lemon juice, and 2 tablespoons (½ ounce) grated Parmesan cheese. Puree until smooth.

**Herbed White Sauce:** Bring 1 cup 1% milk to a simmer in a saucepan. Dissolve 1 tablespoon cornstarch in 2 more tablespoons milk. Add to the saucepan and cook until heated through and thickened. Stir in 2 tablespoons chopped fresh dill, ¼ teaspoon salt, and ¼ teaspoon ground black pepper. For a cheese sauce, stir in ½ cup finely shredded cheese until melted. (Cheddar and Parmesan work well. I also like smoked Gouda.)

# Sesame Vegetable Lo Mein

- **8 ounces Chinese wheat noodles or spaghetti**
- **½ cup vegetable broth**
- **1 tablespoon soy sauce**
- **2 teaspoons vegetarian oyster sauce or black bean sauce**
- **1½ teaspoons sesame oil**
- **2 teaspoons finely chopped fresh ginger**
- **2 cups coarsely chopped bok choy or spinach**
- **1½ cups broccoli florets**
- **1 small carrot, shredded**
- **3 scallions, chopped**
- **½ cup drained canned baby corn, cut into 1" pieces**
- **¼ cup chopped unsalted peanuts (optional)**

Cook the pasta according to package directions. Drain.

Meanwhile, in a small bowl, combine the broth, soy sauce, and oyster or black bean sauce.

Warm the oil in a large nonstick skillet or wok over high heat. Add the ginger. Stir-fry for 1 minute. Add the bok choy or spinach, broccoli, carrot, and scallions. Stir-fry for 3 to 4 minutes, or just until the vegetables are tender.

Stir in the broth mixture. Bring to a boil over high heat. Reduce the heat to low and stir in the noodles and baby corn. Cook for 1 minute to blend the flavors. Sprinkle with the peanuts, if using.

**Makes 4 servings**

***Per serving:*** *328 calories, 12 g. protein, 56 g. carbohydrates, 8 g. fat, 0 mg. cholesterol, 378 mg. sodium, 4 g. dietary fiber*

# Mixed-Mushroom Linguine

- 2 ounces dried porcini mushrooms
- 2 teaspoons butter
- 1 cup thinly sliced white button mushrooms
- 4 large shiitake mushrooms, coarsely chopped
- ½ teaspoon dried thyme
- ¼ teaspoon ground black pepper
- 1 teaspoon cornstarch
- ½ cup vegetable broth
- 2 tablespoons fat-free milk
- 12 ounces fresh linguine
- 2 tablespoons parsley

In a small bowl, soak the porcini mushrooms in hot water to cover for 10 minutes, or until soft. Drain, reserving ¼ cup of the soaking liquid. Coarsely chop the mushrooms.

Melt the butter in a large nonstick skillet over medium-high heat. Add the button mushrooms, shiitake mushrooms, thyme, and pepper. Cook, stirring frequently, for 2 to 3 minutes, or until the mushrooms are tender.

In a small bowl, dissolve the cornstarch in the broth. Stir into the mushroom mixture. Add the milk and the reserved soaking liquid. Cook, stirring frequently, for 2 minutes, or until the sauce thickens slightly.

Meanwhile, cook the linguine in a large pot of boiling water 3 to 5 minutes, or until just tender. Drain and place in a large serving bowl. Pour in the mushroom mixture. Toss to combine. Sprinkle with the parsley.

**Makes 4 servings**

***Per serving:*** *211 calories, 10 g. protein, 36 g. carbohydrates, 3 g. fat, 5 mg. cholesterol, 161 mg. sodium, 5 g. dietary fiber*

**Tip:** You can use 8 ounces dried linguine in place of the fresh. Cook according to package directions.

# Stir-Fried Rice Noodles

- 3½ ounces rice sticks
- 1 cup boiling water
- ½ cup vegetable broth
- 2 tablespoons reduced-sodium teriyaki sauce
- 2 tablespoons Chinese cooking wine or dry sherry
- 1 teaspoon cornstarch
- ½ teaspoon sugar
- 1 teaspoon peanut oil
- 2 cloves garlic, minced
- 1 tablespoon finely chopped fresh ginger
- 2 cups snow peas
- 1 red bell pepper, cut into strips
- 6 scallions, chopped
- ¼ cup chopped unsalted peanuts

PLACE THE RICE STICKS in a medium bowl. Add the water. Let soak for 10 minutes. Drain. Using scissors, cut into 2" lengths.

MEANWHILE, IN A SMALL BOWL, combine the broth, teriyaki sauce, cooking wine or sherry, cornstarch, and sugar. Stir until the cornstarch is dissolved.

WARM THE OIL in a large nonstick skillet or wok over medium-high heat. Add the garlic and ginger. Stir-fry for 1 minute. Add the snow peas, pepper, and scallions. Stir-fry for 4 to 5 minutes, or just until tender. Stir in the broth mixture and rice noodles. Cook, stirring constantly, for 1 to 2 minutes, or until the sauce thickens slightly. Sprinkle with the peanuts.

**Makes 4 servings**

***Per serving:*** *218 calories, 7 g. protein, 34 g. carbohydrates, 6 g. fat, 0 mg. cholesterol, 354 mg. sodium, 4 g. dietary fiber*

**Tip:** Rice sticks are thin, translucent white Chinese noodles sold in nests. Look for them in the international aisle of your supermarket or in an Asian grocery store.

## Quick Conversion

**Stir-Fried Rice Noodles with Chicken:** For a dual vegetarian/nonvegetarian dish, prepare the recipe with the following changes. For the chicken portion, warm ½ teaspoon peanut oil in a large nonstick skillet over medium-high heat for 1 minute. Add ½ pound boneless, skinless chicken breast strips. Cook for 5 to 8 minutes, or until no longer pink and the juices run clear when pierced. Keep warm as you finish the main recipe. Serve half of the completed vegetarian mixture, leaving the remaining half in the skillet or wok. Add the chicken and cook, stirring, for 2 minutes to heat through. (You can also use beef strips instead of chicken in this conversion.)

# Rigatoni with Roasted Garlic Crumbs

- **12** **ounces rigatoni**
- **1** **tablespoon butter**
- **2** **cloves garlic, minced**
- **2** **cups cubed Italian bread**
- **2** **tablespoons chopped fresh basil or 2 teaspoons dried**
- **1** **tablespoon parsley**
- **1** **tablespoon (¼ ounce) grated Parmesan cheese**
- **½** **cup reduced-fat roasted garlic or creamy Caesar salad dressing**
- **2** **tablespoons chopped fresh chives or 2 teaspoons dried**

COOK THE PASTA according to package directions.

MEANWHILE, MELT THE BUTTER in a large nonstick skillet over medium heat. Add the garlic. Cook, stirring frequently, for 1 minute. Add the bread cubes, basil, parsley, and cheese. Cook for 1 minute, or until golden.

DRAIN THE RIGATONI and place in a large serving bowl. Add the dressing and chives. Toss to coat. Sprinkle with the bread cubes.

**Makes 4 servings**

***Per serving:*** *426 calories, 13 g. protein, 78 g. carbohydrates, 7 g. fat, 10 mg. cholesterol, 474 mg. sodium, 3 g. dietary fiber*

# Rotelle with Artichokes and Fennel

- **12 ounces rotelle**
- **2 teaspoons olive oil**
- **1 onion, chopped**
- **1½ cups chopped fennel**
- **1 red bell pepper, cut into strips**
- **1 cup reduced-sodium vegetable broth**
- **¼ cup white wine or nonalcoholic wine**
- **¼ cup 1% milk**
- **½ cup drained marinated artichoke hearts, coarsely chopped**

COOK THE PASTA according to package directions.

WARM THE OIL in a large nonstick skillet over medium-high heat. Add the onion. Cook for 2 to 3 minutes, or until tender. Add the fennel and pepper. Cook for 3 to 5 minutes, or until tender.

STIR IN THE BROTH and wine. Bring to a boil over high heat. Reduce the heat to low. Stir in the milk. Cook for 1 minute. Stir in the artichoke hearts. Cook for 2 minutes, or until the sauce thickens slightly.

DRAIN THE ROTELLE and place in a large serving bowl. Top with the artichoke-fennel mixture.

**Makes 4 servings**

***Per serving:*** *402 calories, 13 g. protein, 73 g. carbohydrates, 5 g. fat, 1 mg. cholesterol, 369 mg. sodium, 5 g. dietary fiber*

# Spaghetti with Caramelized Onions

- **12 ounces thin spaghetti**
- **2 ounces dried porcini mushrooms**
- **1 cup hot water**
- **1 tablespoon butter**
- **1 onion, thinly sliced and separated into rings**
- **1 package (10 ounces) frozen petite peas, thawed**
- **2 tablespoons parsley**
- **2 teaspoons chopped fresh rosemary or ¾ teaspoon dried**

COOK THE PASTA according to package directions.

MEANWHILE, SOAK THE MUSHROOMS in the water for 10 minutes, or until soft. Drain, reserving ½ cup of the soaking liquid.

MELT THE BUTTER in a large nonstick skillet over medium-low heat. Add the onion. Cook, stirring frequently, for 8 to 10 minutes, or until golden.

ADD THE MUSHROOMS, reserved liquid, peas, parsley, and rosemary. Cook for 2 to 3 minutes, or until the peas are heated through.

DRAIN THE SPAGHETTI and place in a large serving bowl. Add the mushroom mixture. Toss to combine.

**Makes 4 servings**

***Per serving:*** *459 calories, 19 g. protein, 83 g. carbohydrates, 5 g. fat, 8 mg. cholesterol, 103 mg. sodium, 9 g. dietary fiber*

**Tip:** To use fresh white button mushrooms instead of the dried porcini mushrooms, cook 2 cups thinly sliced mushrooms along with the onion. Stir in ½ cup vegetable broth in place of the reserved mushroom liquid.

# Fusilli with Peppers and Goat Cheese

- **12 ounces fusilli**
- **2 teaspoons olive oil**
- **1 red bell pepper, cut into strips**
- **1 green bell pepper, cut into strips**
- **1 red onion, thinly sliced and separated into rings**
- **2 cloves garlic, minced**
- **1 cup (4 ounces) crumbled herb-flavored goat cheese**
- **¼ cup coarsely chopped marinated sun-dried tomatoes**

COOK THE PASTA according to package directions.

MEANWHILE, WARM THE OIL in a large nonstick skillet over medium-high heat. Add the red pepper, green pepper, onion, and garlic. Cook, stirring frequently, for 4 to 5 minutes, or until tender.

IN A LARGE SERVING BOWL, combine the cheese and tomatoes. Drain the fusilli and reserve ¼ cup of the cooking liquid. Add the reserved liquid to the cheese mixture. Add the fusilli and pepper mixture. Toss to combine.

**Makes 4 servings**

***Per serving:*** *455 calories, 17 g. protein, 72 g. carbohydrates, 11 g. fat, 13 mg. cholesterol, 131 mg. sodium, 4 g. dietary fiber*

**Tip:** Herb-flavored feta cheese can be used in place of goat cheese for this recipe.

# Crunchy Lo Mein in Peanut Sauce

- 12 ounces Chinese wheat noodles or spaghetti
- ½ cup vegetable broth
- ¼ cup natural peanut butter
- 2 tablespoons fat-free plain yogurt
- 1 tablespoon rice wine vinegar
- 1 tablespoon soy sauce
- 1 tablespoon minced scallions
- ¼ teaspoon sugar
- 2 cups snow peas
- 1 cup bean sprouts

COOK THE PASTA according to package directions.

IN A SMALL BOWL, combine the broth, peanut butter, yogurt, vinegar, soy sauce, scallions, and sugar. Mix until smooth.

PLACE THE SNOW PEAS and bean sprouts in a steamer basket over simmering water. Steam for 3 minutes, or just until tender.

DRAIN THE NOODLES and place in a large serving bowl. Add the peanut mixture, snow peas, and bean sprouts. Toss to combine. Serve hot or cold.

**Makes 4 servings**

***Per serving:*** *441 calories, 16 g. protein, 74 g. carbohydrates, 10 g. fat, 0 mg. cholesterol, 269 mg. sodium, 3 g. dietary fiber*

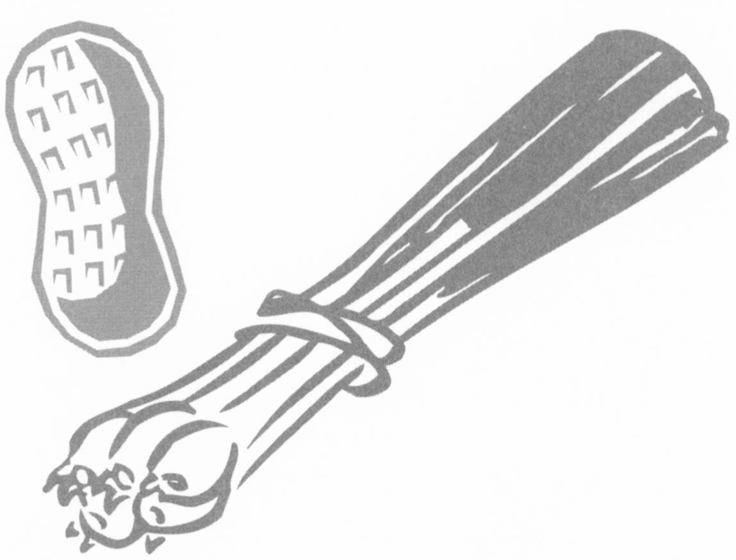

# Baked Elbows with Three Cheeses

- 8 ounces (1½ cups) elbow macaroni
- 2 teaspoons butter
- ½ cup chopped onions
- 2 tablespoons all-purpose flour
- 2 cups 1% milk
- ¾ cup (3 ounces) shredded reduced-fat Swiss cheese
- ¾ cup (3 ounces) shredded reduced-fat Cheddar cheese
- 1 tablespoon (¼ ounce) grated Parmesan cheese
- 1 tablespoon Dijon mustard
- 1 tomato, chopped
- 1 cup frozen mixed vegetables
- 2 tablespoons seasoned dry bread crumbs

Preheat the oven to 375°F. Coat a 1½-quart baking dish with nonstick spray.

Cook the pasta according to package directions. Drain.

Meanwhile, melt the butter in a large nonstick skillet over medium-high heat. Add the onions. Cook, stirring frequently, for 2 to 3 minutes, or until tender. Stir in the flour. Cook for 1 minute. Add the milk. Cook, stirring constantly, for 5 minutes, or until slightly thickened. Remove from the heat and stir in the Swiss, Cheddar, Parmesan, and mustard. Stir until the cheeses have melted. Stir in the tomato and vegetables. Stir in the macaroni.

Spoon into the prepared dish. Sprinkle with the bread crumbs.

Bake for 25 to 30 minutes, or until heated through.

**Makes 4 servings**

***Per serving:*** *425 calories, 22 g. protein, 63 g. carbohydrates, 9 g. fat, 26 mg. cholesterol, 403 mg. sodium, 3 g. dietary fiber*

## Quick Conversion

**Baked Elbows with Three Cheeses and Hot Dogs:** For a dual vegetarian/nonvegetarian dish, prepare the recipe with the following changes. Use two 1-quart baking dishes instead of one 1½-quart baking dish. After stirring in the tomato and vegetables, divide the mixture in half and spoon into the prepared baking dishes. For the hot dog portion, slice 1 beef or chicken hot dog into ½" pieces. Stir into one of the dishes. Top both portions with the bread crumbs and bake for 20 to 25 minutes, or until heated through.

# Broccoli-and-Tofu-Stuffed Shells

- **12** **ounces jumbo pasta shells**
- **8** **ounces firm tofu, drained and squeezed dry**
- **4** **ounces reduced-fat cream cheese or crumbled feta cheese**
- **2** **tablespoons 1% milk**
- **1** **package (10 ounces) frozen chopped broccoli, thawed**
- **1** **tomato, chopped**
- **1** **tablespoon (¼ ounce) grated Parmesan cheese**
- **1** **teaspoon dried basil**
- **¼** **teaspoon freshly ground black pepper**
- **1½** **cups prepared spaghetti sauce**

PREHEAT THE OVEN TO 350°F.

COOK THE SHELLS according to package directions. Drain.

MEANWHILE, IN A FOOD PROCESSOR, combine the tofu, cream cheese or feta, and milk. Process until smooth. Transfer to a medium bowl. Stir in the broccoli, tomato, Parmesan, basil, and pepper. Mix well.

SPREAD ½ CUP OF THE SPAGHETTI SAUCE in a 13" × 9" baking dish. Using a spoon, fill the shells with the tofu mixture. Place, open side up, in the baking dish. Pour the remaining 1 cup sauce over the shells.

BAKE FOR 30 TO 35 MINUTES, or until heated through.

**Makes 8 servings**

***Per serving:*** *281 calories, 12 g. protein, 44 g. carbohydrates, 7 g. fat, 9 mg. cholesterol, 318 mg. sodium, 4 g. dietary fiber*

**Tip:** I sometimes use 1 box (10 ounces) frozen chopped spinach, thawed and squeezed dry, instead of the broccoli.

# Eggplant and Roasted Red Pepper Lasagna

- **1 small eggplant, thinly sliced**
- **1 red bell pepper, thinly sliced**
- **2 zucchini and/or yellow squash, thinly sliced**
- **1 tablespoon olive oil**
- **2 cloves garlic, minced**
- **¼ teaspoon salt**
- **¼ teaspoon black pepper**
- **1 container (16 ounces) reduced-fat ricotta cheese**
- **2 tablespoons finely chopped jarred roasted red peppers**
- **1 jar (25½ ounces) basil-flavored spaghetti sauce**
- **6 oven-ready lasagna noodles**
- **1 cup (4 ounces) shredded reduced-fat mozzarella cheese**

PREHEAT THE OVEN TO 425°F. Coat a roasting pan with nonstick spray.

COMBINE THE EGGPLANT, bell pepper, zucchini or yellow squash, oil, and garlic in the roasting pan. Season with the salt and black pepper. Toss to combine. Bake for 20 to 25 minutes, stirring once, or just until the vegetables are tender.

MEANWHILE, IN A MEDIUM BOWL, combine the ricotta and roasted red peppers. Spread ½ cup of the spaghetti sauce in a 13" × 9" baking dish. Top with 3 lasagna noodles. Layer half the vegetable mixture and half the ricotta mixture over the noodles. Top with 1 cup of the sauce. Repeat the layering with the remaining 3 noodles, vegetables, ricotta, and sauce.

REDUCE THE OVEN TEMPERATURE to 375°F.

COVER THE LASAGNA with foil. Bake for 40 minutes. Sprinkle with the mozzarella. Bake, uncovered, for 10 minutes longer, or until the cheese melts. Let stand for 10 minutes before serving.

**Makes 8 servings**

***Per serving:*** *377 calories, 19 g. protein, 53 g. carbohydrates, 10 g. fat, 25 mg. cholesterol, 664 mg. sodium, 6 g. dietary fiber*

**Tip:** After baking, this dish can be frozen for up to a month. Thaw in the refrigerator before reheating.

# Spaghetti Torte

- 8 ounces spaghetti
- 1 container (16 ounces) reduced-fat ricotta cheese
- 1 package (10 ounces) frozen chopped spinach, thawed and squeezed dry
- 1 can (14 ounces) chopped tomatoes, drained
- ¼ cup (1 ounce) grated Parmesan cheese
- 1 large egg, lightly beaten
- 2 tablespoons chopped fresh basil or 2 teaspoons dried
- ¼ teaspoon ground black pepper
- ½ cup prepared spaghetti sauce
- ¼ cup (1 ounce) shredded reduced-fat mozzarella cheese

PREHEAT THE OVEN TO 350°F. Coat an 8" springform pan with nonstick spray.

COOK THE PASTA according to package directions. Drain well.

IN A LARGE BOWL, combine the ricotta, spinach, tomatoes, Parmesan, egg, basil, and pepper. Stir in the spaghetti. Mix well.

SPOON INTO THE PREPARED PAN. Spread the spaghetti sauce over the top. Sprinkle with the mozzarella.

BAKE FOR 25 TO 30 MINUTES, or until golden. Let stand 10 minutes. Remove the pan sides. Cut into wedges.

**Makes 4 servings**

***Per serving:*** *483 calories, 31 g. protein, 55 g. carbohydrates, 16 g. fat, 148 mg. cholesterol, 563 mg. sodium, 5 g. dietary fiber*

**Tip:** This torte can be assembled early in the day and refrigerated until ready to heat. If refrigerated, add 10 minutes to the cooking time.

# Noodle Frittata

- **1 cup (about 5 ounces) elbow macaroni**
- **2 teaspoons butter**
- **6 scallions, chopped**
- **1 small carrot, shredded**
- **1 package (10 ounces) frozen chopped spinach, thawed and squeezed dry**
- **6 eggs**
- **¼ cup 1% milk**
- **⅓ cup (1⅓ ounces) shredded reduced-fat Cheddar cheese**
- **1 tablespoon (¼ ounce) grated Parmesan cheese**
- **¼ teaspoon salt**
- **¼ teaspoon ground black pepper**

PREHEAT THE BROILER. Cook the pasta according to package directions.

MEANWHILE, MELT THE BUTTER in a large skillet over medium-high heat (use an ovenproof skillet if you have one). Add the scallions and carrot. Cook, stirring frequently, for 4 to 5 minutes, or until tender. Reduce the heat to low.

DRAIN THE MACARONI. In a large bowl, combine the spinach, eggs, milk, Cheddar, Parmesan, salt, and pepper. Mix well. Stir in the macaroni. Pour into the scallion-carrot mixture, stirring gently to combine.

COOK, COVERED, for 6 to 8 minutes, or until the eggs are almost set. (If the skillet is not ovenproof, wrap the handle in several layers of heavy-duty foil.)

PLACE THE SKILLET under the broiler, 4" to 5" from the heat, for 1 to 2 minutes, or until the top is golden.

**Makes 4 servings**

***Per serving:*** *291 calories, 19 g. protein, 28 g. carbohydrates, 12 g. fat, 328 mg. cholesterol, 424 mg. sodium, 4 g. dietary fiber*

## Quick Conversion

**Noodle Frittatta with Bacon:** For a dual vegetarian/nonvegetarian dish, prepare the recipe with the following changes. For the bacon portion, cook 2 strips of bacon in a medium ovenproof skillet over medium-high heat until crisp. Transfer to a plate lined with paper towels, discarding the drippings. Crumble the bacon back into the skillet. Transfer half of the cooked scallion and carrot mixture to the skillet with the bacon. Prepare the egg mixture as directed and divide it between the 2 skillets. Cook the eggs in each skillet for about 4 minutes, or until set. Broil as directed.

# Raisin-Noodle Pudding

PREHEAT THE OVEN TO 350°F. Coat a 13" × 9" baking dish with nonstick spray.

COOK THE PASTA according to package directions. Drain and place in a large bowl.

ADD THE EGGS, cottage cheese, cream cheese, sugar, and cinnamon. Mix well. Stir in the raisins and apricots. Spoon into the prepared dish. Drizzle with the butter.

BAKE FOR 35 TO 40 MINUTES, or until golden.

**Makes 8 servings**

- **12 ounces wide egg noodles**
- **4 eggs**
- **1¼ cups 1% cottage cheese**
- **2⅔ ounces reduced-fat cream cheese**
- **1 tablespoon sugar**
- **½ teaspoon ground cinnamon**
- **½ cup golden raisins**
- **¼ cup finely chopped dried apricots**
- **1 tablespoon butter, melted**

***Per serving:*** *311 calories, 15 g. protein, 45 g. carbohydrates, 8 g. fat, 158 mg. cholesterol, 230 mg. sodium, 2 g. dietary fiber*

# Beans, Grains, and Beyond

*"Don't have a cow, man."*

—Bart Simpson, cartoon character

# Beans, Grains, and Beyond



BEANS AND GRAINS MAKE UP THE HEART of vegetarian cooking. These foods have subtle flavors and soft textures that marry deliciously with a vast array of vegetables, fruits, and seasonings.

This chapter includes my family's favorite dishes made with beans and grains. Some are side dishes, some are main dishes. All are simple. To keep things quick, I call for canned beans. If you cook your own beans, keep in mind that one can of beans (16- to 19-ounce size) equals about 2 cups of cooked beans.

## Recipes

● Kid-Friendly Recipe

● Freezable Recipe

● Microwaveable Recipe

# Golden Risotto

- **2 teaspoons olive oil**
- **1 onion, chopped**
- **1 cup Arborio rice**
- **4½ cups vegetable broth**
- **¼ teaspoon ground saffron or turmeric**
- **½ cup golden raisins**

WARM THE OIL IN A LARGE SAUCEPAN over medium-high heat. Add the onion. Cook for 8 minutes, or until soft. Add the rice. Cook and stir for 1 minute.

WHILE THE ONION IS COOKING, bring the broth to a simmer in a medium saucepan over medium heat. Reduce the heat to low and maintain the simmer.

SLOWLY ADD ½ CUP OF THE BROTH and the saffron or turmeric to the rice mixture, stirring constantly. Cook and stir for 5 minutes, or until the broth is absorbed. Stir in the remaining 4 cups broth, adding ½ cup at a time and stirring constantly for 30 to 40 minutes, or until each addition is absorbed and the rice is creamy but still firm to the bite.

STIR IN THE RAISINS. Cook for 1 minute longer, or until heated through.

**Makes 4 servings**

***Per serving:*** *284 calories, 7 g. protein, 59 g. carbohydrates, 4 g. fat, 0 mg. cholesterol, 1,131 mg. sodium, 2 g. dietary fiber*

**Tips:** The secret to creamy risotto is constant stirring, which encourages the grains to release their starch.

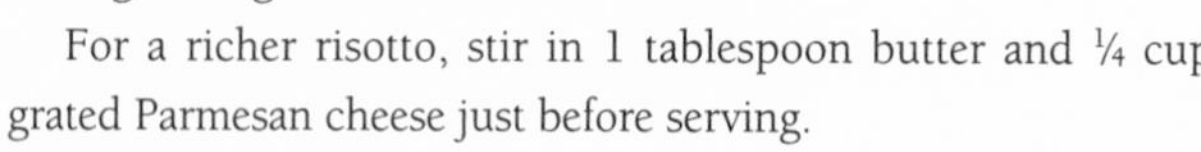

For a richer risotto, stir in 1 tablespoon butter and ¼ cup grated Parmesan cheese just before serving.

# Sesame Quinoa

2 tablespoons sesame seeds
2 teaspoons sesame oil
½ cup chopped red onion
1 tablespoon chopped fresh ginger
2 cups reduced-sodium vegetable broth
½ teaspoon ground cumin
1 cup quinoa, rinsed and drained
½ cup chopped mixed dried fruit

WARM A MEDIUM SAUCEPAN over low heat. Add the sesame seeds. Cook, shaking the pan, for 1 to 2 minutes, or until fragrant and lightly toasted. Remove and set aside.

WARM THE OIL in the same pan over medium-high heat. Add the onion and ginger. Cook, stirring frequently, for 2 to 3 minutes, or until the onion is tender. Stir in the broth and cumin. Bring to a boil. Stir in the quinoa and reduce the heat to low. Cover and simmer for 20 to 25 minutes, or until the liquid has been absorbed. Remove from the heat and stir in the fruit. Cover the saucepan and let stand for 5 minutes.

FLUFF WITH A FORK. Top with the sesame seeds.

**Makes 4 servings**

***Per serving:*** *291 calories, 8 g. protein, 52 g. carbohydrates, 8 g. fat, 0 mg. cholesterol, 516 mg. sodium, 6 g. dietary fiber*

**Tip:** I sometimes use this mixture to stuff peppers or acorn squash halves.

## Quick Conversion

**Chicken Stuffed with Sesame Quinoa:** For a nonvegetarian main dish, prepare the recipe with the following changes. Cut a pocket through the side of four 4-ounce boneless, skinless chicken breasts. Stuff with the completed quinoa and place in an 8" × 8" baking dish. Pour ½ cup chicken broth over the chicken and sprinkle with paprika. Bake at 350°F for 30 to 35 minutes, or until a thermometer inserted in the thickest portion registers 160°F and the juices run clear when pierced.

# Curried Basmati Rice Pilaf

- **2 teaspoons peanut oil**
- **1 onion, chopped**
- **1 teaspoon curry powder**
- **1¼ cups basmati rice**
- **2½ cups vegetable broth**
- **2 tablespoons soy sauce**
- **¼ teaspoon dried red-pepper flakes**
- **1 cup frozen mixed peas and carrots or mixed vegetables**

WARM THE OIL IN A MEDIUM SAUCEPAN over medium-high heat. Add the onion. Cook, stirring frequently, for 2 to 3 minutes, or until tender. Sprinkle with the curry powder. Cook for 1 minute longer. Add the rice and stir to coat it with the oil.

ADD THE BROTH, soy sauce, and pepper flakes. Bring to a boil over high heat. Reduce the heat to low. Cover and simmer for 30 minutes. Stir in the peas and carrots or mixed vegetables. Cover and cook for 5 minutes longer, or until the vegetables are cooked and the liquid has been absorbed.

REMOVE FROM THE HEAT and let stand, covered, for 10 minutes. Fluff with a fork before serving.

**Makes 4 servings**

***Per serving:*** *292 calories, 9 g. protein, 58 g. carbohydrates, 5 g. fat, 0 mg. cholesterol, 917 mg. sodium, 6 g. dietary fiber*

# Tomato-Flavored Bulgur

- 1 cup vegetable broth
- ¼ cup tomato sauce
- 1 cup bulgur
- 2 teaspoons olive oil
- 1 onion, chopped
- 1 small zucchini, chopped
- 2 small yellow squash, chopped
- ¼ teaspoon dried thyme
- ⅛ teaspoon ground black pepper
- 2 tablespoons toasted pine nuts (optional)

IN A MEDIUM SAUCEPAN, bring the broth and tomato sauce to a boil. Stir in the bulgur. Remove from the heat and let stand, covered, for 15 to 20 minutes, or until the bulgur is soft.

MEANWHILE, WARM THE OIL in a large nonstick skillet over medium-high heat. Add the onion, zucchini, and squash. Season with the thyme and pepper. Cook, stirring frequently, for 5 to 6 minutes, or until tender.

IN A LARGE SERVING BOWL, combine the bulgur and squash mixture. Toss to mix. Sprinkle with the pine nuts, if using.

**Makes 4 servings**

***Per serving:*** *174 calories, 7 g. protein, 33 g. carbohydrates, 3 g. fat, 0 mg. cholesterol, 355 mg. sodium, 9 g. dietary fiber*

**Tip:** To toast the pine nuts, place them in a dry skillet over medium heat and shake the pan for 2 minutes, or until fragrant and golden.

# Barley with Spinach and Beans

- 2 cups vegetable broth or vegetable juice
- 1 cup quick-cooking barley
- 1 onion, chopped
- 3 cups chopped fresh spinach
- 1 can (14 ounces) cannellini beans, rinsed and drained
- ¼ cup parsley
- 2 tablespoons (½ ounce) grated Parmesan cheese
- ⅛ teaspoon ground black pepper

IN A MEDIUM SAUCEPAN, combine the broth or vegetable juice, barley, and onion. Bring to a boil over high heat. Reduce the heat to medium-low. Cover and cook for 15 minutes, or until the barley is tender and the liquid is absorbed.

STIR IN THE SPINACH, beans, parsley, cheese, and pepper. Cook for 5 minutes longer, or until the spinach wilts and the beans are heated through.

**Makes 4 servings**

***Per serving:*** *203 calories, 10 g. protein, 40 g. carbohydrates, 3 g. fat, 3 mg. cholesterol, 595 mg. sodium, 9 g. dietary fiber*

**Tip:** Quick-cooking rice can be substituted for the barley.

## The Quicker Grains

There are primarily two types of grains: whole and refined. Whole grains are intact and include the nutritious bran, germ, and endosperm. However, they take longer to cook because they still have hulls. Refined or processed grains have been pretreated in some manner before packaging. Often the hulls are removed or cracked. This process removes the most nutritious parts of the grain, but it also reduces the long cooking time. Thus, refined grains like couscous and white rice are the quickest-cooking.

There is one exception: quinoa. This nutritious whole grain prized by the ancient Incas contains 3 times as much protein as wild rice, has 30 times as much phosphorus as bananas, and cooks in only 20 minutes. It tastes good, too, with a pleasant nutty flavor. Just be sure to rinse quinoa under cold water until the water runs clear before cooking. This removes the bitter *saponin* that naturally coats the surface of the grain.

All of the grains below are ready in 20 minutes or less.

**Basic cooking method:** Bring the liquid to a boil in a medium saucepan. Add the grains and cook for the time specified. Let stand, covered, if necessary. Then fluff with a fork. If no cooking time is listed, pour the hot liquid over the grain and let stand. For liquids, add flavor by using vegetable stock instead of water. I sometimes mix vegetable stock with vegetable juice or fruit juice to vary the flavor.

**To make a pilaf:** Sauté onions, garlic, and finely chopped vegetables in the saucepan first. Then add the grain and cook for 1 minute. Add the liquid and cook as directed. The amounts and times below are figured for 1 cup of raw grain.

| Grain | Liquid (cups) | Cooking Time (min) | Standing Time (min) | Yield (cups) |
|---|---|---|---|---|
| Bulgur (cracked wheat) | 1¼ | None | 15 to 20 | 2½ |
| Couscous | 1½ | None | 5 | 2¼ |
| Kasha (buckwheat) | 2 | 15 to 20 | None | 3 |
| Quick-Cooking Barley | 2 | 10 | 5 | 3 |
| Quick-Cooking Brown Rice | 1¼ | 10 to 15 | 5 | 2 |
| Quick-Cooking Grits | 4 | 5 | None | 4 |
| Quinoa | 2 | 20 | 5 | 3 |
| White Rice | 2 | 20 | 1 | 3 |

# Chickpea Sauté

- **2 teaspoons olive oil**
- **2 large carrots, thinly sliced**
- **1 large rib celery, chopped**
- **1 green bell pepper, chopped**
- **2 cups vegetable broth**
- **1 can (16 ounces) chickpeas, rinsed and drained**
- **2 tablespoons lemon juice**
- **½ teaspoon ground allspice**
- **⅛ teaspoon ground black pepper**

WARM THE OIL IN A LARGE NONSTICK SKILLET over medium heat. Add the carrots, celery, and bell pepper. Cook, stirring frequently, for 3 to 5 minutes, or until the carrots are tender.

STIR IN THE BROTH, chickpeas, lemon juice, allspice, and black pepper. Cover and simmer over medium heat for 15 minutes, or until heated through.

**Makes 4 servings**

***Per serving:*** *170 calories, 6 g. protein, 28 g. carbohydrates, 5 g. fat, 0 mg. cholesterol, 576 mg. sodium, 9 g. dietary fiber*

## Quick Conversion

**Chickpea Sauté with Chicken:** For a dual vegetarian/nonvegetarian dish, prepare the recipe with the following changes. In a large nonstick skillet, cook ½ pound boneless, skinless chicken breast strips in 1 teaspoon of the olive oil until no longer pink and the juices run clear when pierced. Transfer to a platter. Cover with foil to keep warm. Cook half the vegetables in the same skillet. Cook the remaining vegetables in a medium skillet with the remaining 1 teaspoon olive oil. Return the chicken to the large skillet. Divide the broth and other ingredients between the 2 skillets. Simmer both for 15 minutes, or until heated through.

# Black-Eyed Peas and Greens

- 2 cans (15 ounces each) black-eyed peas, rinsed and drained
- 3 cups coarsely chopped fresh spinach and/or kale
- ¼ cup chili sauce
- 1 tablespoon honey
- ⅛ teaspoon ground red pepper
- 1 tablespoon butter
- ¼ cup oats
- 2 tablespoons seasoned dry bread crumbs

PREHEAT THE OVEN TO 350°F. Coat a 2-quart baking dish with nonstick spray.

IN A LARGE BOWL, combine the black-eyed peas, spinach and/or kale, chili sauce, honey, and pepper. Mix well.

MELT THE BUTTER in a small nonstick skillet over medium heat. Add the oats and bread crumbs. Cook, stirring constantly, for 1 to 2 minutes, or until golden.

SPOON THE BLACK-EYED PEA MIXTURE into the baking dish. Top with the oat mixture. Bake for 20 to 25 minutes, or until heated through and the crumbs are browned.

**Makes 4 servings**

***Per serving:*** *176 calories, 8 g. protein, 28 g. carbohydrates, 4 g. fat, 8 mg. cholesterol, 372 mg. sodium, 5 g. dietary fiber*

## Quick Conversion

**Black-Eyed Peas and Greens with Sausage:** For a dual vegetarian/nonvegetarian dish, prepare the recipe with the following changes. Divide the black-eyed pea mixture in half. Cook ½ pound crumbled turkey sausage in a large nonstick skillet over medium heat for 5 to 8 minutes, or until no longer pink. Stir into half the black-eyed pea mixture. Spoon into a 1-quart baking dish. Spoon the remaining vegetarian portion into a 1-quart baking dish. Top each dish with the oat mixture. Bake both for 15 to 20 minutes, or until heated through and the crumbs are browned.

# Baked Lima Beans with Tomato and Basil

- **1 tablespoon olive oil**
- **1 onion, chopped**
- **2 cloves garlic, minced**
- **1 tomato, chopped**
- **½ cup vegetable broth**
- **2 tablespoons chopped fresh basil or 2 teaspoons dried**
- **2 packages (10 ounces each) frozen lima beans**
- **½ cup (2 ounces) shredded reduced-fat mozzarella cheese**
- **2 tablespoons seasoned dry bread crumbs**

PREHEAT THE OVEN TO 350°F. Coat a 1½-quart baking dish with nonstick spray.

WARM THE OIL in a large nonstick skillet over medium-high heat. Add the onion and garlic. Cook, stirring frequently, for 3 to 5 minutes, or until tender. Stir in the tomato. Cook for 2 minutes. Stir in the broth and basil. Simmer for 5 minutes, or until the broth reduces to about ¼ cup. Remove from the heat and stir in the lima beans.

SPOON INTO THE PREPARED BAKING DISH. Sprinkle with the cheese and bread crumbs. Bake for 20 to 25 minutes, or until the cheese is melted and the bean mixture is heated through.

**Makes 4 servings**

***Per serving:*** *165 calories, 10 g. protein, 23 g. carbohydrates, 4 g. fat, 8 mg. cholesterol, 350 mg. sodium, 6 g. dietary fiber*

**Tip:** I've also used a mixture of frozen lima beans and frozen cut green beans.

# Chickpea Pancakes

- 2 teaspoons peanut oil
- 6 scallions, chopped
- 1 small carrot, shredded
- 2 tablespoons chopped fresh cilantro or parsley
- 1 tablespoon lime juice
- ½ teaspoon ground cumin
- 1 can (16 ounces) chickpeas, rinsed and drained
- ¼ cup seasoned dry bread crumbs
- ½ cup fat-free plain yogurt
- 1 egg white
- 1 tablespoon olive oil

WARM THE PEANUT OIL in a large nonstick skillet over medium-high heat. Add the scallions and carrot. Cook, stirring frequently, for 3 to 4 minutes, or just until the carrot is tender. Stir in the cilantro or parsley, lime juice, and cumin. Cook for 1 minute longer.

MASH THE CHICKPEAS in a large bowl. Stir in the bread crumbs, yogurt, egg white, and scallion mixture. Mix well.

WARM THE OIL in the same skillet over medium-high heat for 1 minute. Drop the chickpea mixture ¼ cup at a time into the skillet. If the batter is thick, spread it with a spoon. Cook for 3 to 4 minutes on each side, or until golden brown.

**Makes 12**

***Per pancake:*** *74 calories, 3 g. protein, 10 g. carbohydrates, 3 g. fat, 0 mg. cholesterol, 158 mg. sodium, 3 g. dietary fiber*

**Tip:** Serve with reduced-fat ranch salad dressing, tartar sauce, or salsa.

# Rice-Filled Pot Stickers

**Sauce**

- **¼ cup orange-pineapple juice**
- **2 tablespoons soy sauce**
- **1 tablespoon plum jelly**
- **1 teaspoon finely chopped fresh ginger**
- **½ teaspoon sesame oil**

**Filling**

- **¼ cup long-grain rice**
- **1 cup finely chopped mushrooms**
- **1 cup thawed frozen chopped spinach, squeezed dry**
- **½ cup finely chopped water chestnuts**
- **2 small scallions, chopped**
- **1 tablespoon cornstarch**
- **1 clove garlic, finely minced**
- **1 egg white**
- **16 wonton wrappers**
- **⅔ cup water**

*To make the sauce:*

IN A SMALL BOWL, combine the juice, soy sauce, jelly, ginger, and sesame oil. Mix well. Set aside.

*To make the filling:*

COOK THE RICE according to package directions.

COAT A LARGE NONSTICK SKILLET with nonstick spray and warm over medium-high heat. Add the mushrooms. Cook, stirring frequently, for 2 to 3 minutes, or until tender. Remove from the heat. Stir in the rice, spinach, water chestnuts, scallions, cornstarch, garlic, and egg white. Mix well.

WORKING WITH 1 WRAPPER at a time, spoon about 1 tablespoon rice mixture into the center. With fingertips, moisten the edges of the wrapper with water and bring 2 opposite corners to the center, pinching the points to seal. Bring the remaining 2 corners to the center, again pinching to seal. Pinch the 4 corners together to seal. Place on a baking sheet. Cover loosely with a damp towel to prevent drying. Repeat with the remaining wrappers and rice mixture.

WIPE OUT THE SKILLET. Coat with nonstick spray and warm over medium heat. Place half the pot stickers in the skillet. Cook for 3 to 4 minutes, or until the bottoms are lightly browned. Pour in ⅓ cup water. Cover and cook for 3 minutes, or until the liquid is absorbed. Remove from the skillet and keep warm. Repeat the procedure with the remaining ⅓ cup water and pot stickers.

SERVE with the sauce.

**Makes 16**

***Per pot sticker:*** *52 calories, 2 g. protein, 10 g. carbohydrates, 0.5 g. fat, 1 mg. cholesterol, 128 mg. sodium, 1 g. dietary fiber*

**Tip:** To save time, cook the rice ahead in large quantities and freeze it in ½- or 1-cup batches. Thaw in the refrigerator overnight or in the microwave oven on high power for 1 to 2 minutes. When using cooked rice, use double the amount called for in the recipe and skip the step for cooking it.

## Quick Conversion

**Rice-Filled Pot Stickers with Pork:** For a dual vegetarian/nonvegetarian dish, prepare the recipe with the following changes. Divide the rice filling in half. Brown ½ pound ground pork in a large nonstick skillet over medium heat for 6 to 8 minutes, or until no longer pink. Stir into half the rice filling. Fill half the wonton wrappers with the vegetarian mixture. Fill the remaining half with the pork mixture. Proceed with the recipe as directed.

# Corn Cakes with Mixed-Bean Salsa

**Mixed-Bean Salsa**

- **1** **cup rinsed and drained canned red kidney beans**
- **½** **cup rinsed and drained canned black beans**
- **1** **small tomato, chopped**
- **2** **small scallions, chopped**
- **2** **tablespoons lime juice**
- **2** **tablespoons chopped fresh cilantro**

**Corn Cakes**

- **¾** **cup all-purpose flour**
- **¾** **cup yellow cornmeal**
- **2½** **teaspoons baking powder**
- **1** **tablespoon sugar**
- **½** **teaspoon ground cumin**
- **¼** **teaspoon salt**
- **1** **cup fat-free milk**
- **1** **large egg**
- **½** **cup frozen corn, thawed**

*To make the salsa:*

In a small bowl, combine the kidney beans, black beans, tomato, scallions, lime juice, and cilantro. Toss to mix. Set aside.

*To make the corn cakes:*

In a large bowl, combine the flour, cornmeal, baking powder, sugar, cumin, and salt.

In a medium bowl, combine the milk and egg. Stir in the corn. Add to the flour mixture, stirring just until combined. Batter will be slightly lumpy.

Coat a large nonstick skillet with nonstick spray and warm over medium heat. For each pancake, pour ¼ cup of the batter into the skillet. Cook for 2 to 3 minutes, or until the top bubbles and the bottom is lightly browned. Turn over. Cook for 2 minutes longer, or until the bottom is lightly browned. Transfer to a platter and cover with foil to keep warm. Repeat with any remaining batter.

Serve with the bean salsa.

**Makes 4 servings (3 pancakes each)**

***Per serving:*** *352 calories, 16 g. protein, 67 g. carbohydrates, 3 g. fat, 54 mg. cholesterol, 427 mg. sodium, 11 g. dietary fiber*

# Cabbage Stuffed with Kasha

- **2 cups vegetable broth**
- **1 cup kasha**
- **1 apple, peeled and finely chopped**
- **¼ cup coarsely chopped walnuts**
- **12 large green cabbage leaves**
- **1 teaspoon olive oil**
- **1 tablespoon grated fresh ginger**
- **1 cup crushed pineapple**
- **⅓ cup ketchup**
- **⅓ cup cider vinegar**
- **2 teaspoons cornstarch**

Bring the broth to a boil in a medium saucepan over medium-high heat. Stir in the kasha and apple. Reduce the heat to low. Cover and cook for 15 to 20 minutes, or until the liquid is absorbed. Remove from the heat and let stand for 5 minutes. Stir in the walnuts.

Meanwhile, trim the stiff cores from the cabbage leaves. Steam the cabbage in a basket over gently simmering water for 5 to 8 minutes, or until just soft enough to bend. Set aside.

Warm the oil in a large nonstick skillet over medium heat. Add the ginger. Cook, stirring frequently, for 2 minutes. Stir in the pineapple, ketchup, vinegar, and cornstarch, stirring until the cornstarch is dissolved. Bring to a boil. Reduce the heat to low and cook for 3 to 5 minutes, or until slightly thickened.

Spoon ¼ cup of the kasha mixture in the center of each cabbage leaf. Fold in the sides and roll up, jelly-roll fashion, to enclose the filling. Place in the skillet, seam sides down. Partially cover the skillet. Simmer, occasionally spooning the pineapple sauce over the cabbage rolls, for 10 to 15 minutes, or until heated through.

**Makes 4 servings**

***Per serving:*** *192 calories, 6 g. protein, 33 g. carbohydrates, 7 g. fat, 0 mg. cholesterol, 755 mg. sodium, 5 g. dietary fiber*

## Quick Conversion

**Cabbage Stuffed with Kasha and Beef:** For a dual vegetarian/nonvegetarian dish, prepare the recipe with the following changes. For the beef portion, cook ¼ pound ground beef in a large nonstick skillet over medium heat for 5 minutes, or until no longer pink. Stir into half the kasha mixture. Fill half the cabbage leaves with the vegetarian mixture. Fill the remaining half with the beef mixture. Proceed with the recipe as directed.

# Stuffed Peppers

- 1 cup wild rice or long-grain rice
- 2 teaspoons olive oil
- 2 cups thinly sliced mushrooms
- 6 scallions, chopped
- ½ cup chopped roasted red peppers
- ⅓ cup vegetable broth
- ½ teaspoon dried thyme
- 4 large green and/or red bell peppers
- ¼ cup seasoned dry bread crumbs
- 2 tablespoons (½ ounce) grated Parmesan cheese

COOK THE WILD RICE OR LONG-GRAIN RICE according to package directions.

PREHEAT THE OVEN to 350°F. Coat a 9" × 9" baking dish with nonstick spray.

WARM THE OIL in a large nonstick skillet over medium-high heat. Add the mushrooms and scallions. Cook, stirring frequently, for 4 to 5 minutes, or until the mushrooms are tender. Remove from the heat. Stir in the rice, roasted peppers, broth, and thyme.

SLICE THE TOPS off the bell peppers. Remove and discard the membranes and seeds. Stand the peppers upright, and if necessary, cut a small slice off the bottom to make them stable. Divide the rice mixture among the peppers. Place upright in the prepared dish.

IN A SMALL BOWL, combine the bread crumbs and cheese. Sprinkle over the tops of the peppers.

BAKE FOR 20 TO 25 MINUTES, or until the peppers are tender and the filling is heated through.

**Makes 4**

***Per pepper:*** *277 calories, 11 g. protein, 50 g. carbohydrates, 5 g. fat, 3 mg. cholesterol, 514 mg. sodium, 6 g. dietary fiber*

## Quick Conversion

**Stuffed Peppers with Lamb:** For a dual vegetarian/nonvegetarian dish, prepare the recipe with the following changes. Divide the rice mixture in half. For the lamb portion, brown ¼ pound ground lamb in a medium skillet over medium heat. Stuff 2 peppers with half the completed rice mixture. Add the lamb to the remaining half of the rice mixture and season with salt and pepper. Stuff the other 2 peppers with the lamb-rice mixture. Proceed with the recipe as directed.

# Eggplant Stuffed with Couscous

- **1** **cup couscous**
- **2** **eggplants (about 1 pound each), halved**
- **¼** **teaspoon salt**
- **¼** **teaspoon ground black pepper**
- **1** **tablespoon olive oil**
- **½** **cup finely chopped onions**
- **1** **tomato, chopped**
- **½** **teaspoon dried basil**
- **½** **cup (2 ounces) crumbled feta cheese**

PREHEAT THE OVEN TO 350°F. Cook the couscous according to package directions.

MEANWHILE, CUT OUT THE PULP from each eggplant half, leaving a ½"-thick shell. Finely chop the pulp. Set aside.

COAT THE INSIDE of the eggplant shells with nonstick spray. Season with the salt and pepper. Arrange in a 13" × 9" baking dish. Add ¼" of water. Cover with foil and bake for 15 minutes.

MEANWHILE, WARM THE OIL in a large nonstick skillet. Add the onions. Cook, stirring frequently, for 2 minutes. Stir in the eggplant pulp, tomato, and basil. Cook, stirring frequently, for 5 to 7 minutes, or until the eggplant and tomato are tender. Remove from the heat and stir in the couscous and feta. Spoon into the eggplant shells.

ADD ADDITIONAL WATER to the baking dish to cover the bottom. Cover with foil. Bake for 15 to 20 minutes, or until the tomato-couscous mixture is heated through.

**Makes 4 servings**

***Per serving:*** *314 calories, 11 g. protein, 54 g. carbohydrates, 7 g. fat, 13 mg. cholesterol, 320 mg. sodium, 10 g. dietary fiber*

## Quick Conversion

**Eggplant Stuffed with Couscous and Tuna:** For a dual vegetarian/nonvegetarian dish, prepare the recipe with the following changes. Divide the couscous-feta mixture in half. Add 1 can (3½ ounces) flaked water-packed tuna to half of the filling. Spoon into 2 eggplant shells. Spoon the vegetarian portion into the remaining 2 shells. Proceed with the recipe as directed.

## Sneak in the Beans

Here's a bit of food trivia for you: All beans are legumes, but not all legumes are beans. Beans are merely one type of legume. Legumes are a larger food category comprising any plant species that has a seed pod, including peanuts, peas, lentils, and even clover and alfalfa.

Beans and legumes do have one thing in common, though. They are extremely good for you. They're packed with protein, complex carbohydrates, fiber, and a slew of vitamins and minerals. Studies show that beans can also lower your cholesterol and stabilize blood sugar. Best of all, most beans have very little fat.

But how do you get people to eat them? Sneak 'em in. I add a handful or two of beans to dishes that I know my family loves. That way, they barely taste them but still get the nutritious benefits. And I love the taste of beans, so I sometimes add a few more to my serving.

- Toss into salads.
- Stir into rice or grain dishes.
- Stir into soups.
- Puree and stir into salsas.
- Mix with pasta sauces.
- Mash and combine with mashed potatoes.
- Spoon on top of tacos.
- Sprinkle onto pizzas.
- Puree and stir into dips.

# Rice and Bean Burritos

- ⅓ cup long-grain white or brown rice
- 4 flour tortillas (12" diameter)
- 1 can (16 ounces) black beans, rinsed and drained
- 1 cup canned diced Mexican-style tomatoes, drained
- 3 scallions, chopped
- ¼ cup prepared guacamole or reduced-fat sour cream
- 1 cup salsa
- ½ cup (2 ounces) shredded reduced-fat Cheddar cheese

PREHEAT THE OVEN TO 350°F. Cook the rice according to package directions.

MEANWHILE, WRAP THE TORTILLAS in foil. Place on a nonstick baking sheet. Bake for 10 minutes, or until heated through.

IN A LARGE BOWL, combine the rice, beans, tomatoes, and scallions.

TO ASSEMBLE, divide the bean mixture evenly among the tortillas and spoon down the center of each. Top with 1 tablespoon of the guacamole or sour cream. Fold in the sides of each tortilla and roll up to enclose the filling.

COAT A 13" × 9" BAKING DISH with nonstick spray. Place the burritos, seam side down, in the dish. Spread ¼ cup salsa over each burrito. Sprinkle with the cheese. Bake for 8 to 10 minutes, or until the cheese is melted and the burritos are heated through.

**Makes 4**

***Per burrito:*** *413 calories, 17 g. protein, 70 g. carbohydrates, 8 g. fat, 3 mg. cholesterol, 850 mg. sodium, 10 g. dietary fiber*

## Quick Conversion

**Rice and Chicken Burritos:** For a dual vegetarian/nonvegetarian dish, prepare the recipe with the following changes. Make the burrito filling without the beans. Divide the filling in half. Stir ½ can (about 1 cup) rinsed and drained black beans into the vegetarian portion. Stir 1 cup cooked cubed chicken into the remaining half. Fill 2 tortillas with the bean mixture. Fill the other 2 tortillas with the chicken mixture. Proceed with the recipe as directed.

# Paella with Chickpeas and White Beans

- 1 cup long-grain rice
- 1 tablespoon olive oil
- 1 green bell pepper, chopped
- 1 onion, chopped
- 2 cloves garlic, minced
- 1 can (28 ounces) stewed tomatoes
- ¼ teaspoon ground saffron or turmeric
- 1 large carrot, thinly sliced
- 1 cup frozen peas
- 1 cup rinsed and drained canned chickpeas
- 1 cup rinsed and drained canned white beans
- ½ cup coarsely chopped water-packed artichoke hearts
- ½ cup (2 ounces) shredded Swiss cheese

PREHEAT THE OVEN TO 400°F. Cook the rice according to package directions.

MEANWHILE, WARM THE OIL in a large nonstick skillet over medium-high heat. Add the pepper, onion, and garlic. Cook, stirring frequently, for 4 to 5 minutes, or until tender. Stir in the tomatoes (with juice) and saffron or turmeric. Simmer for 5 minutes.

SPOON THE RICE into a 13" × 9" baking dish. Evenly spread the carrot, peas, chickpeas, white beans, and artichoke hearts over the rice. Spoon the tomato mixture over the vegetables. Top with the cheese. Cover with foil. Bake for 15 minutes. Uncover and bake for 15 minutes longer, or until the cheese melts and the mixture is bubbly.

**Makes 4 servings**

***Per serving:*** *493 calories, 19 g. protein, 87 g. carbohydrates, 11 g. fat, 13 mg. cholesterol, 818 mg. sodium, 16 g. dietary fiber*

## Quick Conversion

**Paella with Shrimp and Clams:** For a dual vegetarian/nonvegetarian dish, prepare the recipe with the following changes. Use two 11" × 7" baking dishes instead of one 13" × 9" dish. Use ½ cup each of chickpeas and white beans instead of 1 cup each. Divide the cooked rice, vegetables, and cheese between the 2 dishes. Cover the dishes with foil. Bake for 10 minutes. Uncover. For the shrimp and clams portion, arrange 6 large peeled and deveined shrimp and 6 to 7 scrubbed littleneck clams over the cheese in one of the dishes. Cook both dishes for 12 to 15 minutes more, or until the shrimp are opaque and the clams open fully. Discard any clams that don't open.

# Stir-Fried Lentils

- **1 cup brown lentils**
- **2 cups water**
- **2 tablespoons hoisin sauce**
- **2 tablespoons soy sauce**
- **1 tablespoon rice wine vinegar**
- **2 teaspoons sesame oil**
- **1¼ teaspoon red-pepper flakes**
- **1 tablespoon peanut oil**
- **2 tablespoons chopped fresh ginger**
- **2 garlic cloves, minced**
- **1 red bell pepper, cut into strips**
- **1 cup snow peas, trimmed**
- **1 cup drained canned baby corn**
- **½ cup drained sliced canned water chestnuts**
- **Crunchy Chinese noodles (optional)**

Sort and rinse the lentils, discarding any that are broken or shriveled. Bring the water to a boil in a medium saucepan over high heat. Reduce the heat to low. Stir in the lentils. Cover and gently simmer for 30 minutes, or until tender. Drain.

In a small bowl, combine the hoisin sauce, soy sauce, vinegar, sesame oil, and pepper flakes. Set aside.

Warm the peanut oil in a wok or nonstick skillet over medium-high heat. Add the ginger and garlic. Stir-fry for 1 minute. Add the bell pepper and snow peas. Stir-fry for 2 minutes, or just until tender.

Stir in the lentils, corn, and water chestnuts. Add the hoisin mixture. Stir-fry for 2 minutes, or until heated through. Serve with Chinese noodles, if using.

**Makes 4 servings**

***Per serving:*** *280 calories, 14 g. protein, 44 g. carbohydrates, 6 g. fat, 0 mg. cholesterol, 505 mg. sodium, 9 g. dietary fiber*

**Tip:** To save time, cook lentils ahead in large quantities and freeze them in 1- or 2-cup batches. Thaw in the refrigerator overnight or in the microwave oven on high power for 1 to 2 minutes. When using cooked lentils, use double the amount called for in the recipe and skip the step for cooking them.

# Polenta Pie

**Polenta**

- 1 cup yellow cornmeal
- 1 cup water
- 2½ cups vegetable broth

**Filling**

- 2 teaspoons olive oil
- 1 onion, chopped
- 1 green bell pepper, chopped
- 1 large tomato, chopped
- 1 can (14½ ounces) red kidney beans, rinsed and drained
- 1 cup drained canned Mexican-style corn
- ¼ cup chopped canned green chiles
- 1 cup reduced-fat sour cream
- 1 egg
- 1 cup (4 ounces) shredded reduced-fat Monterey Jack cheese

*To make the polenta:*

IN A LARGE BOWL, mix the cornmeal and water.

IN A MEDIUM SAUCEPAN, bring the broth to a boil. Gradually add the cornmeal mixture, stirring constantly with a wooden spoon. Cook, stirring constantly, for 25 to 30 minutes, or until the mixture thickens and begins to pull away from the sides of the pan. Coat a 9" pie plate with nonstick spray. Spread the polenta over the bottom and sides of the plate.

*To make the filling:*

PREHEAT THE OVEN TO 350°F.

WARM THE OIL in a large nonstick skillet over medium-high heat. Add the onion and pepper. Cook, stirring frequently, for 4 to 5 minutes, or until tender. Stir in the tomato, beans, corn, and chiles. Cook for 2 minutes, or until heated through.

IN A SMALL BOWL, combine the sour cream, egg, and cheese. Stir into the tomato mixture.

SPOON INTO THE POLENTA SHELL. Bake for 15 to 20 minutes, or until the mixture is bubbly.

**Makes 4 servings**

***Per serving:*** *511 calories, 28 g. protein, 68 g. carbohydrates, 16 g. fat, 93 mg. cholesterol, 796 mg. sodium, 14 g. dietary fiber*

**Tip:** Store-bought prepared polenta can be substituted for the homemade variety.

# Taco Bean Burgers

- **1** **can (8 ounces) red kidney beans or chickpeas, rinsed and drained**
- **1** **can (8 ounces) black beans or white beans, rinsed and drained**
- **1** **cup seasoned dry bread crumbs**
- **½** **cup finely chopped red onions**
- **½** **cup salsa**
- **1** **egg white**
- **1** **tablespoon chili powder**
- **1** **tablespoon lime juice**
- **4** **taco shells**
- **½** **cup chopped avocado**
- **½** **cup (2 ounces) shredded reduced-fat Cheddar cheese**

PREHEAT THE BROILER. Coat a broiler pan with nonstick spray.

IN A LARGE BOWL, mash the kidney beans or chickpeas and black beans or white beans. Add the bread crumbs, onions, salsa, egg white, chili powder, and lime juice. Mix well.

SHAPE INTO 4 PATTIES. Arrange in the prepared pan. Broil 3" from the heat for 4 to 5 minutes on each side, or until browned.

WARM THE TACO SHELLS according to package directions. Cut each patty in half and arrange in the shells. Top with equal amounts of avocado and cheese.

**Makes 4 servings**

***Per serving:*** *367 calories, 17 g. protein, 56 g. carbohydrates, 9 g. fat, 3 mg. cholesterol, 769 mg. sodium, 12 g. dietary fiber*

# Lentil and Vegetable Shepherd's Pie

- ¾ cup lentils
- 1¾ cups vegetable broth
- 1½ pounds potatoes (about 4 medium), peeled and chopped
- ½–1 cup fat-free milk
- 1 tablespoon olive oil
- 1 small fennel bulb, sliced
- 1 carrot, sliced
- 2 ribs celery, sliced
- 1 cup sliced parsnips
- ½ teaspoon dried thyme
- 1 can (14½ ounces) stewed tomatoes

SORT AND RINSE THE LENTILS, discarding any that are broken or shriveled. Place the lentils in a medium saucepan. Add the broth and bring to a boil over medium-high heat. Reduce the heat to low. Cover and simmer for 25 to 30 minutes, or until tender. Drain.

MEANWHILE, PLACE THE POTATOES in a large saucepan and cover with water. Bring to a boil over medium-high heat. Reduce the heat to medium-low. Cover and simmer for 10 to 15 minutes, or until the potatoes are tender when pierced with a fork. Drain well. Mash with a potato masher until fluffy, adding the milk as needed.

PREHEAT THE OVEN to 350°F. Warm the oil in a large nonstick skillet over medium heat for 1 minute. Add the fennel, carrot, celery, and parsnips. Cook, stirring frequently, for 2 to 3 minutes, or just until the vegetables are tender. Sprinkle with the thyme. Cook for 5 minutes longer. Remove from the heat and stir in the lentils and stewed tomatoes (with juice). Spoon into a 4-cup gratin dish or an 11" × 7" baking dish. Spread the potatoes over the top.

BAKE FOR 20 TO 25 MINUTES, or until the mixture is bubbly.

**Makes 4 servings**

***Per serving:*** *437 calories, 19 g. protein, 84 g. carbohydrates, 5 g. fat, 1 mg. cholesterol, 950 mg. sodium, 22 g. dietary fiber*

## Quick Conversion

**Lentil and Vegetable Shepherd's Pie with Beef:** For a dual vegetarian/non-vegetarian dish, prepare the recipe with the following changes. Cook the lentils using half the amount of lentils and half the amount of broth (use the same measuring cups, but measure half of each). For the beef portion, combine 1 tablespoon flour, ⅛ teaspoon salt, and ⅛ teaspoon ground black pepper. Coat ½ pound beef cubes with the seasoned flour. Add to a warmed nonstick skillet coated with nonstick spray. Cook for 5 to 10 minutes, or until browned. Before adding the lentils and tomatoes to the cooked vegetable mixture, transfer half of the mixture to the skillet with the beef. Stir in half of the tomatoes. Add the lentils to the remaining half of the cooked vegetable mixture. Spoon each mixture into separate 2-cup gratin dishes or small baking dishes. Spread half the mashed potatoes over each. Bake for 15 to 20 minutes, or until bubbly.

*"Good bread is the most fundamentally satisfying of all foods; and good bread with fresh butter, the greatest of feasts."*

—James Beard, cookbook author

# *Oven-Fresh Breads and Crisps*

HAVE YOU EVER WONDERED why supermarkets place bakeries near the entrance? The strategy is simple. Bread is the queen of comfort foods. It has the power to warm our souls. To satisfy our appetites. To make us feel comfy, cozy, and at home. For supermarket managers, the thinking is, if we get a whiff of some seductive aromas, we feel happy and we buy.

I've included 16 of my easiest bread recipes here. Some are quick breads like muffins and biscuits that come hot from the oven in less than 30 minutes. Others start with store-bought doughs so that they're ready to bake in nothing flat. There's even an easy recipe for Cheddar Crisps. And the yeast breads? When you have a few moments, give one a try. Kneading bread is a wonderful way to relax and unwind. If there's no time to knead by hand, let your bread machine do the work.

## Recipes

● Kid-Friendly Recipe

● Freezable Recipe

● Microwaveable Recipe

# Cheddar Crisps

- **⅔ cup all-purpose flour**
- **¼ cup yellow cornmeal**
- **½ teaspoon sugar**
- **¼ teaspoon baking soda**
- **¼ teaspoon salt**
- **¼ cup chilled unsalted butter**
- **¾ cup (3 ounces) shredded reduced-fat extra-sharp Cheddar cheese**
- **¼ cup cold water**
- **1 tablespoon distilled white vinegar**
- **1 tablespoon poppy seeds, sesame seeds, or minced dried onions**

IN A LARGE BOWL, combine the flour, cornmeal, sugar, baking soda, and salt. With a pastry blender or fork, cut in the butter until the mixture resembles coarse crumbs. Stir in the cheese, water, and vinegar. Combine just until the mixture forms a dough. Shape the dough into a ball and wrap with plastic wrap. Freeze for 30 minutes, or until well chilled.

PREHEAT THE OVEN to 375°F. Coat a large baking sheet with nonstick spray.

LIGHTLY SPRINKLE A WORK SURFACE with flour. Place half the dough on the work surface, returning the other half to the freezer. Roll into a paper-thin 12" circle. Sprinkle with 1½ teaspoons of the seeds or onions and lightly roll over the dough to press into place. Cut into 8 wedges. Place on the prepared baking sheet. Sprinkle the work surface with more flour if needed. Repeat with the remaining dough half.

BAKE FOR 8 TO 10 MINUTES, or until golden brown and crisp. Remove to a rack to cool.

**Makes 16 wedges**

***Per wedge:*** *64 calories, 2 g. protein, 6 g. carbohydrates, 4 g. fat, 9 mg. cholesterol, 90 mg. sodium, 0 g. dietary fiber*

# Parmesan Cheese Flatbread

- **1 tablespoon olive oil**
- **1 red onion, thinly sliced and separated into rings**
- **1 teaspoon dried basil**
- **¼ teaspoon ground black pepper**
- **1 tube (10 ounces) refrigerated pizza dough**
- **2 tablespoons (½ ounce) grated Parmesan cheese**

PREHEAT THE OVEN TO 350°F. Coat a large baking sheet with nonstick spray.

WARM 1 TEASPOON OF THE OIL in a medium nonstick skillet over medium-high heat. Add the onion. Cook, stirring frequently, for 10 to 12 minutes, or until very soft and golden brown. Stir in the basil and pepper.

UNROLL THE PIZZA DOUGH and place on the baking sheet. Stretch into a 16" × 7" rectangle. Brush the remaining 2 teaspoons oil over the dough. Spread the onion mixture over the dough, leaving a ½" border. Sprinkle with the cheese. Bake for 10 to 15 minutes, or until the crust is golden brown.

REMOVE FROM THE BAKING SHEET. Cool on a rack for 5 minutes. Cut into rectangles.

**Makes 8 servings**

***Per serving:*** *125 calories, 4 g. protein, 20 g. carbohydrates, 3 g. fat, 1 mg. cholesterol, 246 mg. sodium, 1 g. dietary fiber*

**Tips:** This flatbread can be double-wrapped in foil and frozen for up to 1 month. To use, thaw in the refrigerator, then bake at 350°F for 10 minutes, or until heated through.

To vary the flavor, experiment with different seasonings in the topping. Try stirring 2 tablespoons sesame seeds or poppy seeds into the onion mixture.

This makes a wonderful sandwich bread (with the caramelized onions on the inside).

# Skillet Oat Bread

- **2 cups all-purpose flour**
- **⅓ cup quick-cooking oats**
- **1 tablespoon grated lemon peel**
- **½ teaspoon salt**
- **½ teaspoon baking soda**
- **¼ cup + 1 tablespoon chilled unsalted butter**
- **1 cup 1% buttermilk**
- **1 large egg, lightly beaten**
- **2 tablespoons sugar**
- **1 tablespoon lemon juice**

PREHEAT THE OVEN TO 425°F. Coat a heavy-bottomed 9" skillet with nonstick spray. (Use a skillet with a handle that can withstand oven heat, or wrap the handle in several layers of foil to protect it from the heat.)

IN A LARGE BOWL, combine the flour, 4 tablespoons of the oats, lemon peel, salt, and baking soda. With a pastry blender or fork, cut in ¼ cup butter until the mixture resembles coarse crumbs.

IN A MEDIUM BOWL, whisk together the buttermilk, egg, sugar, and lemon juice. Add to the flour mixture. Stir just until combined.

SPREAD OVER THE BOTTOM of the prepared skillet. Melt the remaining 1 tablespoon butter. Sprinkle the remaining oats over the dough. Drizzle with the butter.

BAKE FOR 20 TO 25 MINUTES, or until golden brown. Cut into 8 wedges and serve warm.

**Makes 8 wedges**

***Per wedge:*** *224 calories, 6 g. protein, 31 g. carbohydrates, 9 g. fat, 47 mg. cholesterol, 266 mg. sodium, 1 g. dietary fiber*

**Tips:** This bread can be removed from the skillet, double-wrapped in foil, and frozen for up to 1 month. To use, thaw in the refrigerator, then bake at 400°F for 10 to 15 minutes, or until heated through.

Stir 1 tablespoon poppy seeds into the flour mixture.

# Multigrain Streusel-Topped Muffins

**Muffins**

- 1 cup all-purpose flour
- ½ cup cornmeal
- ⅓ cup oat bran
- ¼ cup honey-flavored wheat germ
- ¼ cup packed brown sugar
- 1 tablespoon baking powder
- ½ teaspoon baking soda
- ¾ cup 1% milk
- 1 egg
- 3 tablespoons canola oil
- 2 tablespoons molasses

**Topping**

- ¼ cup packed brown sugar
- 1 tablespoon quick-cooking oats
- 1 tablespoon all-purpose flour
- ¼ teaspoon ground cinnamon
- 1 tablespoon chilled unsalted butter

*To make the muffins:*

PREHEAT THE OVEN TO 400°F. Coat 12 muffin cups with nonstick spray.

IN A LARGE BOWL, combine the flour, cornmeal, oat bran, wheat germ, brown sugar, baking powder, and baking soda.

IN A MEDIUM BOWL, combine the milk, egg, oil, and molasses. Stir into the flour mixture just until moistened. (The batter will be very thick. Don't overmix it, or the muffins will be dense.) Divide the batter evenly among the prepared cups.

*To make the topping:*

IN A SMALL BOWL, combine the brown sugar, oats, flour, and cinnamon. With a pastry blender or fork, cut in the butter until the mixture resembles coarse crumbs. Sprinkle over the muffins.

BAKE FOR 15 TO 20 MINUTES, or until a toothpick inserted in the center comes out clean. Cool in the pan on a rack for 10 minutes. Remove the muffins and let cool completely on the rack.

**Makes 12**

***Per muffin:*** *139 calories, 4 g. protein, 20 g. carbohydrates, 6 g. fat, 21 mg. cholesterol, 132 mg. sodium, 1 g. dietary fiber*

**Tip:** These muffins can be double-wrapped in foil and frozen for up to 1 month. To use, thaw in the refrigerator, then bake at 350°F for 10 minutes, or until heated through.

# Lemon Muffins

| | |
|---|---|
| **⅔** | **cup (about 5 ounces) fat-free lemon yogurt** |
| **⅓** | **cup 1% milk** |
| **¼** | **cup canola oil** |
| **1** | **egg** |
| **1¾** | **cups all-purpose flour** |
| **⅓** | **cup sugar** |
| **2½** | **teaspoons baking powder** |
| **½** | **teaspoon baking soda** |
| **¼** | **teaspoon salt** |

PREHEAT THE OVEN TO 400°F. Coat the bottoms only of 12 muffin cups with nonstick spray or line the cups with paper liners.

IN A LARGE BOWL, with a mixer on medium speed, beat the yogurt, milk, oil, and egg for 1 minute, or until blended.

IN A MEDIUM BOWL, combine the flour, sugar, baking powder, baking soda, and salt. Add to the yogurt mixture. Stir, by hand, just until combined.

DIVIDE THE BATTER evenly among the prepared cups. Bake for 15 to 20 minutes, or until a toothpick inserted in the center comes out clean.

COOL IN THE PAN on a rack for 10 minutes. Remove the muffins and let cool completely on the rack.

**Makes 12**

***Per muffin:*** *135 calories, 3 g. protein, 20 g. carbohydrates, 5 g. fat, 0 mg. cholesterol, 163 mg. sodium, 0 g. dietary fiber*

**Tips:** Before baking, stir in ¾ cup fresh whole blueberries or chopped strawberries or ½ cup chopped dried fruit.

These muffins can be double-wrapped in foil and frozen for up to 1 month. To use, thaw in the refrigerator, then bake at 350°F for 10 minutes, or until heated through.

# Buttermilk-Fruit Scones

- 2 cups all-purpose flour
- ¼ cup + 1 teaspoon sugar
- 1 tablespoon baking powder
- ¼ teaspoon baking soda
- 1 tablespoon grated orange peel
- 2 tablespoons chilled unsalted butter
- ½ cup chopped mixed dried fruit
- 1 cup 1% buttermilk
- 1 teaspoon vanilla extract

PREHEAT THE OVEN TO 425°F. Coat a large baking sheet with nonstick spray.

IN A MEDIUM BOWL, combine the flour, ¼ cup sugar, baking powder, baking soda, and orange peel. With a pastry blender or fork, cut in the butter until the mixture resembles coarse crumbs. Stir in the dried fruit. Add the buttermilk and vanilla. Stir just until combined.

SPRINKLE A WORK SURFACE with flour. Turn the dough onto the work surface. Knead 10 to 12 times. Roll into a 10" circle. Sprinkle with the remaining 1 teaspoon sugar. Using a floured knife, cut into 12 triangles.

BAKE FOR 12 TO 15 MINUTES, or until golden brown. Serve warm.

**Makes 12**

***Per scone:*** *166 calories, 3 g. protein, 34 g. carbohydrates, 2 g. fat, 6 mg. cholesterol, 71 mg. sodium, 2 g. dietary fiber*

**Tips:** Dried cranberries or chopped dried apricots can be substituted for the mixed dried fruit.

These scones can be double-wrapped in foil and frozen for up to 1 month. To use, thaw in the refrigerator, then bake at 375°F for 10 minutes, or until heated through.

## 8 Bread Machine Tips

Homemade yeast breads were once a luxury that could be afforded only by those with time and skill. Bread machines have changed all that. Now, anybody can have fresh bread. Any time of day. I love nothing more than waking up to the intoxicating aroma of fresh bread baking in my kitchen. Of course, the bread my family now enjoys is not exactly what emerged from my machine the first time I used it. I went through at least half a dozen dense, fallen, or failed breads before producing the perfect high-rising loaf with a tender, airy crumb. It takes a bit of trial and error because all bread machines are different. Here are a few rules of thumb to help you produce the perfect loaf from your machine. For specific troubleshooting tips, see page 274.

1. Familiarize yourself completely with the manufacturer's directions for your machine.
2. The first time you use your machine, follow one of the manufacturer's suggested bread recipes to get comfortable with the necessary terminology.
3. Determine whether your machine makes 1-pound loaves or 1½- to 2-pound loaves. The recipes in this book are written to make 1½-pound loaves, the size produced by most bread machines.
4. Add the ingredients in the order specified for your machine. This step is essential to producing a properly mixed dough.
5. If you keep your yeast in the freezer or refrigerator, bring it to room temperature before using. Cold yeast may not allow the dough to rise properly.
6. Know the time cycles of your machine. Many machines take from 2 to 4 hours.
7. Remove bread from the machine immediately after it is done cooking. Bread left in the machine will get steamed and soggy.
8. Let bread cool completely before slicing. A serrated knife or an electric knife will give you the best results.

# Yeast Wheat Biscuits

- ½ cup 1% buttermilk
- 1 package (¼ ounce) quick-rising yeast
- 1½ cups all-purpose flour
- 1 cup whole wheat flour
- 1 tablespoon sugar
- 1¼ teaspoons baking powder
- ¼ teaspoon salt
- 3 tablespoons chilled unsalted butter
- ½ cup cinnamon-flavored applesauce

PREHEAT THE OVEN TO 400°F. Coat a large baking sheet with nonstick spray.

PLACE THE BUTTERMILK in a small bowl. Microwave on high power until warm (105°–115°F). Add the yeast.

IN A LARGE BOWL, combine the all-purpose flour, whole wheat flour, sugar, baking powder, and salt. With a pastry blender or fork, cut in the butter until the mixture resembles coarse crumbs. Stir in the buttermilk mixture and applesauce.

SPRINKLE A WORK SURFACE with all-purpose flour. Turn the dough onto the work surface. Knead 3 to 5 times. Roll to ½" thickness. Cut into biscuits with a floured 2" biscuit cutter or drinking glass. Place on the prepared baking sheet. Cover loosely with plastic wrap. Let stand in a warm place for 15 minutes.

BAKE FOR 10 TO 12 MINUTES, or until golden brown.

**Makes 12**

***Per biscuit:*** *131 calories, 4 g. protein, 22 g. carbohydrates, 3 g. fat, 8 mg. cholesterol, 85 mg. sodium, 2 g. dietary fiber*

**Tip:** Before rolling out the biscuit dough, knead in 1 tablespoon sesame seeds.

# Whole Wheat–Caraway Biscuit Squares

- 1 cup all-purpose flour
- 1 cup whole wheat flour
- ¼ cup honey-flavored wheat germ
- 1 tablespoon baking powder
- 1 teaspoon caraway seeds
- ¼ teaspoon salt
- 1¼ cup chilled unsalted butter
- ⅔ cup 1% milk

PREHEAT THE OVEN TO 450°F.

IN A MEDIUM BOWL, combine the all-purpose flour, whole wheat flour, wheat germ, baking powder, seeds, and salt. With a pastry blender or fork, cut in the butter until the mixture resembles coarse crumbs. Stir in the milk until the dough leaves the sides of the bowl and forms a ball. If the dough seems dry, add 1 to 2 tablespoons water.

SPRINKLE A WORK SURFACE with flour. Turn the dough onto the work surface. Coat gently with the flour. Knead 1 or 2 times. Press to form a ½"-thick rectangle. Using a floured knife, cut into 12 squares. Place on an ungreased baking sheet.

BAKE FOR 10 TO 12 MINUTES, or until golden brown. Remove from the baking sheet and cool on a rack.

**Makes 12**

***Per biscuit:*** *121 calories, 4 g. protein, 17 g. carbohydrates, 5 g. fat, 11 mg. cholesterol, 115 mg. sodium, 2 g. dietary fiber*

**Tip:** For round biscuits, press or roll dough to ½" thickness and use a biscuit cutter or drinking glass to cut circles.

# Cheddar Cheese Bread

- 1½ cups yellow cornmeal
- 1¼ cups 1% buttermilk
- ½ cup all-purpose flour
- 2 eggs
- ¼ cup softened unsalted butter
- 1½ teaspoons baking powder
- 1 tablespoon sugar
- ½ teaspoon baking soda
- 1 cup shredded reduced-fat taco-flavored or plain Cheddar cheese
- 1 tablespoon chopped green chiles

PREHEAT THE OVEN TO 450°F. Coat an 8" × 8" baking pan with nonstick spray.

IN A LARGE BOWL, combine the cornmeal, buttermilk, flour, eggs, butter, baking powder, sugar, and baking soda. Beat vigorously with a wooden spoon until well-mixed. Gently stir in the cheese and chiles. Spoon into the prepared pan.

BAKE FOR 20 TO 25 MINUTES, or until golden brown. Cool 10 minutes in the pan. Cut into squares and serve warm or at room temperature.

**Makes 8 servings**

***Per serving:*** *228 calories, 9 g. protein, 28 g. carbohydrates, 9 g. fat, 73 mg. cholesterol, 273 mg. sodium, 2 g. dietary fiber*

**Tip:** This bread can be removed from the pan, double-wrapped in foil, and frozen for up to 1 month. To use, thaw in the refrigerator, then bake at 375°F for 10 to 15 minutes, or until heated through.

# Applesauce-Zucchini Bread

- **¾ cup finely shredded zucchini**
- **1½ cups all-purpose flour**
- **½ cup sugar**
- **½ teaspoon baking soda**
- **½ teaspoon ground cinnamon**
- **¼ teaspoon salt**
- **¼ teaspoon baking powder**
- **⅓ cup cinnamon-flavored applesauce**
- **1 large egg, lightly beaten**
- **2 tablespoons vegetable oil**
- **1 teaspoon vanilla extract**

PREHEAT THE OVEN TO 350°F. Coat an 8" × 4" loaf pan with nonstick spray.

PLACE THE ZUCCHINI in a fine mesh strainer and let drain for 10 minutes.

IN A LARGE BOWL, combine the flour, sugar, baking soda, cinnamon, salt, and baking powder.

IN A MEDIUM BOWL, mix the zucchini, applesauce, egg, oil, and vanilla. Add to the flour mixture. Stir just until combined. Spoon into the prepared pan.

BAKE FOR 50 TO 60 MINUTES, or until a toothpick inserted in the center comes out clean. Cool in the pan on a rack for 10 minutes. Remove from the pan and let cool completely on the rack.

**Makes 16 slices**

***Per slice:*** *93 calories, 2 g. protein, 17 g. carbohydrates, 2 g. fat, 13 mg. cholesterol, 84 mg. sodium, 1 g. dietary fiber*

**Tips:** My kids love making this bread. Spread it with cream cheese for a wonderful quick breakfast.

This bread can be double-wrapped in foil and frozen for up to 1 month. To use, thaw in the refrigerator, then bake at 325°F for 10 minutes, or until heated through.

# Apple–Sweet Potato Bread

- 2⅓ cups all-purpose flour
- ¾ cup packed brown sugar
- 1¼ teaspoons baking powder
- ½ teaspoon baking soda
- ¼ teaspoon ground cinnamon
- ⅛ teaspoon ground nutmeg
- ½ cup canned mashed unsweetened sweet potatoes
- 2 eggs
- ¼ cup unsweetened apple juice
- 3 tablespoons melted unsalted butter
- 1 cup chopped dried apples

PREHEAT THE OVEN TO 350°F. Coat a 9" × 5" loaf pan with nonstick spray.

IN A LARGE BOWL, combine the flour, brown sugar, baking powder, baking soda, cinnamon, and nutmeg.

IN A MEDIUM BOWL, combine the sweet potatoes, eggs, apple juice, and butter. Add to the flour mixture. Stir just until combined. Gently stir in the apples. Spoon into the prepared pan.

BAKE FOR 1 HOUR, or until a toothpick inserted in the center comes out clean. Cool in the pan on a rack for 10 minutes. Remove from the pan and let cool completely on the rack.

**Makes 16 slices**

***Per slice:*** *128 calories, 3 g. protein, 22 g. carbohydrates, 3 g. fat, 32 mg. cholesterol, 87 mg. sodium, 1 g. dietary fiber*

**Tips:** Orange juice can be substituted for the apple juice and chopped dried apricots for the dried apples.

This bread can be double-wrapped in foil and frozen for up to 1 month. To use, thaw in the refrigerator, then bake at 325°F for 10 to 15 minutes, or until heated through.

# Cinnamon Pull-Apart Bread

- **1 pound frozen bread dough, thawed**
- **¼ cup packed brown sugar**
- **1 teaspoon ground cinnamon**
- **¼ cup honey**
- **2 tablespoons orange juice**
- **1 tablespoon unsalted butter**

PREHEAT THE OVEN TO 350°F. Coat a 9" or 10" round cake pan with nonstick spray.

CUT THE DOUGH into 12 equal pieces. On a large piece of waxed paper, stir together the brown sugar and cinnamon. Roll the dough pieces in the sugar mixture. Place, with sides touching, in the prepared pan. Cover loosely and let the dough rise in a warm spot for 30 minutes, or until almost double in size.

IN A SMALL SAUCEPAN, mix the honey, orange juice, and butter. Bring just to a boil over medium-high heat, stirring frequently. Drizzle over the dough.

BAKE FOR 20 TO 25 MINUTES, or until the bread is golden brown. Cool in the pan on a rack for 10 minutes. Remove from the pan and place on a platter. Serve warm, pulling apart pieces of the bread with your fingers.

**Makes 12 servings**

***Per serving:*** *138 calories, 4 g. protein, 26 g. carbohydrates, 3 g. fat, 3 mg. cholesterol, 213 mg. sodium, 1 g. dietary fiber*

**Tip:** This bread will get stickier as it stands.

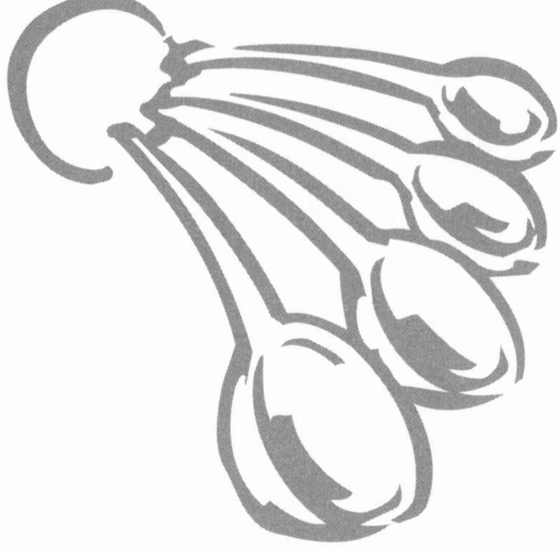

# Dried-Cherry Spiral Bread

- 1 pound frozen bread dough, thawed
- 6 ounces reduced-fat cream cheese
- 2 tablespoons confectioners' sugar
- ½ teaspoon almond extract
- ¼ cup dried cherries
- ¼ cup raisins
- 1 tablespoon 1% milk
- 1 tablespoon honey

PREHEAT THE OVEN TO 375°F. Coat a 15" × 10" jelly-roll pan with nonstick spray. Roll the dough to a 12" × 8" rectangle.

IN A SMALL BOWL, combine the cream cheese, sugar, and almond extract. Mix well. Spread in a 4" column down the center of the dough. Top with the cherries and raisins.

ON THE LONG SIDES OF THE RECTANGLE, score the dough starting from the cream cheese filling to the edge of the dough to make twelve 1"-wide strips. Fold the strips, alternating sides, at an angle across the cream cheese filling. Cover the dough loosely and let rise in a warm spot for 30 minutes, or until almost double in size.

BRUSH THE MILK over the dough and drizzle with the honey. Bake for 20 to 25 minutes, or until golden brown. Remove to a rack and cool.

**Makes 12 servings**

***Per serving:*** *193 calories, 6 g. protein, 34 g. carbohydrates, 5 g. fat, 8 mg. cholesterol, 259 mg. sodium, 2 g. dietary fiber*

**Tip:** For a glaze, mix together ¼ cup confectioners' sugar, 1 tablespoon water, and 1 teaspoon lemon juice. Drizzle over the warm bread.

# Secrets of Successful Bread

Baking bread really isn't that difficult. Whether you bake bread by hand or in a machine, here is everything you need to turn out a perfect loaf every time.

## HANDMADE BREAD

Kneading bread can be a wonderful way to relax. Best of all, you get to enjoy warm, homemade bread, fresh from your oven. Here are the basics and a few tricks.

**Tools:** Dough scraper, dry measuring cups, bread board or countertop, oven thermometer (to check your oven's temperature for accuracy), large mixing bowl, mixing spoons, and one pair of strong hands.

**Flour:** Use bread flour for best results. On very moist days, dough may need additional flour during kneading. Add flour 1 to 2 tablespoons at a time.

**Rising:** To prevent rising dough from sticking to the bowl, coat the bowl with nonstick cooking spray. Cover the bowl with a towel and let the dough rise in a warm place (80°–90°F). An electric oven with the light on or a gas oven with a pilot is a good place.

**Doubling:** Most recipes require bread dough to rise until doubled in size. To test for doubling, gently press a fingertip into the dough. If a dent remains, the dough has doubled. If it fills in quickly, let the dough rise longer.

**Punching down:** When dough has doubled, punch it down by pushing your fist deep into the center. Turn the dough over in the bowl and let it rest for a few minutes.

**Kneading:** Shape the dough into a ball and place on a lightly floured surface. Fold the dough over itself toward you. Using the heels of your hands, push the dough away with a rolling motion, then give it a quarter turn. Continue in this fashion 8 to 10 times.

**Elastic dough:** Properly kneaded dough should be smooth and pliable. If dough becomes too elastic and "shrinks back" during kneading, give it a rest for 10 minutes. Overworked dough will result in tough bread.

**For better texture:** Make a sponge. Combine the yeast, liquid, and half the flour. Mix well, cover, and set aside for 30 minutes to rise. Proceed with recipe.

**For a crispy crust:** Use a metal pan. Recipes with more fat and liquid will also produce a darker crust.

**Baking stones:** These re-create the tile-lined ovens found in bakeries. The stone absorbs moisture, creating a crisp crust. Baking stones are available in kitchen stores. You can also use unglazed quarry tiles.

**Well-shaped loaves:** To prevent loaves from losing their shape during rising, wrap a thin band of foil around the bread and remove halfway during baking.

## BREAD MACHINE TROUBLESHOOTING

When changing bread machine recipes, make one adjustment at a time so that you can isolate the problem. For instance, if the bread didn't rise, increase the yeast by ¼ teaspoon the next time you make it. The hints below will help.

**Loaf didn't rise**

- Add ¼ teaspoon yeast.
- Add 1 teaspoon sugar.
- Subtract ¼ teaspoon salt.
- Subtract 1 teaspoon fat.
- Add 1 tablespoon liquid.
- Be sure yeast has not expired.

**Overrisen or collapsed loaf**

- Subtract ¼ teaspoon yeast.
- Subtract 1 teaspoon sugar.
- Add ¼ teaspoon salt.
- Subtract 1 tablespoon liquid.
- Humidity too high; bake during coolest time of day.
- Remove bread from machine immediately after cooking.

**Crust too dark**

- Subtract 1 teaspoon sugar.
- Subtract 1 teaspoon fat.
- Use light crust setting on machine.
- Decrease sugary ingredients (e.g., fruit).

**Crust too light**

- Add 1 teaspoon sugar.
- Add 1 teaspoon fat.
- Use dark crust setting on machine.

**Gummy or underbaked center**

- Add 1 tablespoon flour.
- Subtract 1 tablespoon liquid.
- Replace some whole grain flour (if using) with bread flour.
- Decrease wet ingredients (e.g., fresh fruit, eggs).

**Short loaf**

- Add ¼ teaspoon yeast.
- Add 1 teaspoon sugar.
- Use bread flour.
- Replace some whole grain flour (if using) with bread flour.

**Mushroomlike top**

- Subtract ¼ teaspoon yeast.
- Subtract ¼ teaspoon sugar.
- Add ¼ teaspoon salt.
- Subtract 1 tablespoon liquid.
- Decrease sugary ingredients (e.g., fruit).

**Too many holes in texture**

- Subtract ¼ teaspoon yeast.
- Add ¼ teaspoon salt.
- Subtract 1 tablespoon liquid.
- Drain and pat dry fruit or vegetables.

**Dense, heavy texture**

- Subtract 1 tablespoon flour.
- Add ¼ teaspoon yeast.
- Add 1 teaspoon sugar.
- Subtract 1 tablespoon liquid.
- Replace some whole grain flour (if using) with bread flour.

# Good-for-Toasting Wheat Bread

- **1⅔ cups whole wheat flour**
- **1½ cups all-purpose flour**
- **3 tablespoons packed brown sugar**
- **1½ teaspoons active dry yeast**
- **1 teaspoon salt**
- **½ cup 1% milk**
- **½ cup water**
- **1 tablespoon canola oil**

COAT A MEDIUM BOWL WITH NONSTICK SPRAY. Coat a 9" × 5" loaf pan with nonstick spray.

IN A LARGE BOWL, combine the whole wheat flour, 1 cup all-purpose flour, brown sugar, yeast, and salt.

IN A SMALL SAUCEPAN, mix the milk, water, and oil. Warm over medium heat to 125° to 130°F. Pour slowly into the flour mixture, beating with a wooden spoon. Add enough of the remaining ½ cup all-purpose flour to form a soft dough (all may not be needed).

LIGHTLY SPRINKLE A WORK SURFACE with all-purpose flour. Turn the dough onto the work surface. Knead for 8 to 10 minutes, or until the dough is smooth and elastic, incorporating a little flour if the dough becomes too sticky. Form into a ball and place in the prepared medium bowl, turning to coat both sides with the nonstick spray.

COVER THE BOWL with plastic wrap and a kitchen towel. Place in a warm spot (80°–90°F) for 1 hour, or until double in size. Punch down the dough and let it rest for 5 minutes.

TURN THE DOUGH onto the floured work surface and gently stretch and press into a 9"-long rectangle. Starting at a narrow end of the rectangle, roll up the dough. Pinch the seams closed on either side and turn them underneath

the dough. Place in the prepared loaf pan. Cover with plastic wrap and a towel. Let rise for 30 minutes, or until about ½" above the top of the pan. Remove the plastic wrap and towel.

PREHEAT THE OVEN to 400°F.

BAKE FOR 20 TO 25 MINUTES, or until golden brown. Remove from the pan and cool on a rack.

**Makes 1½-pound loaf (12 slices)**

***Per slice:*** *119 calories, 4 g. protein, 23 g. carbohydrates, 2 g. fat, 0 mg. cholesterol, 202 mg. sodium, 2 g. dietary fiber*

**Tip:** To freeze the bread, wrap it in plastic wrap, then place in a food-storage bag in the freezer for up to 3 months. To use, thaw in the refrigerator. If desired, toast slices of the bread or warm in a 300°F oven until heated through.

## Bread Machine Recipe

**Quick Good-for-Toasting Wheat Bread:** Place the ingredients in the bread machine pan in the order recommended by the manufacturer. All bread machines differ, so it is very important to follow the ingredient order recommended for your machine. Select the appropriate bake cycle and start the machine. When baking is done, remove promptly. Cool on a rack.

# Honey-Rye Bread

- **2¼ cups bread flour**
- **1 cup rye flour**
- **1 package (¼ ounce) active dry yeast**
- **½ teaspoon salt**
- **¾ cup water**
- **¼ cup 1% milk**
- **2 tablespoons vegetable oil**
- **3 tablespoons honey**
- **½ cup golden raisins**

Coat a medium bowl with nonstick spray. Coat a 9" × 5" loaf pan with nonstick spray.

In a large bowl, combine 1¾ cups bread flour, the rye flour, yeast, and salt.

In a small saucepan, combine the water, milk, oil, and honey. Cook over medium-low heat until warm (about 125°F). Pour slowly into the flour mixture, stirring with a wooden spoon. Add enough of the remaining ½ cup bread flour to form a soft dough (all may not be needed).

Lightly sprinkle a work surface with bread flour. Turn the dough onto the work surface. Knead for 8 to 10 minutes, or until the dough is smooth and elastic, adding in the raisins and incorporating a little flour if the dough becomes too sticky. Form into a ball and place in the prepared medium bowl, turning to coat both sides with the nonstick spray.

Cover the bowl with plastic wrap and a kitchen towel. Place in a warm spot (80°–90°F) for 1 hour, or until double in size. Punch down the dough and let it rest for 5 minutes.

Turn the dough onto the floured work surface and gently stretch and press into a 9"-long rectangle. Starting at a narrow end of the rectangle, roll up the dough. Pinch the seams closed on either side and turn them underneath

the dough. Place in the prepared loaf pan. Cover with plastic wrap and a towel. Let rise for 30 minutes, or until about ½" above the top of the pan. Remove the plastic wrap and towel.

PREHEAT THE OVEN to 400°F.

BAKE FOR 20 TO 25 MINUTES, or until golden brown. Remove from the pan and cool on a rack.

**Makes 1½-pound loaf (15 slices)**

***Per slice:*** *156 calories, 4 g. protein, 30 g. carbohydrates, 2 g. fat, 0 mg. cholesterol, 43 mg. sodium, 2 g. dietary fiber*

**Tip:** To freeze the bread, wrap it in plastic wrap, then place in a food-storage bag in the freezer for up to 3 months. To use, thaw in the refrigerator. If desired, toast slices of the bread or warm in a 300°F oven until heated through.

## Bread Machine Recipe

**Quick Honey-Rye Bread:** Place the ingredients in the bread machine pan in the order recommended by the manufacturer. All bread machines differ, so it is very important to follow the ingredient order recommended for your machine. Select the appropriate bake cycle and start the machine. When baking is done, remove promptly. Cool on a rack.

# Molasses-Corn Yeast Bread

- **3 cups bread flour**
- **1¼ teaspoons active dry yeast**
- **½ teaspoon salt**
- **½ cup warm water**
- **½ cup 1% milk**
- **½ cup yellow cornmeal**
- **3 tablespoons butter or margarine**
- **2 tablespoons molasses**
- **2 tablespoons packed brown sugar**
- **1 large egg, lightly beaten**
- **1 teaspoon grated orange peel**

COAT A MEDIUM BOWL WITH NONSTICK SPRAY. Coat a 9" × 5" loaf pan with nonstick spray.

IN A LARGE BOWL, combine 2½ cups of the flour, the yeast, and salt.

IN A MEDIUM BOWL, combine the water and milk. Microwave on high power for 4 minutes, or until warm (125°F). Stir in the cornmeal, butter or margarine, molasses, brown sugar, egg, and orange peel, mixing well. Pour slowly into the flour mixture, beating with a wooden spoon and adding enough of the remaining ½ cup flour to form a soft dough (all may not be needed).

LIGHTLY SPRINKLE A WORK SURFACE with bread flour. Turn the dough onto the work surface. Knead for 8 to 10 minutes, or until the dough is smooth and elastic, incorporating a little flour if the dough becomes too sticky. Form into a ball and place in the prepared bowl, turning to coat both sides with the nonstick spray.

COVER THE BOWL with plastic wrap and a kitchen towel. Place in a warm spot (80°–90°F) for 1 hour, or until double in size. Punch down the dough and let it rest for 5 minutes.

TURN THE DOUGH onto the floured work surface and gently stretch and press into a 9"-long rectangle. Starting at a narrow end of the rectangle, roll up the dough. Pinch the seams closed on either side and turn them underneath the dough. Place in the prepared loaf pan. Cover with plastic wrap and a towel. Let rise for 30 minutes, or until about ½" above the top of the pan. Remove the plastic wrap and towel.

PREHEAT THE OVEN to 400°F.

BAKE FOR 20 TO 25 MINUTES, or until golden brown. Remove from the pan and cool on a rack.

**Makes 1½-pound loaf (15 slices)**

***Per slice:*** *150 calories, 4 g. protein, 25 g. carbohydrates, 3 g. fat, 21 mg. cholesterol, 73 mg. sodium, 1 g. dietary fiber*

**Tip:** To freeze the bread, wrap it in plastic wrap, then place in a food-storage bag in the freezer for up to 3 months. To use, thaw in the refrigerator. If desired, toast slices of the bread or warm in a 300°F oven until heated through.

## Bread Machine Recipe

**Quick Molasses-Corn Yeast Bread:** In a medium bowl, combine the water and milk. Microwave on high power until warm (125°F). Stir in the cornmeal, butter or margarine, molasses, brown sugar, egg, and orange peel. Mix well.

Place the cornmeal mixture, flour, yeast, and salt in the bread machine pan in the order recommended by the manufacturer. All bread machines differ, so it is very important to follow the ingredient order recommended for your machine. Select the appropriate bake cycle and start the machine. When baking is done, remove promptly. Cool on a rack.

# Dips, Dunks, and Slathers

*"The full use of taste is an act of genius."*

—John La Farge, U.S. artist and writer

# Dips, Dunks, and Slathers

SOMETIMES THE TYPICAL ketchup, mustard, or mayo just doesn't cut it. I want more flavor. More tingly sensations on my tastebuds. I came up with these spreads and sauces to fill that need. They add that last-minute splash of color, texture, spice, or sweetness. And they're great make-aheads. Most of these recipes make enough for several meals, and they keep in the refrigerator or freezer for months. All are ultra-light and no big deal to whip up. They also make great gifts. I like to place the chutney, fruit butter, and fruit vinegar in decorative jars and tie on the recipe with ribbon. For more dips and spreads, see Great Little Bites beginning on page 49.

## Recipes

● Kid-Friendly Recipe

● Freezable Recipe

● Microwaveable Recipe

# Citrus-Flavored BBQ Sauce

- **2 teaspoons olive oil**
- **3 scallions, chopped**
- **2 cloves garlic, minced**
- **1 cup tropical-flavored juice blend**
- **¾ cup tomato puree**
- **2 tablespoons packed brown sugar**
- **1 tablespoon steak sauce**
- **1 tablespoon cider vinegar**

Warm the oil in a small saucepan over medium-high heat for 1 minute. Add the scallions and garlic. Cook, stirring frequently, for 2 to 3 minutes, or until the scallions are tender. Stir in the juice blend, tomato puree, brown sugar, steak sauce, and vinegar. Bring to a boil over high heat. Reduce the heat to low and cook for 10 to 15 minutes longer to blend the flavors.

**Makes 2 cups**

***Per tablespoon:*** *17 calories, 0 g. protein, 3 g. carbohydrates, 0.5 g. fat, 0 mg. cholesterol, 6 mg. sodium, 0 g. dietary fiber*

**Tips:** Use this sauce for marinating firm tofu and fresh vegetables (which taste great grilled on skewers). Or spoon it over steamed broccoli.

To make the sauce in a microwave oven, heat the oil in a microwaveable bowl on high power for 1 minute. Add the scallions and garlic. Cook on high power, stirring once, for 1 to 2 minutes, or until the scallions are tender. Stir in the remaining ingredients. Cook on high power for 5 minutes longer.

# Mexican Marinara Sauce

- **1 tablespoon olive oil**
- **2 cloves garlic, minced**
- **1 tablespoon chili powder**
- **1 tablespoon unsweetened cocoa powder**
- **1 jar (16 ounces) marinara sauce**
- **¼ cup sliced canned black olives**
- **1 teaspoon sugar**
- **½ teaspoon dried Italian seasoning**

WARM THE OIL IN A LARGE NONSTICK SKILLET over medium-high heat for 1 minute. Add the garlic and chili powder. Cook, stirring frequently, for 1 to 2 minutes, or until the garlic is tender. Stir in the cocoa. Cook for 1 minute longer.

STIR IN THE MARINARA SAUCE, olives, sugar, and Italian seasoning. Bring to a boil over high heat. Reduce the heat to low and simmer, partially covered, for 10 minutes to blend the flavors.

**Makes 2½ cups**

***Per ½ cup:*** *104 calories, 2 g. protein, 16 g. carbohydrates, 6 g. fat, 0 mg. cholesterol, 648 mg. sodium, 1 g. dietary fiber*

**Tips:** Chopped fresh spinach can be stirred in along with the olives.

Serve over pasta or a baked potato.

The sauce can be frozen in a tightly covered container for up to 3 months. Reheat on the stove top over medium heat or in a microwave oven on high power.

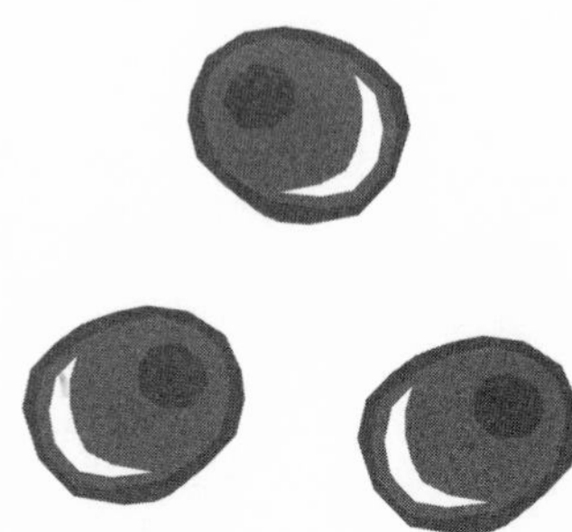

# Sesame Dipping Sauce

- ¼ cup vegetable or beef broth
- 2 tablespoons chopped fresh chives or 2 teaspoons dried
- 2 tablespoons teriyaki sauce
- 2 tablespoons rice wine vinegar
- 2 teaspoons grated fresh ginger
- 1 teaspoon toasted sesame seeds

IN A SMALL BOWL, combine the broth, chives, teriyaki sauce, vinegar, ginger, and sesame seeds. Mix well. Cover and refrigerate for at least 30 minutes to blend the flavors.

**Makes ½ cup**

***Per tablespoon:*** *7 calories, 0 g. protein, 1 g. carbohydrates, 0.5 g. fat, 0 mg. cholesterol, 204 mg. sodium, 0 g. dietary fiber*

**Tips:** To toast the sesame seeds, place them in a dry skillet over medium heat and shake the pan for 2 minutes, or until fragrant and golden.

Serve with Chinese pancakes or wontons. Or spoon over salad greens, especially bitter greens like arugula.

# Berry Vinegar

- ¾ cup fresh raspberries
- ¾ cup fresh strawberries
- 1 cup rice wine vinegar or cider vinegar
- ¼ cup orange juice
- 2 tablespoons grated lemon peel
- 2 tablespoons grated orange peel

IN A LARGE GLASS BOWL, combine the raspberries, strawberries, vinegar, orange juice, lemon peel, and orange peel. Let stand, uncovered, for 1 to 3 days at room temperature.

USING A STRAINER or sieve, strain the vinegar into a jar with a tight-fitting lid, pressing the vinegar from the berries. Discard the berries or save for another use. Store in the refrigerator for up to 3 months.

**Makes 1¼ cups**

***Per tablespoon:*** *6 calories, 0 g. protein, 1 g. carbohydrates, 0 g. fat, 0 mg. cholesterol, 0 mg. sodium, 1 g. dietary fiber*

**Tips:** Use the vinegar to splash on a salad or to make a vinaigrette.

For a sweeter vinegar, add a pinch of sugar.

## Easy Food Gifts

Handmade gifts have a specialness all their own. They say "I took the time to make this for you." Just how much time? Less than 15 minutes of hands-on time in the recipes below. That's less time than it takes to stand in line at some stores! Give one of these recipes a try. Use decorative jars and attach the recipe.

### Tomato Salsa

- **3 medium tomatoes, chopped**
- **1 medium onion, chopped**
- **2 chile peppers, seeded and finely chopped**
- **2 tablespoons chopped fresh cilantro**
- **1 tablespoon lime juice**
- **¼ teaspoon salt**

In a medium bowl, combine the tomatoes, onion, peppers, cilantro, lime juice, and salt. Mix well. Spoon into a decorative jar. Cover tightly and refrigerate. Keeps refrigerated for 1 week.

**Tip:** To alter the basic salsa, try adding sautéed tomatillos and garlic. Chopped bell peppers add a crunchy twist. To make fruit salsa, add chopped mango and papaya.

### Mixed-Herb Vinegar

- **2 cups white wine vinegar or red wine vinegar**
- **4 sprigs fresh thyme**
- **2 sprigs fresh rosemary**
- **2 sprigs fresh tarragon**

In a pint-size glass jar with a tight-fitting lid, combine the vinegar, thyme, rosemary, and tarragon. Cover tightly and let stand at room temperature for 1 week. Refrigerate up to 6 months.

**Tip:** To vary the flavor, use sherry vinegar or your favorite herbs, or add in strips of fresh lemon peel.

### Mustard

- **½ cup mustard powder**
- **⅓ cup cold water**
- **¾ cup all-purpose flour**
- **⅓ cup cider vinegar**
- **2 teaspoons packed brown sugar**
- **1 teaspoon salt**
- **½ teaspoon ground black pepper**

In a small bowl, whisk together the mustard and water. Let stand at room temperature for 15 minutes. Whisk in the flour, vinegar, brown sugar, salt, and pepper. Let stand at room temperature for 15 minutes. Refrigerate in a tightly sealed jar for up to 6 months.

**Tip:** To make honey mustard, stir in 2 tablespoons honey after the mustard and water have been standing.

# Apple-Nut Chutney

- **2 apples, peeled and chopped**
- **½ cup golden raisins**
- **½ cup unsweetened apple juice**
- **1 tablespoon packed brown sugar**
- **1 tablespoon balsamic vinegar**
- **¼ teaspoon ground ginger**
- **¼ cup chopped toasted walnuts**

IN A MEDIUM SAUCEPAN, combine the apples, raisins, apple juice, brown sugar, vinegar, and ginger. Bring to a boil over high heat. Reduce the heat to low and simmer, stirring frequently, for 20 to 30 minutes, or until the fruit is tender and the mixture is thickened. Stir in the walnuts. Cook for 2 minutes, or until the nuts are heated through.

**Makes 1½ cups**

***Per tablespoon:*** *44 calories, 1 g. protein, 10 g. carbohydrates, 1 g. fat, 0 mg. cholesterol, 2 mg. sodium, 1 g. dietary fiber*

**Tips:** To toast the walnuts, place them in a dry skillet over medium heat and shake the pan for 2 minutes, or until fragrant and golden.

Serve over grilled vegetables or meats.

Pears can be substituted for the apples.

# Pepper Salsa

- 2 medium red and/or yellow bell peppers, chopped
- 1 medium tomato, chopped
- 3 scallions, chopped
- 2 tablespoons chopped canned green chiles
- 2 tablespoons chopped fresh cilantro or 2 teaspoons dried
- 1 tablespoon lime juice
- 2 teaspoons olive oil
- ¼ teaspoon ground cumin
- Pinch of ground red pepper

In a medium bowl, combine the bell peppers, tomato, scallions, chiles, cilantro, lime juice, oil, cumin, and red pepper. Mix well. Cover and refrigerate for at least 30 minutes to blend the flavors.

**Makes 2 cups**

***Per tablespoon:*** *6 calories, 0 g. protein, 1 g. carbohydrates, 0.5 g. fat, 0 mg. cholesterol, 4 mg. sodium, 0 g. dietary fiber*

**Tips:** Spoon over baked potatoes or toss with hot cooked pasta.

Red onions can be substituted for the scallions. Parsley can stand in for the cilantro.

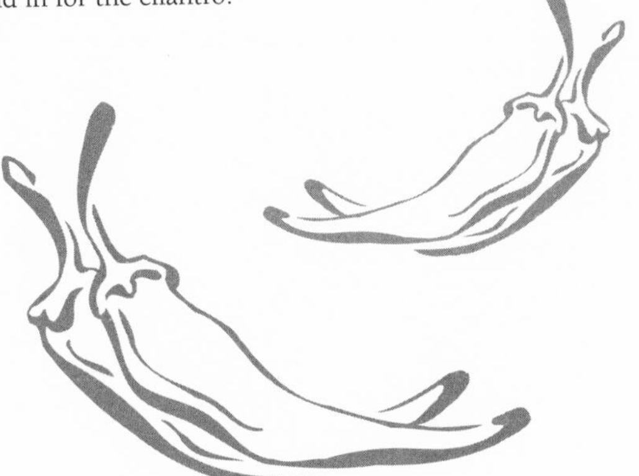

# Lemon-Herb Pesto

- 2 cups packed fresh spinach leaves
- ¼ cup packed fresh flat-leaf parsley
- ¼ cup packed fresh basil leaves
- 3 cloves garlic
- 2 tablespoons pine nuts
- 1 tablespoon grated lemon peel
- ½ teaspoon salt-free lemon-herb seasoning
- ¼ cup olive oil
- ¼ cup vegetable broth

IN A BLENDER OR FOOD PROCESSOR, combine the spinach, parsley, basil, garlic, pine nuts, lemon peel, and lemon-herb seasoning. Blend or process until finely chopped.

WITH THE BLENDER or processor running, gradually pour in the oil and broth. Blend or process until well-combined.

**Makes 1 cup**

***Per tablespoon:*** *41 calories, 1 g. protein, 1 g. carbohydrates, 4 g. fat, 0 mg. cholesterol, 28 mg. sodium, 1 g. dietary fiber*

**Tips:** Stir into grains or soups. Or spread on bread in place of mayonnaise or mustard.

Pesto can be frozen for up to 3 months.

# Dried Fruit Butter

2 **packages (1 ounce each) mixed dried fruit**

¼ **cup water**

2 **tablespoons thawed apple juice concentrate**

1 **tablespoon honey**

1 **tablespoon grated orange peel**

1 **stick cinnamon**

IN A MEDIUM SAUCEPAN, combine the fruit, water, juice concentrate, honey, orange peel, and cinnamon. Stir to mix. Bring to a boil over high heat. Reduce the heat to low and simmer, stirring frequently, for 30 to 45 minutes, or until the fruit is very tender. Remove and discard the cinnamon.

TRANSFER THE SAUCE to a blender or food processor. Blend or process until the mixture is smooth. Refrigerate until well chilled.

**Makes 2 cups**

***Per tablespoon:*** *73 calories, 1 g. protein, 19 g. carbohydrates, 0.5 g. fat, 0 mg. cholesterol, 5 mg. sodium, 2 g. dietary fiber*

**Tip:** Use as a fruit filling for pastries.

# Yogurt-Cheese Tomato Spread

- **2 cups (16 ounces) fat-free plain yogurt**
- **½ cup dry-pack sun-dried tomatoes**
- **2 tablespoons chopped fresh basil**
- **1 tablespoon olive oil**
- **¼ teaspoon ground black pepper**

PLACE A COFFEE FILTER in a small stainless steel or plastic strainer and set over a medium bowl. Spoon the yogurt into the filter. Let drain in the refrigerator, covered with a paper towel, for 3 hours, or until the liquid (whey) drains into the bowl and the remaining cheese is firm.

WHILE THE YOGURT IS DRAINING, in a small bowl, soak the tomatoes in hot water to cover for 10 minutes, or until soft. Drain and finely chop.

DISCARD THE WHEY and place the cheese in a small bowl. Add the tomatoes, basil, oil, and pepper. Stir to combine.

**Makes 1¼ cups**

***Per tablespoon:*** *25 calories, 1 g. protein, 3 g. carbohydrates, 1 g. fat, 1 mg. cholesterol, 46 mg. sodium, 0 g. dietary fiber*

**Tip:** Kids love to see what happens to the yogurt after it is placed in the filter. Draining the yogurt may take as long as 12 hours. I usually do it overnight.

# Eggplant Spread

- 1 medium eggplant (about 1 pound)
- 1 medium tomato, chopped
- ½ cup chopped jarred roasted red peppers
- 1 tablespoon chopped parsley
- 1 tablespoon rinsed and drained capers (chopped if large)
- 1 tablespoon olive oil
- 1 tablespoon balsamic vinegar
- ¼ teaspoon ground black pepper

COAT A GRILL RACK OR BROILER PAN with nonstick spray. Preheat the grill or broiler. Place the eggplant on the grill or under the broiler. Grill or broil, turning frequently, for 10 to 15 minutes, or until charred all over.

LET THE EGGPLANT COOL ENOUGH TO HANDLE. Cut in half. Scoop out the pulp and place it in a strainer over a bowl. Discard the skin. Let the pulp stand for 10 minutes. Discard the liquid.

FINELY CHOP THE PULP and place in a medium bowl. Stir in the tomato, red peppers, parsley, capers, oil, vinegar, and black pepper. Let stand, uncovered, for 30 minutes at room temperature to blend the flavors. After 30 minutes, cover and refrigerate. Bring to room temperature before using.

**Makes 2 cups**

***Per tablespoon:*** *9 calories, 0 g. protein, 1 g. carbohydrates, 0 g. fat, 0 mg. cholesterol, 9 mg. sodium, 0 g. dietary fiber*

**Tip:** Spread on a grilled tomato and mozzarella cheese sandwich for a unique twist.

Index

# Index

Underscored page references indicate sidebars and tables. **Boldface** references indicate illustrations.

# C

## D



## E

# F



# G

# H



# I



# K



# L

# M

# N



# O



# P

# Q

# T

## V



## W

## Y



## Z

## Conversion Chart

These equivalents have been slightly rounded to make measuring easier.

VOLUME MEASUREMENTS

| *U.S.* | *Imperial* | *Metric* |
|---|---|---|
| ¼ tsp | – | 1.25 ml |
| ½ tsp | – | 2.5 ml |
| 1 tsp | – | 5 ml |
| 1 Tbsp | – | 15 ml |
| 2 Tbsp (1 oz) | 1 fl oz | 30 ml |
| ¼ cup (2 oz) | 2 fl oz | 60 ml |
| ⅓ cup (3 oz) | 3 fl oz | 80 ml |
| ½ cup (4 oz) | 4 fl oz | 120 ml |
| ⅔ cup (5 oz) | 5 fl oz | 160 ml |
| ¾ cup (6 oz) | 6 fl oz | 180 ml |
| 1 cup (8 oz) | 8 fl oz | 240 ml |

WEIGHT MEASUREMENTS

| *U.S.* | *Metric* |
|---|---|
| 1 oz | 30 g |
| 2 oz | 60 g |
| 4 oz (¼ lb) | 115 g |
| 5 oz (⅓ lb) | 145 g |
| 6 oz | 170 g |
| 7 oz | 200 g |
| 8 oz (½ lb) | 230 g |
| 10 oz | 285 g |
| 12 oz (¾ lb) | 340 g |
| 14 oz | 400 g |
| 16 oz (1 lb) | 455 g |
| 2.2 lb | 1 kg |

LENGTH MEASUREMENTS

| *U.S.* | *Metric* |
|---|---|
| ¼" | 0.6 cm |
| ½" | 1.25 cm |
| 1" | 2.5 cm |
| 2" | 5 cm |
| 4" | 11 cm |
| 6" | 15 cm |
| 8" | 20 cm |
| 10" | 25 cm |
| 12" (1') | 30 cm |

PAN SIZES

| *U.S.* | *Metric* |
|---|---|
| 8" cake pan | 20 × 4-cm sandwich or cake tin |
| 9" cake pan | 23 × 3.5-cm sandwich or cake tin |
| 11" × 7" baking pan | 28 × 18-cm baking pan |
| 13" × 9" baking pan | 32.5 × 23-cm baking pan |
| 2-qt rectangular baking dish | 30 × 19-cm baking dish |
| 15" × 10" baking pan | 38 × 25.5-cm baking pan (Swiss roll tin) |
| 9" pie plate | 22 × 4 or 23 × 4-cm pie plate |
| 7" or 8" springform pan | 18 or 20-cm springform or loose-bottom cake tin |
| 9" × 5" loaf pan | 23 × 13-cm or 2-lb narrow loaf pan or pâté tin |
| 1½-qt casserole | 1.5-l casserole |
| 2-qt casserole | 2-l casserole |

TEMPERATURES

| *Fahrenheit* | *Centigrade* | *Gas* |
|---|---|---|
| 140° | 60° | – |
| 160° | 70° | – |
| 180° | 80° | – |
| 225° | 110° | – |
| 250° | 120° | ½ |
| 300° | 150° | 2 |
| 325° | 160° | 3 |
| 350° | 180° | 4 |
| 375° | 190° | 5 |
| 400° | 200° | 6 |
| 450° | 230° | 8 |
| 500° | 260° | – |